AMERICAN WOMEN
IN TRANSITION

THE POPULATION OF THE UNITED STATES IN THE 1980s

A Census Monograph Series

AMERICAN WOMEN IN TRANSITION

Suzanne M. Bianchi
and
Daphne Spain

for the
National Committee for Research
on the 1980 Census

RUSSELL SAGE FOUNDATION / NEW YORK

The Russell Sage Foundation

The Russell Sage Foundation, one of the oldest of America's general purpose foundations, was established in 1907 by Mrs. Margaret Olivia Sage for "the improvement of social and living conditions in the United States." The Foundation seeks to fulfill this mandate by fostering the development and dissemination of knowledge about the political, social, and economic problems of America. It conducts research in the social sciences and public policy, and publishes books and pamphlets that derive from this research.

The Board of Trustees is responsible for oversight and the general policies of the Foundation, while administrative direction of the program and staff is vested in the President, assisted by the officers and staff. The President bears final responsibility for the decision to publish a manuscript as a Russell Sage Foundation book. In reaching a judgment on the competence, accuracy, and objectivity of each study, the President is advised by the staff and selected expert readers. The conclusions and interpretations in Russell Sage Foundation publications are those of the authors and not of the Foundation, its Trustees, or its staff. Publication by the Foundation, therefore, does not imply endorsement of the contents of the study.

Library of Congress Cataloging-in-Publication Data
Bianchi, Suzanne M.
    American women in transition.

(The Population of the United States in the 1980s)
"For the National Committee for Research on the 1980 Census."

Bibliography: p.
Includes index.
1. Women—United States—Social conditions—1945–
2. Women—United States—Economic conditions—1945–
3. Women—United States. I. Spain, Daphne. II. National Committee for
Research on the 1980 Census. III. Title. IV. Series.
HQ1420.B484 1986   305.4'2'0973   85-62809
ISBN 0-87154-111-4
ISBN 0-87154-112-2 (pbk.)

Cover and text design: HUGUETTE FRANCO

10 9 8 7 6 5 4 3

The National Committee for Research on the 1980 Census

The committee is sponsored by the Social Science Research Council, the Russell Sage Foundation, and the Alfred P. Sloan Foundation, in collaboration with the U.S. Bureau of the Census. The opinions, findings, and conclusions or recommendations expressed in the monographs supported by the Committee are those of the author(s) and do not necessarily reflect the views of the Committee or its sponsors.

Foreword

American Women in Transition is the first in an ambitious series of
volumes aimed at converting the vast statistical yield of the 1980 census into authoritative analyses of major changes and trends in American
life. This series, "The Population of the United States in the 1980s,"
represents an important episode in social science research and revives a
long tradition of independent census analysis. First in 1930, and then
again in 1950 and 1960, teams of social scientists worked with the U.S.
Bureau of the Census to investigate significant social, economic, and
demographic developments revealed by the decennial censuses. These
census projects produced three landmark series of studies, providing a
firm foundation and setting a high standard for our present undertaking.

There is, in fact, more than a theoretical continuity between those
earlier census projects and the present one. Like those previous efforts,
this new census project has benefited from close cooperation between
the Census Bureau and a distinguished, interdisciplinary group of schol-
ars. Like the 1950 and 1960 research projects, research on the 1980
census was initiated by the Social Science Research Council and the
Russell Sage Foundation. In deciding once again to promote a coordi-
nated program of census analysis, Russell Sage and the Council were
mindful not only of the severe budgetary restrictions imposed on the
Census Bureau's own publishing and dissemination activities in the
1980s, but also of the extraordinary changes that have occurred in so
many dimensions of American life over the past two decades.

The studies constituting "The Population of the United States
in the 1980s" were planned, commissioned, and monitored by the
National Committee for Research on the 1980 Census, a special committee appointed by the Social Science Research Council and sponsored by
the Council, the Russell Sage Foundation, and the Alfred P. Sloan
Foundation, with the collaboration of the U.S. Bureau of the Census.
This committee includes leading social scientists from a broad range of
fields—demography, economics, education, geography, history, political

science, sociology, and statistics. It has been the committee's task to select the main topics for research, obtain highly qualified specialists to carry out that research, and provide the structure necessary to facilitate coordination among researchers and with the Census Bureau.

The topics treated in this series span virtually all the major features of American society—ethnic groups (blacks, Asian Americans, Hispanics, foreign-born, Native Americans); spatial dimensions (migration and immigration, neighborhoods, housing, regional and metropolitan growth and decline); and status groups (income levels, work, families and households, children, women, the elderly). Authors were encouraged to draw not only on the 1980 Census but also on previous censuses and on subsequent national data. Each individual research project was assigned a special advisory panel made up of one committee member, one member nominated by the Census Bureau, one nominated by the National Science Foundation, and one or two other experts. These advisory panels were responsible for project liaison and review and for recommendations to the National Committee regarding the readiness of each manuscript for publication. With the final approval of the chairman of the National Committee, each report was released to the Russell Sage Foundation for publication and distribution.

The debts of gratitude incurred by a project of such scope and organizational complexity are necessarily large and numerous. The committee must thank, first, its sponsors—the Social Science Research Council, headed until recently by Kenneth Prewitt; the Russell Sage Foundation, under the direction of president Marshall Robinson; and the Alfred P. Sloan Foundation, led by Albert Rees. The long-range vision and day-to-day persistence of these organizations and individuals sustained this research program over many years. The active and willing cooperation of the Bureau of the Census was clearly invaluable at all stages of this project, and the extra commitment of time and effort made by Bureau economist James R. Wetzel must be singled out for special recognition. A special tribute is also due to David L. Sills of the Social Science Research Council, staff member of the committee, whose organizational, administrative, and diplomatic skills kept this complicated project running smoothly.

The committee also wishes to thank those organizations that contributed additional funding to the 1980 Census project—the Ford Foundation and its deputy vice president, Louis Winnick, the National Science Foundation, the National Institute on Aging, and the National Institute of Child Health and Human Development. Their support of the research program in general and of several particular studies is gratefully acknowledged.

The ultimate goal of the National Committee and its sponsors has been to produce a definitive, accurate, and comprehensive picture of the U.S. population in the 1980s, a picture that would be primarily descriptive but also enriched by a historical perspective and a sense of the challenges for the future inherent in the trends of today. We hope our readers will agree that the present volume takes a significant step toward achieving that goal.

CHARLES F. WESTOFF
Chairman and Executive Director,
National Committee for Research
on the 1980 Census

*This volume is dedicated to our
grandmothers, mothers,
sisters, and daughter.*

Acknowledgments

Research support for this monograph was provided by the National Committee for Research on the 1980 Census and the U.S. Bureau of the Census. We are particularly grateful to William P. Butz, the Bureau's Associate Director for Demographic Fields, and James R. Wetzel and Larry H. Long of the Bureau's Center for Demographic Studies, for providing encouragement, comments, and a supportive research environment for the completion of this project.

We would also like to thank the myriad reviewers whose comments, criticisms, and suggestions strengthened the final version of the book. In particular, Charles F. Westoff, Chairman and Executive Director of the National Committee for Research on the 1980 Census, read and commented on numerous drafts of the manuscript. Isabel V. Sawhill, Carolyn C. Rogers, and Donald J. Treiman served on the advisory panel for this volume and provided extremely useful, detailed comments which were incorporated in the final version. Herbert C. Morton provided editorial guidance. Frank Levy and Reynolds Farley, both engaged in writing their own monographs, devoted time to reviewing selected chapters and provided comments that were very helpful in revising chapters 2, 6, and 7. We are particularly appreciative of the assistance provided by Nancy F. Rytina in developing the analysis of occupations included in chapter 5. Steven L. Nock also provided comments on drafts of the manuscript at various stages. Finally, many individuals at the Bureau of the Census reviewed selected chapters and made suggestions that were included in the final manuscript.

The work could not have been completed without the assistance of the research support staff within the Center for Demographic Studies of the Bureau of the Census. We thank Ruth Breads for creating the data extracts from the 1960, 1970, and 1980 censuses and for programming assistance throughout the project. Darlene Young and Tom Cochran provided invaluable assistance with the tables, figures, and bibliography.

Peggy Glorius typed and retyped each revision of the manuscript and provided some much appreciated editorial assistance along the way.

In 1982, as a first step in this project, we wrote a short overview of topics that have subsequently been developed in this book. Published in 1983 by the Bureau of the Census, under the title *American Women: Three Decades of Change*, the report was in such demand that it quickly required a second printing. This report was very useful in helping us focus on the theme of this book *American Women in Transition:* transition and balance in women's lives. We are hopeful that this comprehensive review of demographic and socioeconomic changes affecting women will provide a useful reference for readers interested in women's changing lives.

SUZANNE M. BIANCHI
DAPHNE SPAIN

Contents

List of Tables

List of Figures

AMERICAN WOMEN
IN TRANSITION

INTRODUCTION

A s WOMEN have taken on more roles outside the home, they have transformed society as well as their own lives. This monograph traces women's transition from the private domains of marriage and family life to the more public domains of higher education and paid employment. Fertility is at a historic low, while women's educational attainment and labor force participation are at an all-time high. These trends are the hallmark of an industrialized society and thus somewhat predictable. Yet the timing of the shift is important.

In the twenty years between the 1960 and 1980 censuses, the average number of children per American woman declined from over three to fewer than two (below replacement level), the proportion of women with a college degree doubled, and the proportion of women in the labor force increased dramatically. The greatest changes in labor force participation took place among women with children: In 1960, very few wives with children were in the labor force; by the early 1980s, one-half of wives with preschoolers and over three-fifths of wives with school-age children were working outside the home.

From both society's and the individual's standpoint, the structure of the family and the labor market have changed. Families are smaller and demands for child care are greater than they were in the past. Some traditionally male occupations are increasingly female. Greater participation in the labor force has resulted in different expectations and demands by women, which in turn have produced efforts at social change. The women's movement of the 1960s gave birth to the Equal Rights Amendment legislation of the 1970s, but the ERA had been defeated by the time this book was completed in 1985.

The typical adult woman now works for wages in addition to caring for a husband, children, and home. For the past century, nearly 90 percent of all women have married by age 30 and between 80 and 90 percent have become mothers by age 40, but the addition of labor force duties is relatively new. For the majority of women, time is now split between family obligations and work responsibilities. Women's time is also split in ways that men's time is not: Wives who are employed full time spend nearly twice as many hours per week on housework as husbands do.

If taking care of a family and home are traditionally important tasks to society and the individual, and if paid labor force participation is becoming increasingly important, how do women combine both successfully? Many women refer to their lives as a "balancing act" between family and work responsibilities. The ability to juggle competing demands often depends on taking traditionally female jobs, such as teaching and nursing, to ensure working hours compatible with childrearing. Approximately half of all employed women work part time or for only part of the year, another possible adaptation to the conflicting needs for income and for family caretaking.

Delayed age at marriage and delayed childbearing may be other adaptations to competing roles. By remaining single longer, women can pursue schooling and work without family responsibilities. Average age at first marriage rose from 20 to 23 between 1960 and 1983, suggesting that women were beginning to take advantage of increased opportunities in education and in the labor force. The proportion of women in their early 20s who had never married almost doubled between 1960 and 1980 and continued to increase sharply through 1983.

More young women are also remaining childless. Only 25 percent of ever-married women aged 20 to 24 were childless in 1960, but that figure had risen to 42 percent by 1980. Later childbearing allows women more time to establish themselves in the labor force and is associated with increased economic assets for couples.

Those who see women's work outside the home as contributing to marital instability might argue that divorce is another adaptation to conflicting roles for women. Divorce rates have risen, and 7 percent of all women were currently divorced in 1980 compared with just 3 percent in 1960. But women who are divorced from their husbands are seldom divorced from their children; most children of divorced parents live with their mother. If anything, the divorced woman is likely to have more problems reconciling work and home life than a married woman. Also, women usually experience a reduction in their standard of living following divorce.

Whether by choice of later marriage or necessity due to divorce or widowhood, an increasing proportion of women are maintaining their own households. The proportion of households maintained by a woman increased from about 17 percent in 1960 to 25 percent in 1980. Older widowed women have one of the highest rates of maintaining separate households: In 1960, 60 percent of unmarried women aged 65 and over, most of whom are widowed, lived independently; that figure had risen to approximately 80 percent by 1980.

Women have made great strides in educational attainment: The proportion of women who were college educated doubled from 6 to 13 percent between 1960 and 1980. This improvement is somewhat tempered by the fact that there is still a fairly large discrepancy between the proportion of men and women who complete four or more years of college. In 1960 there was a 4 percentage point difference between men and women, but by 1980 that gap had widened to almost 8 percentage points. Nevertheless, women's rates of college enrollment were equal to those of men by 1980, a promising sign for future equality in graduation trends.

Increasing educational achievements are partly responsible for women's increased labor force participation. Between 1960 and 1980, the proportion of women in the labor force increased from 38 to 52 percent. Since 1970, women have become much less likely to leave the labor force once they have entered, which suggests that women are becoming more committed to working outside the home. The greatest changes occurred among married women with children, a group traditionally the least likely to be employed.

Changes for women in marital status, fertility, living arrangements, education, and labor force participation have all been more dramatic than changes in earnings. The ratio of female earnings to male earnings has remained remarkably stable over time. Whether one uses annual earnings, weekly earnings, or annual income, women on average make 70 percent or less of what men make when both are working full time. Common explanations for this difference are that women enter and leave the labor force more frequently than men, resulting in less work experience; women's skills, education, and training are not equal to those of men; and women are concentrated in relatively low-paying occupations compared with men. Some researchers believe that earnings differences may also arise from sex discrimination.

Whatever the reason for the discrepancy between men's and women's income, its persistence makes the balancing act particularly difficult for women who maintain independent households. Part-time employment may not be a financial option for women who support dependents by themselves, and increased work responsibilities are complicated by the lack of a husband to help with child care. Add to this the fact that most working women do not earn as much as most working men and that fewer than one-half of divorced mothers who were awarded child support in 1981 received the full amount due, and it becomes apparent why the average female householder often faces serious economic difficulty. Poverty rates among women who maintain households are higher than for households maintained by men or by husband-wife couples, and women and their children constitute an increasing proportion of the poverty population.

In sum, this volume documents a period of history in which large numbers of women are moving rapidly into the paid labor force and independent living arrangements, but are not giving up traditional homemaking and mothering roles. Many Americans still expect women to be unpaid caretakers in the home, but now also expect them to be paid workers outside the home. Just as research has shown that American families are "here to stay,"[1] it appears that working women are also here to stay. The challenge for the future is to find a reconciliation between the roles of wife and mother and that of wage earner.

Overview

Previous series of Census monographs have not included a separate volume on women. A wide variety of data for women were

---

[1]Mary Jo Bane, *Here to Stay: American Families in the Twentieth Century* (New York: Basic Books, 1976).

available in monographs on the family, education, and the labor force, but not until 1980 were changes in women's roles considered sufficiently important to warrant the introduction of a specialized volume. Indeed, in the past, a woman's arena was primarily in the home and was almost synonymous with "marriage and the family." But extensive social changes have taken place between the monographs written after the 1940 census and today; much of that change occurred since the last monographs based on the 1960 census were published. This book summarizes the major demographic and social changes for women in the post–World War II period and presents them in one integrated reference work.

The monograph is organized around the theme of women's transition from the private spheres of home and family to the more public spheres of education and work for pay. Chapters 1 through 3 review changes in marital status, fertility, and household living arrangements, documenting the trend toward delayed marriage, higher divorce rates, lower and later fertility, and greater independence in living arrangements. These chapters cover the roles of wife, mother, and caregiver traditionally held by women. They show that the vast majority of women continue to marry and have children, but do so at later ages than they did in the past. Partly due to delayed marriage and higher divorce rates, more women are maintaining their own households now. While chapters 1 and 2 show support for continued commitment to marriage and the family, chapter 3 challenges the assumption that most women are cared for by others, first by their fathers and then by their husbands. The increase in the proportion of households maintained by women reflects today's more independent lifestyles.

These changes in living arrangements set the stage for chapters 4, 5, and 6, which focus on the increasingly public roles women are playing by attending college, participating in the labor force, and earning a living. Historically, women have had higher rates of high school graduation than men, but lower rates of college enrollment and completion. Women have now caught up with men in college enrollment rates and continue their progress in earning degrees (although completion rates are still lower than men's). Partly due to greater educational attainment, women's labor force participation rates have increased dramatically in the past twenty years. Changes in education and the labor force, however, have been more significant than changes in earnings: Women continue to earn considerably less than men, and this earnings difference has a particularly harsh impact on households in which women are the primary earners.

Chapters 7 and 8 examine the outcome of the overlap between women's private and public roles by reviewing the relationship between household living arrangements, income, and poverty and between fertility and labor force participation. The concluding chapter speculates on the balance struck by women in their attempt to integrate private and public roles. We say "speculate" because the census data which form the core of this book do not address sociological or psychological correlates of the demographic changes summarized. Our framework focuses on transition and balance: The subtitle of the book could be "The Balancing Act" to reflect the challenge of competing roles that women face today.

Data and Analysis

Sources of Data

We rely primarily on three types of data. First, we rely on data collected in the decennial census of 1980. We also rely quite heavily on the 1960 and 1970 and, to a lesser extent, the 1940 and 1950 Censuses of Population. Microdata tapes from the 1960, 1970, and 1980 censuses are used to supplement information available in published form. Although microdata tapes from the 1940 and 1950 censuses now exist, they were not available at the beginning of this project. Thus, as a practical measure, we restrict many of our analyses to the 1960–80 period. The 1960s and 1970s were decades of very rapid change in women's lives, which makes this period a particularly relevant time frame for analysis. Also, because the last census monographs were produced after the 1960 census, there is greater need to document changes that have occurred since that time.

Second, at various points in the analysis, we use Current Population Survey (CPS) data to add to the picture afforded by the decennial censuses at ten-year intervals and to extend trends through the early 1980s. The CPS is a monthly household survey which has been conducted since the late 1940s. It is primarily designed to produce information on employment and unemployment, but information on a variety of additional topics is collected in regular supplements to the survey. For example, marital history supplements to the June

1971, 1975, and 1980 CPS provide information that augments the picture of changing marriage patterns during the 1970s, a decade of particularly rapid increase in divorce. School enrollment supplements to the October CPS enrich the analysis of educational change for women; fertility supplements to the June CPS aid in understanding recent changes in the timing of childbearing; and income and child support supplements to the March and April CPS provide information on the economic well-being of families, in particular those maintained by women.

In addition to the census and CPS, data collected by federal agencies other than the Bureau of the Census are utilized where relevant. For example, data from the vital registration system of birth, deaths, marriages, and divorces, collected by the National Center for Health Statistics (NCHS), complement information on marital status, age at first marriage, number of times married, and children ever born collected in the decennial censuses. Data on the conferral of college degrees, collected by the National Center for Educational Statistics (NCES), augment data on school enrollment and educational attainment collected in the census and CPS.

The advantages of multiple sources of information must, of course, be weighed against the disadvantages, the major one being that information collected in the CPS or through registration of vital events is not always consistent with information provided by the decennial censuses. For example, labor force information is collected in both the decennial censuses and the CPS and, although definitions used are similar in the two sources, the resultant CPS and census labor force participation rates differ. Typically, rates obtained from the census are sightly lower than rates from the CPS. Major trends appear regardless of which source is used, but we rely on the more sensitive, year-to-year readings provided by CPS data. In general, because the CPS is devoted to monitoring the labor force, we consider it the superior data source. Throughout the monograph, when data from other sources are clearly superior to the census or when information is not collected in the census but is available from either vital statistics or the CPS, we turn to the auxiliary source.

Period Versus Cohort Analysis

In order to interpret trends presented in subsequent chapters, it is important to distinguish between period and cohort measures. A cohort is a group of people who experience the same event (birth, marriage, entry into the labor force) during the same period of time. Persons born between 1950 and 1959 form the core of the "baby boom" cohort, for example. All persons who marry during a given year can be thought of as a marriage cohort.

A cohort effect is any feature of a group of people that distinguishes their experiences from those of other cohorts. For example, women who reached childbearing age during the Depression had very low fertility, with consequences which persisted throughout their lives. Cohort analysis describes a group's experience of an event over time: If, for instance, we use the 1960 census to calculate the proportion of persons aged 20 who had never married, the 1970 census to calculate the proportion of persons aged 30 who remained single, and the 1980 census to calculate the proportion of persons aged 40 who still had not married, we would be doing cohort analysis. That is, we would be tracking the actual first marriage experience of the birth cohort of 1940.

Whereas cohort analysis provides a "lifetime picture" of an event, period analysis provides a "snapshot" of an event at a particular point in time. That is, period analysis describes an event as represented by many groups at one point in time: For example, if we used the 1980 census to calculate the proportion of persons aged 20, 30, and 40 who had not yet married, we again would be focusing on first-marriage experience but as represented by several birth cohorts (those born in 1960, 1950, and 1940). The first-marriage rates calculated would be period rates.

Period and cohort data often differ only in the way the data are grouped. Sometimes period analysis is all that is feasible because adequate historical data necessary for cohort analysis are missing. For example, many of the tables in subsequent chapters provide only a "snapshot" at ten-year intervals. By covering three (sometimes five) census dates in this monographs, however, it is possible to conduct limited cohort analysis. We attempt to provide a cohort perspective, or at least a discussion of the ways in which the period data may be misleading, wherever possible.

1

MARRIAGE PATTERNS

WHY BEGIN a monograph on women's *changing* lives by focusing first on their most traditional role as wives? Because, with the exception of motherhood, no other status is so universally assumed by women. Today, 90 percent of American women marry by age 30, a proportion that has remained fairly constant for the past century.[1]

It is also true that nearly 90 percent of adult men marry, but marriage has different implications for women and men. Early childhood socialization places more emphasis on marriage for girls than for boys,[2] and young women are more likely than young men to evaluate "having a good marriage and family life" as extremely important.[3] Marital and family status has greater economic consequences for women, since marriage is more often a source of financial secu-

[1] Andrew Cherlin, *Marriage, Divorce, Remarriage* (Cambridge, MA: Harvard University Press, 1981); and John Modell, Frank Furstenberg, and Douglas Strong, "The Timing of Marriage in the Transition to Adulthood: Continuity and Change, 1860–1975," in John Demos and Sarane Spence Boocock, eds., *Turning Points* (Chicago: University of Chicago Press, 1978), pp. S120–50.

[2] Kay Schaffer, *Sex Roles and Human Behavior* (Cambridge, MA: Winthrop, 1981); and Shirley Weitz, *Sex Roles: Biological, Psychological, and Social Foundations* (New York: Oxford University Press, 1977).

[3] Arland Thornton and Deborah Freedman, "Changing Attitudes toward Marriage and Single Life," *Family Planning Perspectives* 14 (November-December 1982):297–303.

rity for women than men. Historically, most married women never worked outside the home because their husbands were expected to support them financially, implicitly in exchange for domestic caretaking.[4] Opinion polls conducted in 1939 reported that one-half to two thirds of Americans did not approve of married women working if their husbands earned a sufficient income to support the family.[5] Attitudes have changed, but marriage continues to influence women's economic activities. In 1981, wives were less likely to be in the labor force than unmarried women, regardless of age or presence of children.[6]

The vast majority of women marry, but the timing and duration of marriages have changed over time. For example, the median age at first marriage has risen, and the average duration of a marriage in the early 1970s was four years less than in the early 1960s.[7] More variation in marriage patterns exists today than was true in the past. Cohabitation before marriage, delaying marriage, and not marrying at all are becoming more socially acceptable.[8] Divorce is more common now, and remarriage follows divorce or widowhood for an increasing number of women.

All of these changes combine to alter the centrality of marriage for women at different stages of the life cycle. Such shifts also have important implications for society. Changes in women's marital status are linked to changes in labor force participation and fertility. Those linkages will be explored more fully in later chapters. First, however, basic trends in the first marriage, divorce, remarriage, and widowhood experiences of American women are reviewed.

First Marriage

Women are now marrying two and one-half years later, on average, than they did twenty years ago. Median age at first marriage,

---

[4]Gary S. Becker, "A Theory of Marriage," in Theodore W. Schultz, ed., *Economics of the Family* (Chicago: University of Chicago Press, 1974), pp. 299–344; and David M. Heer, "The Measurement and Bases of Family Power: An Overview," *Journal of Marriage and the Family* 25 (May 1963):133–39.

[5]Valerie K. Oppenheimer, *The Female Labor Force in the United States* (Westport, CT: Greenwood Press, 1970).

[6]Kristin A. Moore, Daphne Spain, and Suzanne M. Bianchi, "Working Wives and Mothers," *Marriage and Family Review* 7 (Fall-Winter 1984):77–98.

[7]Thomas J. Espenshade, "Marriage, Divorce, and Remarriage from Retrospective Data: A Multiregional Approach," *Environment and Planning A* 15 (December 1983):1633–52.

[8]Arland Thornton and Deborah Freedman, "The Changing American Family," *Population Bulletin*, vol. 38, no. 4 (Washington, DC: Population Reference Bureau, 1983).

which was 20.3 for women in 1960, gradually increased during the 1960s, but by 1970 it was still only 20.8. By 1983 it had jumped to 22.8, higher for women than it has been at any time in American history.[9]

A better indicator of delayed marriage is the increase in the proportion of young adults who remain single. Between 1950 and 1983, the proportion of women aged 20 to 24 who had never married rose substantially (from 32 to 56 percent). (See Table 1.1.) Men have also been delaying entry into marriage. By 1983, almost three quarters of men aged 20 to 24 had never married compared with about one-half of women. At ages 25 to 29, almost two-fifths of men compared with one-quarter of women were still single in 1983.

Because they marry at younger ages than men, women continue to have fewer years than men do prior to marriage in which to complete higher education and establish themselves in the labor force or in an independent household. However, women's age-at-marriage patterns have become more like those of men during the last two decades, partly as a result of their increased college enrollment and labor force participation.

One-quarter of women marry by the age of 19 or 20, and this has not changed since the early 1960s. But the age by which three-quar-

[9]The median ages at first marriage which are reported are approximations derived indirectly from census and CPS tabulations of marital status and age. The proportion ever married among persons 45 to 54 years old is used to estimate the proportion of young people who will eventually marry. One-half of this expected proportion is calculated and the current age of young men and women who are at this halfway mark is computed. See U.S. Bureau of the Census, "Marital Status and Living Arrangements: March 1983," *Current Population Reports,* series P-20, no. 389 (Washington, DC: U.S. Government Printing Office, 1984), table A.

An alternative series of median ages of brides and grooms at first marriage, based on marriage records from States participating in the Marriage Registration Area (MRA), is published by the National Center for Health Statistics (NCHS). Although trends are similar, median ages differ from those estimated from the census and the CPS. For example, the registration data indicate a somewhat smaller rise in median age at first marriage than do CPS figures. According to the vital registration data, the median age of brides at first marriage rose from 20.3 to 22.0 between 1963 and 1980. For the series, extending from 1963 to 1981, see National Center for Health Statistics, "Advance Report of Final Marriage Statistics, 1981," *Monthly Vital Statistics Report,* vol. 32, no. 11, supplement (Washington, DC: U.S. Government Printing Office, 1984), table 5.

We have chosen to report the census/CPS median ages for two reasons. First, the series extends back to 1890 allowing for a longer historical perspective. Second, the NCHS series is unadjusted for changes in the age distribution of the population. Median ages are based on the absolute numbers of men and women who marry in a given year. In recent years, as the large baby boom cohorts have reached young adult ages, the number of marriages accounted for by younger age groups has increased disproportionately. Thus, median ages estimated from the number of marriages in recent years may be artificially low, in part accounting for the differences between vital registration data on age of brides and grooms and census/CPS estimates of median age at first marriage.

TABLE 1.1

Changes in the Percentage of Americans Who Have Never Married

Race and Age	Women					Men				
	1950	1960	1970	1980	1983	1950	1960	1970	1980	1983
ALL RACES										
Total, 15 Years and Over	18.5%	17.3%	20.6%	22.9%	22.9%	24.9%	23.2%	26.4%	29.7%	30.0%
15–19 Years	82.9	83.9	88.1	91.2	93.4	96.7	96.1	95.9	97.2	98.1
20–24 Years	32.3	28.4	36.3	51.2	55.5	59.0	53.1	55.5	68.2	73.2
25–29 Years	13.3	10.5	12.2	21.6	24.8	23.8	20.8	19.6	32.1	38.2
30–34 Years	9.3	6.9	7.4	10.6	13.0	13.2	11.9	10.7	14.9	19.6
35 Years and Over	8.2	7.2	6.5	5.7	5.2	8.8	7.8	7.1	6.3	6.1
WHITE										
Total, 15 Years and Over	18.5	17.0	19.9	21.2	21.1	24.7	22.6	25.6	28.0	28.4
15–19 Years	83.5	83.9	88.0	90.7	92.8	96.8	96.1	95.9	97.2	97.9
20–24 Years	32.4	27.4	35.1	48.6	52.2	59.5	52.6	54.9	66.9	71.1
25–29 Years	13.1	9.8	10.8	19.2	21.8	23.6	20.0	18.7	30.5	35.5
30–34 Years	9.3	6.6	6.7	9.1	10.9	13.1	11.3	10.0	13.8	18.3
35 Years and Over	8.5	7.4	6.4	5.3	4.8	8.9	7.6	6.8	5.8	5.8
BLACK										
Total, 15 Years and Over	18.8	20.0	26.2	34.1	36.0	26.6	28.3	32.9	40.6	42.4
15–19 Years	78.9	83.8	88.6	95.1	96.9	95.6	96.2	95.5	98.0	99.6
20–24 Years	31.2	35.4	43.6	67.5	75.3	54.7	57.1	58.4	77.8	85.2
25–29 Years	14.1	15.7	21.3	37.0	42.6	25.2	27.6	25.4	42.6	56.6
30–34 Years	8.9	9.6	12.8	21.5	27.2	14.4	17.2	16.1	23.1	29.3
35 Years and Over	5.2	6.1	7.1	8.4	9.0	7.9	9.5	9.5	9.8	8.8

NOTE: Data for 1983 are from the Current Population Survey and not strictly comparable to census data for earlier years; data for 1950 and 1960 are for nonwhites.

SOURCE: U.S. Bureau of the Census, *Census of Population: 1950, vol. 2, pt. 1,* U.S. Summary, table 104; *Census of Population: 1960, vol. 1, pt. 1,* U.S. Summary, table 176; *Census of Population: 1970, vol. 1, pt. 1,* U.S. Summary, table 203; *Census of Population: 1980, vol. 1, chap. D,* U.S. Summary, table 264; "Marital Status and Living Arrangements: March 1983," *Current Population Reports,* series P-20, no. 389, table 1.

ters of a cohort of women have married increased from 23 to 27 years between 1963 and 1982, with most of this upward movement occurring during the 1970s. In the early 1960s, there was a span of about four years, between ages 19 and 23, in which most women married compared with a span of about six years, between ages 20 and 26, in which most men married. By the early 1980s, the span of years over which most women entered a first marriage had lengthened by about three years compared with an increase of a little over one year for men. Most women were marrying between ages 20 and 27; men were marrying between ages 22 and 29 or 30. As a result, the length of time it took a cohort of women to marry became much closer to the length of time it took for a cohort of men to marry.[10]

A 23-year-old woman in 1963 who had not yet married was in the minority; for every such unmarried woman, there were three married women. By 1982, a woman of the same age who was not married was almost as typical as one who had married.

International Comparisons

The United States is similar to other industrialized nations in the trend toward delayed marriage.[11] Teenage marriages are now fairly rare, and at least one-half of all persons aged 20 to 24 have not yet married in Western nations. Table 1.2 presents international data for the most recent years available.

In the United States, Canada, France, and Great Britain, the proportion of persons aged 20 to 24 who are unmarried is similar. In all four nations, about one-half of women and three-quarters of men are still single at age 20 to 24. A common factor among all industrialized nations is an improved educational status for women and growing rates of female labor force participation.

Scandinavian countries have the highest proportion of young women who have never married, possibly because of high rates of cohabitation.[12] Among Swedes aged 20 to 24 in 1981, 85 percent of

---

[10]U.S. Bureau of the Census, "Marital Status and Living Arrangements: March 1982," *Current Population Reports*, series P-20, no. 380 (Washington, DC: U.S. Government Printing Office, 1983), table C.

[11]Ann K. Blanc, "The Impact of Changing Family Patterns on Reproductive Behavior: Nonmarital Cohabitation and Fertility in Norway," paper presented at the annual meeting of the Population Association of America, Minneapolis, May 2–5, 1984; and Charles F. Westoff, "Marriage and Fertility in the Developed Countries," *Scientific American* 239 (June 1978):51–57.

[12]Blanc, "Changing Family Patterns"; and Cherlin, *Marriage, Divorce, Remarriage.*

TABLE 1.2

Percentage of the Population Never Married, for Selected Countries

	Women			Men		
Country and Date	15–19 Years Old	20–24 Years Old	45–49 Years Old	15–19 Years Old	20–24 Years Old	45–49 Years Old
United States, 1982	92.0%	53.4%	4.1%	97.5%	72.0%	5.4%
Canada, 1980	95.6	55.2	5.7	99.1	76.1	7.3
France, 1980	95.4	51.4	7.3	99.6	74.3	10.8
West Germany, 1980	96.4	60.1	6.4	99.6	84.2	7.3
Sweden, 1981	99.3	84.8	7.1	99.9	95.0	12.8
Denmark, 1982	99.1	78.3	5.1	99.9	92.4	9.1
Norway, 1981	97.9	64.6	5.2	99.8	85.7	10.6
United Kingdom, 1981	95.5	53.7	5.7	98.9	74.8	8.9
Japan, 1980	99.0	77.7	4.4	99.6	91.5	3.1
Hungary, 1981	85.7	30.9	3.7	98.2	66.1	5.3
East Germany, 1980	95.1	39.1	6.0	99.1	67.7	3.5

SOURCE: United Nations, *Demographic Yearbook 1982* (New York: United Nations, 1984), table 24.

women and 95 percent of men were still single. The relatively low proportion of older Scandinavians not married suggests that cohabitation is one stage in a life cycle that eventually includes marriage.

Japan has a similarly high proportion of unmarried young people, but the explanation in Japan is that delayed marriage became part of the "multiphasic response" to demographic pressures after the war.[13] Rather than cohabit, the Japanese live at home longer with their parents before marriage.

In contrast to Western European, Scandinavian, and North American countries, members of Eastern bloc nations marry early. In Hungary and in East Germany only 30 to 40 percent of young women were single in the early 1980s. These countries are pronatalist and encourage early marriage and childbearing to offset current and future population losses.

Black-White Differences in First-Marriage Patterns

For individual birth years from 1880 to 1960, Thornton and Rodgers have calculated the quartiles of the first-marriage distribu-

[13]Kingsley Davis, "The Theory of Change and Response in Modern Demographic History," *Population Index* 29 (October 1963):345–65.

tion of White and Black women in the United States.[14] During this period, one-quarter of White women married by age 18 and one-half married by age 23, while one-quarter of Black women married by age 17 and one-half by age 25. Black women thus have a wider range of ages at first marriage than White women. The age at which three-quarters of all women were married was as late as 29 for both Blacks and Whites among women born in the last century. The age steadily declined and reached a low of 23 for White women and 24 for Black women born in the 1930s (that is, those of marriageable age during the 1950s), before beginning to rise again for women born during the baby boom. Black women are now delaying marriage (though not motherhood) longer than White women. For women born in 1953, three-quarters of White women were married by age 26 and three-quarters of Black women were married by age 28.[15]

Lifetime Singlehood

The recent increase in the proportion of adults in their 20s and early 30s who have never married combined with increasingly favorable attitudes toward single life have led to speculation that a higher proportion of adults are remaining single throughout life now than was true in the past.[16]

It is unlikely that women born in the 1950s and early 1960s will end up with as high a proportion married as women born in the 1930s who came of marriageable age after World War II. However, it is still unclear whether the proportion who never marry will rise above the historical maximum of 10 percent. Table 1.1 shows that among persons aged 35 and over, the proportion never married declined between the censuses of 1950 and 1980, at least for Whites. Among women over 65, about 9 percent had never married in 1950 compared with 7 percent in 1980. (See Appendix Table 1.A at the end of this chapter.) These differences are admittedly small, but the trend is the same for each five-year age group over 39 for men as

[14]Arland Thornton and Willard Rodgers, "Changing Patterns of Marriage and Divorce in the United States," final report prepared for the National Institute of Child Health and Human Development (Ann Arbor: Institute for Social Research, 1983); Willard L. Rodgers and Arland Thornton, "Changing Patterns of First Marriage in the United States," *Demography* 22 (May 1985): 265–79.

[15]Thornton and Rodgers, "Changing Patterns of Marriage."

[16]U.S. Bureau of the Census, "Marital Status: March 1982," p. 1; and Thornton and Freedman, "The Changing American Family."

well as women. These trends do not suggest that lifetime singlehood is increasing, but it is difficult to speculate since the data reflect a mix of cohort and period experiences.

Causes and Correlates of Delayed Marriage

There are numerous explanations for the current postponement of marriage. The 1970s were a period of great social change for women. The reincarnation of the women's movement, which emerged in the late 1960s and gained strength in the early 1970s, was one agent of these changes. A goal of the movement was to demonstrate that women had alternatives to being wives and mothers. Whether an individual woman considered herself a "feminist" or not, the climate created by the movement opened new educational, occupational, and legal options for all women.

Heer and Grossbard-Shechtman propose that the women's movement operated in conjunction with various other demographic and social factors to increase the attractiveness of alternatives to the traditional roles of wife and mother.[17] Advances in contraceptive technology contributed to the ability to avoid unplanned pregnancies,[18] which in turn led to more favorable attitudes toward sex before marriage and cohabitation as an alternative.

Demographers such as Glick and Norton and Shoen also point to the "marriage squeeze" as a factor in delayed marriage.[19] That is, women typically marry men a few years older than themselves. As successive cohorts have increased in size, there has been a relative dearth of young men for women to marry. As children of the "baby bust" grow older this situation will reverse and there will be a relative shortage of young women in the future. However, it is not clear how much a factor this is—in response to changes in the pool of eligible men, women probably adjust not only the age at which they

[17]David M. Heer and Amyra Grossbard-Schechtman, "The Impact of the Female Marriage Squeeze and the Contraceptive Revolution on Sex Roles and the Women's Liberation Movement in the United States, 1960 to 1975," *Journal of Marriage and the Family* 43 (February 1981):49–66.

[18]Charles F. Westoff and Norman B. Ryder, *The Contraceptive Revolution* (Princeton, NJ: Princeton University Press, 1977); and Charles F. Westoff, "The Decline of Unplanned Births in the United States," *Science* 191 (January 9, 1976):38–41.

[19]Paul C. Glick and Arthur J. Norton, "Marrying, Divorcing, and Living Together in the U.S. Today," *Population Bulletin*, vol. 32, no. 5 (Washington, DC: Population Reference Bureau, 1977); and Robert Schoen, "Measuring the Tightness of a Marriage Squeeze," *Demography* 20 (February 1983):61–78.

marry but also their expectations about the age difference that should separate brides from grooms.

Economic factors may have contributed to the delay in marriage. Easterlin has proposed that the depressed economic conditions of the 1970s combined with the labor market entry problems of the large baby boom cohort reaching adulthood made it difficult for young people to marry and start a family while maintaining the standard of living they had come to expect from growing up in relatively affluent homes.[20]

Schooling is also related to age at marriage: The higher a woman's educational attainment, the older she tends to be when she first marries.[21] College enrollment rates have increased for women over the last two decades and hence more women are still in school in their late teens and early 20s. Typically, marriage does not occur until after schooling is finished, although this "normative ordering" may be violated as persons stay in school longer.[22] Causality probably runs in both directions: Early marriage often leads a woman to curtail her schooling. Conversely, a college education exposes a woman to a variety of experiences, in particular greater employment opportunities, which may reduce her interest in an early marriage.

Another correlate of delayed marriage is parental resources. Waite and Spitze found that the higher a family's educational and occupational status (and hence their potential financial resources), the later their daughters tend to marry.[23]

Data on the substitution of work for marriage are contradictory. In an aggregate analysis, Preston and Richards found that areas with attractive employment for women had lower proportions of young women ever married.[24] Waite and Spitze, however, found that em-

---

[20]Richard A. Easterlin, "What Will 1984 Be Like? Sociological Implications of Recent Twists in Age Structure," *Demography* 15 (November 1978):379–432.

[21]Andrew Cherlin, "Postponing Marriage: The Influence of Young Women's Work Expectations," *Journal of Marriage and the Family* 42 (May 1980):355–65; Margaret M. Marini, "The Transition to Adulthood: Sex Differences in Educational Attainment and Age at Marriage," *American Sociological Review* 43 (August 1978):483–507; and James A. Sweet, "Demography and the Family," in Alex Inkeles, ed., *Annual Review of Sociology*, vol. 3 (Palo Alto, CA: Annual Reviews, 1977), pp. 363–406.

[22]Dennis P. Hogan, "The Variable Order of Events in the Life Course," *American Sociological Review* 43 (August 1978):573–86; and Dennis P. Hogan, "The Transition to Adulthood as a Career Contingency," *American Sociological Review* 45 (April 1980):261–75.

[23]Linda J. Waite and Glenna D. Spitze, "Young Women's Transition to Marriage," *Demography* 18 (November 1981):681–94.

[24]Samuel H. Preston and Alan T. Richards, "The Influence of Women's Work Opportunities on Marriage Rates," *Demography* 12 (May 1975):209–22.

ployment can act to increase a single woman's contacts with eligible men and thus increase the likelihood of marriage.[25] Some family theorists have suggested that women's labor force participation actually encourages earlier marriage by increasing the household's potential resources.[26] On the other hand, the increase in female labor force participation means that more women are financially independent and do not view marriage as a way of being cared for. Some would argue that marriage, therefore, may provide less economic utility to women—and to men—in a situation in which both partners work outside the home versus one in which husbands specialize in market work and wives in nonmarket work.[27]

Future plans and preferences to work later in life appear to result in a postponement of marriage. Young women are much more likely now than they were in the past to say that they want to work instead of being housewives. The proportion of women in their early 20s who planned to be housewives (versus those who planned to work outside the home) declined from about one-half to one-quarter for Whites and from about one-half to one-fifth for Blacks between 1969 and 1975. Changes in work plans were greatest for women with the most education.[28]

Attitudinal and lifestyle variables may also be related to the delay in marriage and more independent living. The high divorce rate may dissuade people from early marriage, and lifetime singlehood may be a more acceptable option now than it was in the past. Attitudinal data spanning the past two decades show that people have become less negative toward remaining single and are less likely to choose the married state as preferable to the single state.[29]

The demographic consequences of later marriage are fairly clear.

[25]Waite and Spitze, "Young Women's Transition to Marriage."

[26]Kingsley Davis, "The American Family in Relation to Demographic Change," in Charles F. Westoff and Robert Parke, eds., *Demographic and Social Aspects of Population Growth*, Commission on Population Growth and the American Future, vol. 1 (Washington, DC: U.S. Government Printing Office, 1972), pp. 235–65; William F. Goode, *World Revolution and Family Patterns* (New York: Free Press, 1963); and Judith Sklar, "Marriage Regulation and the California Birth Rate," in Kingsley Davis and Frederick G. Styles, eds., *California's Twenty Million: Research Contributions to Population Policy* (Berkeley: Institute of International Studies, University of California, 1971), pp. 165–206.

[27]Becker, "Theory of Marriage;" Gary S. Becker, Elizabeth M. Landes, and Robert T. Michael, "An Economic Analysis of Marital Instability," *Journal of Political Economy* 85 (December 1977):1141–87; and Gary S. Becker, *A Treatise on the Family* (Cambridge, MA: Harvard University Press, 1981).

[28]Cherlin, "Postponing Marriage"; and Waite and Spitze, "Young Women's Transition to Marriage."

[29]Thornton and Freedman, "Changing Attitudes Toward Marriage."

Later marriage tends to lower the risk of divorce[30] and result in later childbearing and smaller families.[31] For example, women aged 50 to 54 in 1980 who had married at age 18 or 19 averaged 3.3 children, while women who had married in their early 30s averaged 1.9 children.[32] Later age at marriage may also provide more time to consider life choices like motherhood and labor force participation.

Cohabitation

Current delays in marriage are similar to turn-of-the-century patterns. What is unusual from a historical standpoint is the current alternative to early marriage: cohabitation. The practice of men and women living together before (or instead of) marriage is a growing trend which may account for part of the delay in age at first marriage.[33] The actual number of unmarried couples living together more than tripled between 1960 and 1983, from 439,000 to 1.9 million (see Figure 1.1). About 4 percent of all couples in 1981 were unmarried, a figure that had doubled in five years.

Living together as husband and wife without legal sanction of marriage has become more socially acceptable in the past twenty years, primarily among younger adults. One-quarter of men and nearly two-fifths of cohabiting women in 1981 were under age 25.[34] Unmarried cohabitation appears to have gained momentum among college students in the 1960s.[35] By the mid-1970s, estimates were

[30]Larry L. Bumpass and James A. Sweet, "Differentials in Marital Instability: 1970," *American Sociological Review* 37 (December 1972):754–66; Kristin A. Moore and Linda J. Waite, "Marital Dissolution, Early Motherhood, and Early Marriage," *Social Forces* 60 (September 1981):20–40; and Elwood Carlson and Kandi Stinson, "Motherhood, Marriage Timing, and Marital Stability: A Research Note," *Social Forces* 61 (September 1982):258–67.

[31]Larry L. Bumpass, Ronald R. Rindfuss, and Richard B. Janosik, "Age and Marital Status at First Birth and the Pace of Subsequent Fertility," *Demography* 15 (February 1978):75–86; Westoff and Ryder, *Contraceptive Revolution*; and Margaret M. Marini and Peter J. Hodsdon, "Effects of the Timing of Marriage and First Birth on the Spacing of Subsequent Births," *Demography* 18 (November 1981):529–48.

[32]U.S. Bureau of the Census, "Fertility of American Women: June 1980," *Current Population Reports*, series P-20, no. 375 (Washington, DC: U.S. Government Printing Office, 1982), table 17.

[33]Paul C. Glick and Graham Spanier, "Married and Unmarried Cohabitation in the United States," *Journal of Marriage and the Family* 42 (February 1980):19–30.

[34]Graham Spanier, "Married and Unmarried Cohabitation in the United States: 1980," *Journal of Marriage and the Family* 45 (May 1983):277–88.

[35]Eleanor D. Macklin, "Heterosexual Cohabitation among Unmarried College Students," *Family Coordinator* 21 (October 1972):463–72.

FIGURE 1.1

Trend in Cohabitation

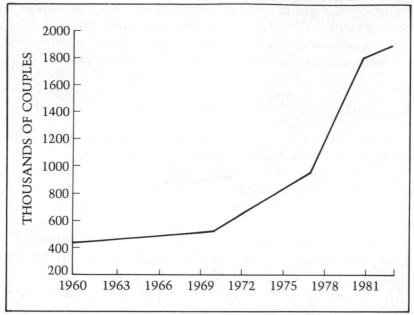

NOTE: Numbers for 1961–69 and 1971–75 are interpolated.

SOURCE: U.S. Bureau of the Census, *Census of Population: 1960*, PC(2)-4B, "Persons by Family Characteristics," table 15; *Census of Population: 1970*, PC(2)-4B, "Persons by Family Characteristics," table 11; "Marital Status and Living Arrangements," *Current Population Reports*, series P-20, no. 389, table G, no. 380, table G, no. 372, table F, no. 349, table E, no. 338, table D.

that almost one-quarter of college undergraduates had cohabited and another one-half would have done so if presented with the opportunity; only one-quarter objected to the practice on moral or religious grounds.[36] Spanier found that never-married women in a cohabiting relationship were more likely to have a college degree than either married women or cohabiting men and were most likely to be living with highly educated men. Young cohabiting women were also more likely to be in the labor force than young married women in 1980.[37] This evidence suggests that cohabitation is seen as an alternative or precursor to marriage for less traditional women interested in higher education and careers.

[36]Eleanor D. Macklin, "Nonmarital Heterosexual Cohabitation," *Marriage and Family Review* 1 (Spring 1978):1–12.
[37]Spanier, "Married and Unmarried Cohabitation."

Cohabitation may play a role in postponing second marriages as well as first marriages. Approximately one-half of all cohabiting individuals in 1981 had been previously married. Among women, the proportion never married (55 percent) somewhat exceeded those ever married (45 percent). Cohabitation that occurs after a previous marriage may involve children, although the majority of cohabiting couples do not have children and the proportion with children declined between 1970 and 1981.[38] The timing of cohabitation after (or between) marriages may reflect its flexibility as an option that suits people best at different stages of the life cycle. Cohabitation can provide the emotional security of an intimate relationship without the legal and economic ties of marriage.

Perhaps another attraction of cohabitation is that ending the relationship is easier legally than ending a marriage. Since there are no statistics on the number of cohabiting couples who split up, it is difficult to assess the relative frequency or style in which cohabiting relationships end. In contrast, there is no shortage of statistics on divorce. In recent years, it has become more common for marriages to end in divorce than through the death of a spouse.[39]

Divorce

Researchers agree that the incidence of divorce has reached an all-time high.[40] As shown in Figure 1.2, the divorce rate peaked after World War II but then declined to levels only slightly higher than prewar levels during the 1950s. However, rates began to increase rapidly during the late 1960s and 1970s. The actual number of divorces increased from 393,000 in 1960 to 1.2 million in 1981. In 1982 the number of divorces declined slightly for the first time in two decades (to 1.18 million), but the level remains very high by historical standards.[41] The divorce rate more than doubled, from 2.2 to 5.3 per

[38]Spanier, "Married and Unmarried Cohabitation."

[39]Cherlin, *Marriage, Divorce, Remarriage.*

[40]Cherlin, *Marriage, Divorce, Remarriage*; Thornton and Rodgers, "Changing Patterns of Marriage"; Paul C. Glick and Arthur J. Norton, "Perspectives on the Recent Upturn in Divorce and Remarriage," *Demography* 10 (August 1973):301–14; Samuel H. Preston and John McDonald, "The Incidence of Divorce Within Cohorts of American Marriages Contracted Since the Civil War," *Demography* 16 (February 1979):1–25; and Robert T. Michael, "The Rise in Divorce Rates, 1960–1974: Age-Specific Components," *Demography* 15 (May 1978):177–82.

[41]National Center for Health Statistics, "Annual Summary of Births, Deaths, Marriages, and Divorces: United States, 1982," *Monthly Vital Statistics Report*, vol. 31, no. 13 (Washington, DC: U.S. Government Printing Office, 1983), p. 9.

FIGURE 1.2

Trend in U.S. Divorce Rates

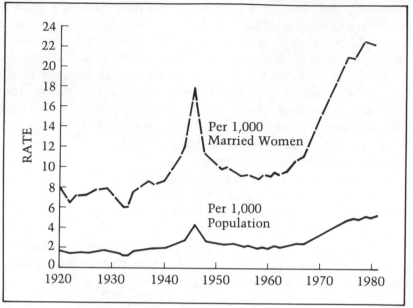

SOURCE: National Center for Health Statistics, "Advance Report of Final Divorce Statistics, 1981," *Monthly Vital Statistics Report,* vol. 32, no. 9, supplement (2) (January 1984), tables 1 and 10; U.S. Bureau of the Census, *Historical Statistics of the United States: Colonial Times to 1970,* Bicentennial Edition (Washington, DC: U.S. Government Printing Office, 1975), series B216-220.

1,000 persons, between 1960 and 1981 and then declined slightly to 5.0 in 1983.[42] If the denominator is refined to include only currently married women, between 1960 and 1981, the rate increased from 9.2 to 22.6 divorces per 1,000 married women aged 15 and over.[43] (See Figure 1.2.) The proportion of women who reported themselves as currently divorced rose from 2.9 percent of all those aged 15 and over in 1960 to 7.1 percent in 1980. Proportions are highest for women in their 30s and early 40s (see Appendix Table 1.A).

The total rate of marital dissolutions (number of marriages end-

[42]National Center for Health Statistics, "Annual Summary of Births, Deaths, Marriages, and Divorces: United States, 1983," *Monthly Vital Statistics Report,* vol. 32, no. 9 (Washington, DC: U.S. Government Printing Office, 1984), p. 1.

[43]The divorce rate per 1,000 married women reached its highest level, 28.8, in 1979. See National Center for Health Statistics, "Advance Report of Final Divorce Statistics, 1981," *Monthly Vital Statistics Report,* vol. 32, no. 9, supplement (Washington, DC: U.S. Government Printing Office, 1984), p. 12.

FIGURE 1.3

Percentage of Marriages Projected to End in Divorce

SOURCE: James A. Weed, "National Estimates of Marriage Dissolution and Survivorship: United States," *Vital and Health Statistics*, series 3, Analytical Studies, no. 19 (Washington, DC: National Center for Health Statistics, 1980), table A.

ing in divorce or death in a given year per 1,000 existing marriages) has not changed much over the past century. In the 1860s, for example, the combined rate was 34.5 dissolutions per 1,000 existing marriages, with death being the primary cause of dissolution.[44] By 1978 the total dissolution rate had risen slightly to 40.5. However, death rates have declined at the same time divorce rates have risen and, as a result, divorce has become the more important component. The 1970s were the first time in American history that more marriages ended every year in divorce than through death of a spouse.[45]

Figure 1.3 shows the steady increase in the proportion of mar-

[44]Mary Jo Bane, *Here to Stay: American Families in the Twentieth Century* (New York: Basic Books, 1976).
[45]Cherlin, *Marriage, Divorce, Remarriage.*

TABLE 1.3
Crude Divorce Rates for Selected Countries

Country	1963	1973	1981	1982
United States	2.3	4.3	5.3	5.1
Canada	0.4	1.7	2.8	—
France	0.6	1.0	1.6[a]	—
West Germany	0.9	1.4	1.8	—
East Germany	1.4	2.3	2.9	—
Sweden	1.1	2.0	2.4	2.6
Denmark	1.4	2.5	2.8	2.9
Norway	0.7	1.2	1.7	—
United Kingdom	0.7	2.1	2.9	—
Japan	0.7	1.0	1.3	—
Hungary	1.8	2.4	2.6	—
Australia	0.7	1.2	2.8	—
USSR	1.3	2.7	3.5	3.3

NOTE: Number of divorces per 1,000 population; [a] = 1979 data.

SOURCE: United Nations, *Demographic Yearbook 1982* (New York: United Nations, 1984), table 33.

riages projected to end in divorce.[46] Among marriages contracted in 1960, 39 percent are predicted to end through divorce, and current estimates are that almost 50 percent of marriages contracted during the 1970s will end in divorce.[47]

International Comparisons

The United States historically has had the highest divorce rate of any industralized nation, as Table 1.3 demonstrates. Although other countries experienced similar rises in rates over the past twenty years, none has reached the American level. The Soviet Union is second highest with a rate of 3.5 divorces per 1,000 population in 1981 and has recently experienced a slight decline similar to that in the United States.

Reasons for the high American divorce rate are the subject of

[46]For a full discussion of the techniques used to compute the projections of marriages ending in divorce, see James A. Weed, "National Estimates of Marriage Dissolution and Survivorship: United States," National Center for Health Statistics, *Vital and Health Statistics*, series 3, Analytic Studies, no. 19 (Washington, DC: U.S. Government Printing Office, 1980).

[47]Paul C. Glick, "Marriage, Divorce, and Living Arrangements," *Journal of Family Issues* 5 (March 1984):7–26; Samuel H. Preston, "Estimating the Proportion of American Marriages That End in Divorce," *Sociological Methods and Research* 3 (May 1975):435–60; and James A. Weed, "National Estimates."

extensive debate. One argument is that as more women enter the labor force and wives' earnings increase, the likelihood of divorce increases. Scandinavian countries, however, have a higher proportion of women in the labor force and a lower divorce rate than the United States, possibly because cohabitation is more prevalent. The Japanese divorce rate is currently lower than for any other industrialized nation, perhaps due to the traditionally high value placed on family stability.[48]

Rates like these point up the difficulties in making cross-cultural comparisons of divorce statistics. Marriage and divorce have different consequences depending on the society. The one common denominator in the steady rise of divorce rates around the world appears to be the growing tendency for both men and women to have equal rights to divorce.[49]

Black-White Differences in Divorce

Marital dissolution is more common among Blacks than Whites, whether dissolution is defined as separation or legal divorce. The divorce ratio (number of currently divorced persons per 1,000 currently married persons) for Black women in 1983 was 297 versus 126 for White women.[50] In other words, there were nearly 3 divorced Black women for every 10 intact Black marriages and just over 1 divorced White woman for every 10 intact White marriages in 1983. Black women are also about twice as likely as White women to be separated from their husbands and they tend to remain separated, without divorcing, longer than Whites.[51]

One of the reasons for higher Black marital dissolution rates is the higher rate of Black teenage and premarital pregnancies. Women whose first birth is out of wedlock are more likely to separate than those whose first birth occurred within marriage, and Black women are more likely than White women to give birth outside of marriage (see chapter 2 on childbearing). Thus young Black women face nu-

[48]Goode, *World Revolution.*
[49]Goode, *World Revolution.*
[50]U.S. Bureau of the Census, "Marital Status: March 1983," table C.
[51]James McCarthy, "A Comparison of the Probability of the Dissolution of First and Second Marriages," *Demography* 15 (August 1978):345–59; James McCarthy and Jane Menken, "Marriage, Remarriage, Marital Disruption and Age at First Birth," *Family Planning Perspectives* 11 (January-February 1979):21–30; and Martin O'Connell and Carolyn Rogers, "Out-of-Wedlock Births, Premarital Pregnancies, and Their Effect on Family Formation and Dissolution," *Family Planning Perspectives* 16 (July-August 1984):157.

merous obstacles to a long-lasting marriage: Compared with White women, they run a higher risk of a teenage pregnancy, a premarital pregnancy, an early marriage, and a separation or divorce.

Causes and Correlates of Divorce

One explanation for increasing rates of divorce is a change in attitudes: People have become more tolerant of divorce and less tolerant of unhappy marriages. Divorce no longer carries the stigma it once did when few couples divorced. However, as with all relationships between attitudes and behavior, the direction of causality is unclear. Cherlin cites public opinion poll data for 1945 and 1966 that showed little change in attitudes toward the fairness of current divorce laws, despite the rise in divorce rates in the early 1960s. By the early 1970s, the proportion of adults who believed that divorce should be "easier to obtain" had increased. Cherlin proposes that in this case liberalized attitudes followed changes in actual behavior.[52]

The more important factor in the rise in divorce rates may be changes in the female labor force during the past two decades. In recent years, the most dramatic increase in labor force participation has been among young, married women. Younger women are more likely than older women to divorce, and married women who are employed are more likely to divorce than those who are housewives.[53] Husbands' and wives' thoughts of divorce increase with the wife's work experience, and a wife's earnings are positively correlated with marital dissolution.[54] While the wife's employment is not usually a direct cause of divorce, employment for women does provide an economic alternative to an unhappy marriage by reducing the wife's dependence on her spouse.

Research has shown repeatedly that age at first marriage is one of the most powerful predictors of separation and divorce. The youn-

[52]Cherlin, Marriage, Divorce, Remarriage, p. 46.
[53]Cherlin, Marriage, Divorce, Remarriage, pp. 53–54.
[54]Michael T. Hannan, Nancy B. Tuma, and Lyle P. Groeneveld, "Income and Marital Events: Evidence from an Income-Maintenance Experiment," American Journal of Sociology 82 (May 1977):1186–211; Heather L. Ross and Isabel V. Sawhill, Time of Transition: The Growth of Families Headed by Women (Washington, DC: The Urban Institute, 1975); Andrew Cherlin, "Work Life and Marital Dissolution," in George Levinger and Oliver C. Moles, eds., Divorce and Separation: Context, Causes, and Consequences (New York: Basic Books, 1979), pp. 151–66; and Joan Huber and Glenna Spitze, "Considering Divorce: An Expansion of Becker's Theory of Marital Instability," American Journal of Sociology 86 (July 1980):75–89.

ger the age at first marriage, the greater is the risk of divorce. The negative association between age at marriage and marital stability is so strong that it cannot be explained by earlier childbearing or lower levels of educational attainment characteristic of young marriages.[55] As the age at first marriage rises, we may see a decline in the divorce rate.

Length of marriage is also influential in predicting divorce. Numerous studies have shown that divorce and thoughts of divorce decline with marital duration.[56] The median duration of marriage was 7 years in 1981, which does not mean that most couples divorce after 7 years of marriage. The number of divorces peaks at about 2 years of married life and declines gradually thereafter.[57] As shown in Table 1.4, the probability that a marriage will end in divorce declines steadily with marital duration. Whereas one-half of all marriages will eventually end in divorce, only two-fifths of those which survive 5 years of marriage will divorce. For couples celebrating a tenth wedding anniversary, the likelihood of divorce in the years ahead is a little over 25 percent. By the time couples reach their silver wedding anniversary, only 7 percent will eventually divorce.

The relationship between economic status and marital dissolution is complex. Couples commonly argue about income and spending,[58] but not every couple with money problems gets divorced. Becker, Landis, and Michael argue that the probability of divorce is lowered by increases in men's earnings.[59] Carter and Glick found that men with lower incomes were more likely to be divorced.[60] Other studies have shown that a sudden loss of income is more dam-

[55]Bumpass and Sweet, "Marital Instability"; Moore and Waite, "Marital Dissolution"; Ross and Sawhill, *Time of Transition*; Jane Menken, James Trussell, Debra Stempel, and Ozer Babakol, "Proportional Hazards Life Table Models: An Illustrative Analysis of Socio-Demographic Influences on Marriage Dissolution in the United States," *Demography* 18 (May 1981):181–200; Arland Thornton, "Marital Instability Differentials and Interactions: Insights from Multivariate Contingency Table Analysis," *Sociology and Social Research* 62 (July 1978):572–95.

[56]Paul H. Jacobson, "Differentials in Divorce by Duration of Marriage and Size of Family," *American Sociological Review* 15 (April 1950):235–44; Robert Schoen, "California Divorce Rates by Age at First Marriage and Duration of First Marriage," *Journal of Marriage and the Family* 37 (August 1975):548–55; and Huber and Spitze, "Considering Divorce."

[57]National Center for Health Statistics, "Final Divorce Statistics, 1981," p. 3.

[58]Yankelovich, Skelly, and White, Inc., *The General Mills American Family Report, 1974–75* (Minneapolis: General Mills, 1975).

[59]Becker, Landis, and Michael, "Marital Instability."

[60]Hugh Carter and Paul C. Glick, *Marriage and Divorce: A Social and Economic Study*, rev. ed. (Cambridge, MA: Harvard University Press, 1976).

TABLE 1.4

Likelihood That Marriages of a Given Duration Will End Eventually in Divorce

Number of Years a Couple Has Been Married	Percentage Who Will Divorce at Some Point in the Future
0	49.6%
1	48.8
2	46.8
3	44.2
4	41.5
5	38.8
6	36.2
7	33.7
8	31.2
9	29.0
10	26.8
15	17.8
20	11.4
25	6.6
30	3.5
35	1.8
40	0.9
50	0.6

SOURCE: James A. Weed, "National Estimates of Marriage Dissolution and Survivorship: United States," *Vital and Health Statistics*, series 3, Analytical Studies, no. 19 (Washington, DC: U.S. Government Printing Office, 1980), table 1.

aging to the marital relationship than actual income level.[61] Data from the Seattle and Denver Income Maintenance Experiments show that increases in income raise the overall rate of marital dissolution for low-income populations,[62] although contradictory results from the National Longitudinal Survey of Labor Market Experience found that direct supplements had little effect on marital stability.[63]

Conflicting results make it difficult to assess the effects of children on marriages. One economic theory is that investments in

[61]Ross and Sawhill, *Time of Transition*; Jeffrey Liker and Glen Elder, "Economic Hardship and Marital Relations in the 1930s," *American Sociological Review* 48 (June 1983):343–59.

[62]Michael T. Hannan, Nancy B. Tuma, and Lyle P. Groeneveld, "Income and Independence Effects on Marital Dissolution: Results from the Seattle and Denver Income-Maintenance Experiments," *American Journal of Sociology* 84 (November 1978):611–33; and Hannan, Tuma, and Groeneveld, "Income and Marital Events."

[63]Richard Galligan and Steven J. Bahr, "Economic Well-Being and Marital Stability: Implications for Income Maintenance Programs," *Journal of Marriage and the Family* 40 (May 1978):283–90.

children tend to strengthen a marriage.[64] Bumpass and Sweet and Morgan and Rindfuss found that childless women have considerably higher disruption rates than women with children, while Chester found that divorcing couples had higher fertility than nondivorcing couples.[65] Cherlin found that only pre-school-age children were a deterrent to separation and divorce, presumably because the high costs in time, money, and effort necessary for small children tend to discourage parental break-ups.[66] Findings by Huber and Spitze support Cherlin's conclusions. Wives whose youngest child was in school were most likely to consider a divorce, and husbands were least likely to consider divorce when children under age 6 were in the household.[67] Koo and Janowitz, on the other hand, found no relationship between presence of children and marital instability.[68]

One recent change that has clearly not contributed to higher rates of divorce is the institution of no-fault divorce laws. The California Family Law Act, instituted in 1970, was the country's first no-fault divorce law. By 1980 only two states (Illinois and South Dakota) still had traditional divorce laws that attributed guilt to one of the spouses.[69] Studies of divorce before and after no-fault became available showed no increase in the rate of marital dissolution,[70] and little change in the types of settlement granted.[71] The only pronounced change was an increase in the proportion of husbands who took the initiative in filing for divorce.[72]

[64]Becker, Landis, and Michael, "Marital Instability."

[65]Bumpass and Sweet, "Marital Instability"; S. Philip Morgan and Ronald R. Rindfuss, "Marital Disruption: Structural and Temporal Dimensions," *American Journal of Sociology* 90 (March 1985):1055–77; and R. Chester, "Is There a Relationship between Childlessness and Marriage Breakdown?" in Ellen Peck and Judith Senderowitz, eds., *Pronatalism: The Myth of Mom and Apple Pie* (New York: Crowell, 1974), pp. 114–26.

[66]Andrew Cherlin, "The Effects of Children on Marital Dissolution," *Demography* 14 (August 1977):265–72.

[67]Huber and Spitze, "Considering Divorce."

[68]Helen P. Koo and Barbara K. Janowitz, "Interrelationships between Fertility and Marital Dissolution: Results of a Simultaneous Logit Model," *Demography* 20 (May 1983):129–45.

[69]Charles E. Welch and Sharon Price-Bonham, "A Decade of No-Fault Divorce Revisited: California, Georgia and Washington," *Journal of Marriage and the Family* 45 (May 1983):411–18.

[70]Steven J. Bahr, "Marital Dissolution Laws: Impact of Recent Changes for Women," *Journal of Family Issues* 4 (September 1983):455–66; Robert Schoen, Harry N. Greenblatt, and Robert B. Mielke, "California's Experience with Non-Adversary Divorce," *Demography* 12 (May 1975):223–44; Ruth B. Dixon and Lenore J. Weitzman, "When Husbands File for Divorce," *Journal of Marriage and the Family* 44 (February 1982):103–15.

[71]Dixon and Weitzman, "When Husbands File"; and Welch and Price-Bonham, "No-Fault Divorce."

[72]B. G. Gunter and Doyle Johnson, "Divorce Filing as Role Behavior: Effect of No-Fault Law on Divorce Filing Patterns," *Journal of Marriage and the Family* 40 (August 1978):571–74.

Thornton and Rodgers attribute the current high divorce rates to the times we live in, or what they call the period effects of historical time.[73] They point to two previous periods in history with high divorce rates: the economic depression of the early 1930s and the World War II dislocations of the mid-1940s. Despite their inability to isolate any one factor that made the 1960s and 1970s a similarly disruptive time for marriages, Thornton and Rodgers propose a combination of factors such as women's employment, changes in values and attitudes, contraceptive technology, economic cycles, and the aging baby boom as being responsible for current high rates of divorce.

Consequences of Divorce

The nearly unanimous conclusion of researchers who analyze data on the economic consequences of divorce is that the economic status of men improves after divorce while that of women deteriorates.[74] Because children usually stay with their mother, a divorced woman has a larger household to support than a divorced man, and most wives' earnings are only a fraction of their husbands' earnings. Many divorced women do not receive child support, and those to whom it is legally granted often do not collect the full amount. (See chapter 7.)[75] Men's economic status may improve because of smaller

---

[73]Thornton and Rodgers, "Changing Patterns of Marriage."

[74]Mary Corcoran, "The Economic Consequences of Marital Dissolution for Women in the Middle Years," *Sex Roles* 5 (June 1979):343–53; Greg J. Duncan and Saul D. Hoffman, "The Economic Consequences of Marital Instability," paper presented at the NBER Income and Wealth Conference on Horizontal Equity, Uncertainty and Well-Being, Baltimore, December 1983; Thomas Draper, "On the Relationship between Welfare and Marital Stability: A Research Note," *Journal of Marriage and the Family* 43 (May 1981):293–99; Thomas J. Espenshade, "The Economic Consequences of Divorce," *Journal of Marriage and the Family* 41 (August 1979):615–25; Robert Hampton, "Marital Disruption: Some Social and Economic Consequences," in Greg J. Duncan and James N. Morgan, eds., *Five Thousand American Families: Patterns of Economic Progress*, vol. 3 (Ann Arbor: Institute for Social Research, 1975), pp. 163–86; and Saul Hoffman, "Marital Instability and the Economic Status of Women," *Demography* 14 (February 1977):67–76.

[75]Carol Jones, Nancy Gordon, and Isabel V. Sawhill, "Child Support Payments in the United States", Working Paper no. 992-03 (Washington, DC: Urban Institute, 1976); Ruth A. Brandwein, Carol A. Brown, and Elizabeth M. Fox, "Women and Children Last: The Social Situation of Divorced Mothers and Their Families," *Journal of Marriage and the Family* 36 (August 1974):498–14; and U.S. Bureau of the Census, "Child Support and Alimony: 1981 (Advance Report)," *Current Population Reports, Special Studies*, series P-23, no. 124 (Washington, DC: U.S. Government Printing Office, 1983), p. 1.

household size and fewer contributions to family members not in residence, while women's status declines concomitantly.[76] No-fault divorce laws have been accompanied by fewer and smaller property, alimony, and child-support awards for women.[77] The overall effect of these recent changes in divorce law has been to increase the economic inequality between men and women following divorce.[78]

Espenshade argues that divorced women fare "marginally better than their former husbands" in ownership of durables and stocks (for example, a house) and that the gap in economic well-being is narrowed by women's ability to shop more wisely than men.[79] One could argue that divorced women have little choice but to be thrifty when their income is severely reduced: by nearly one-third according to Hoffman.[80]

A divorced woman's alternatives to loss of husband's income are to go to work, go on welfare, or move in with others. Most women choose work. In the Panel Study of Income Dynamics sample of 5,000 families, 80 percent of White women and 70 percent of Black women either continued or returned to work after divorce. Six percent of White separated or divorced women went on welfare compared with 16 percent of Black women. Black women were more likely to be in living arrangements where other earners helped recoup lost income. Although Blacks, on average, were originally worse off economically than Whites, Black women were able to reconstitute 96 percent of their lost income by going to work, receiving transfer payments, and relying on contributions from others in the household. White women, in contrast, were able to recoup only 50 percent of lost income by these measures.[81] The fact that divorce is not as economically debilitating for Black women as it is for White women may help explain the higher divorce and separation rate of Black women.

---

[76]Hoffman, "Marital Instability"; and Duncan and Hoffman, "Economic Consequences."

[77]Karen Seal, "A Decade of No-Fault Divorce: What It Has Meant Financially for Women in California," *Family Advocate* 1 (Spring 1979):10–15; and Lenore J. Weitzman, "The Economics of Divorce: Social and Economic Consequences of Property, Alimony, and Child Support Awards," *UCLA Law Review* 28 (August 1981):1181–268.

[78]Bahr, "Marital Dissolution Laws."

[79]Espenshade, "Economic Consequences"; see also Hampton, "Marital Disruption."

[80]Hoffman, "Marital Instability."

[81]Hoffman, "Marital Instability."

Widowhood

If a marriage does not end through divorce over the course of the life cycle, it inevitably ends through the death of one spouse. A husband is likely to die before his wife and hence widowhood typifies the later stages of a woman's life. Elderly women are decidedly less likely to be married than elderly men. In both 1960 and 1983 about one-half of all women aged 65 and over were widowed. In contrast, the proportion of elderly men who were widowed declined from 19 to 13 percent (Figure 1.4).

Differences in the proportion of widows and widowers at older ages is even more pronounced. Among persons aged 75 and over, 68 percent of women and 22 percent of men were widowed in 1981. As with persons aged 65 and over, this difference between the sexes has widened over time. In 1960, 32 percent of men aged 75 and over and 68 percent of women were currently widowed.[82] In other words, among those aged 75 and over, the proportion of men who are currently widowed has declined, and older men are much less likely than older women to be widowed.

Work by Espenshade shows that women are widowed twice as often as men. Women also tend to be widowed at younger ages, spend twice as many years widowed, and remarry half as often as widowed men.[83] Among young women widowed before age 40, the median length of widowhood exceeds 15 years.[84]

Between 1960 and 1983 the number of widows increased from 8.3 to 10.9 million, while the number of widowers actually dropped slightly from 2.3 to 1.9 million. This decline in the number of widowers and increase in the number of widows has resulted in a current ratio of nearly six widows for every widower.[85]

The life expectancy of women at age 65 now exceeds that of

[82]Jacob S. Siegel and Maria Davidson, "Demographic and Socioeconomic Aspects of Aging in the United States," *Current Population Reports, Special Studies*, series P-23, no. 138, U.S. Bureau of the Census (Washington, DC: U.S. Government Printing Office, 1984), p. 94.

[83]Espenshade, "Marriage, Divorce, and Remarriage."

[84]U.S. Bureau of the Census, "Marriage, Divorce, Widowhood, and Remarriage by Family Characteristics: June 1975," *Current Population Reports*, series P-20, no. 312 (Washington, DC: U.S. Government Printing Office, 1977), p. 15.

[85]U.S. Bureau of the Census, "Marital Status and Living Arrangements: March 1983," table 1; and Noreen Goldman and Graham Lord, "Sex Differences in Life Cycle Measures of Widowhood," *Demography* 20 (May 1983):177–96.

FIGURE 1.4

*Percentage of Women and Men Aged 65 and Over Who Are Widowed,
Selected Years*

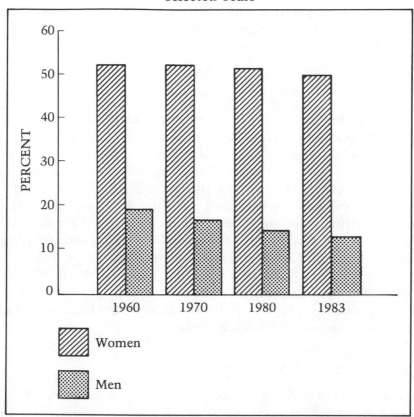

SOURCE: Appendix Table 1.A; U.S. Bureau of the Census, "Marital Status and Living Arrangements: March 1983," *Current Population Reports*, series P-20, no. 389 (Washington, DC: U.S. Government Printing Office, 1983), table 1.

men by 4.5 years.[86] This, in part, explains why there are so many more elderly widows than widowers. Married men have death rates two to three times higher than married women of the same age. In addition, a wife is typically three or four years younger than her husband which increases the likelihood that she will survive him. Another factor contributing to the higher proportion of widows is the higher remarriage

[86]National Center for Health Statistics, "Advance Report of Final Mortality Statistics, 1982," *Monthly Vital Statistics Report*, vol. 33, no. 9, supplement (Washington, DC: U.S. Government Printing Office, 1984), p. 3.

rate among widowed men. Widowers over 65 are eight times as likely to remarry as widows.[87] Social norms encourage the marriage of older men to younger women while discouraging the marriage of older women to younger men. Given the large pool of eligible women (that is, those younger, widowed, divorced, or never married) and the shortage of men, it is easier for older men to remarry.

Black-White Differences in Widowhood

Black and White women are almost equally likely to become widows: 69 percent of White and 65 percent of Black women outlive their husbands.[88] The proportion of marriages likely to end in widowhood is about the same for Black and White women: approximately 50 percent.[89] Overall mortality is higher for Blacks (except at the oldest ages), and life expectancy at birth is seven years less for Blacks, resulting in a lower mean age at widowhood for Blacks; in 1970 it was 56.6 years for Black women compared with 64.2 years for White women. The mean length of time spent as a widow was 22.6 years for Blacks and 18.6 years for Whites in 1970.[90] Using a different data set, Espenshade's results are slightly different, but support the general findings of younger age at widowhood and longer duration of widowhood for Black women.[91]

Consequences of Widowhood

The effects of widowhood are similar to the effects of divorce on a woman's economic well-being. Most studies have shown that households maintained by widows have low family income[92] and that women experience a drop in real income after becoming widowed.[93]

[87]Siegel and Davidson, "Demographic and Socioeconomic Aspects of Aging," p. 86.
[88]Goldman and Lord, "Widowhood."
[89]Espenshade, "Marriage, Divorce, and Remarriage."
[90]Goldman and Lord, "Widowhood."
[91]Espenshade, "Marriage, Divorce, and Remarriage."
[92]Leslie A. Morgan, "A Re-Examination of Widowhood and Morale," *Journal of Gerontology* 31 (November 1976):687–95; and Helena Z. Lopata, *Widowhood in an American City* (Cambridge, MA: Schenckman, 1973).
[93]Helena Z. Lopata, *Women as Widows: Support Systems* (New York: Elsevier, 1979); Saul Hoffman and John Holmes, "Husbands, Wives, and Divorce," in Greg J. Duncan and James N. Morgan, eds., *Five Thousand American Families: Patterns of Economic Progress*, vol. 4 (Ann Arbor: Institute for Social Research, 1976), pp. 23–76; and James N. Morgan, Katherine Dickinson, Jonathan Dickinson, Jacob Benus, and Greg J. Duncan, *Five Thousand American Families: Patterns of Economic Progress*, vol. 1 (Ann Arbor: Institute for Social Research, 1974).

Most conclusions about pronounced economic differences between married and widowed women are based on cross-sectional analysis which does not allow for the household's past income. In the National Longitudinal Survey sample of widows aged 30 to 44, Morgan found little change in the economic status of women widowed early in life.[94] Partly because of lower family income before widowhood and partly because of contributions from Social Security and the woman's earnings, there was not such a radical shift in economic well-being as suggested by other studies. Morgan's conclusion was that "widows unquestionably experience lower financial well-being than their still-married peers, but the event of widowhood is not the turning point in creating these differences."[95]

Remarriage

As the number of marriages that end through divorce has increased, so has the incidence of remarriage. Approximately 45 percent of all marriages in 1981 involved persons previously married compared with 31 percent in 1970.[96] The number of women who remarried increased from 197,000 in 1960 to 616,000 in 1981.[97] Figure 1.5 illustrates the trend in first-marriage, divorce, and remarriage rates.

First-marriage rates have shown a steady decline since 1960, while divorce and remarriage rates have climbed. Remarriage rates steadily increased from 33 in 1960 to 40 in 1975, dipped slightly between 1975 and 1980, and then returned to 40 in 1981. The majority of remarriages occur after divorce rather than widowhood. In 1981 slightly more than three-quarters of remarried women and men had been previously divorced.[98] The declining median age of remarried women (from 36 in 1963 to 32 in 1981) reflects the shift from remarriage after widowhood to remarriage after divorce. In 1981 the average age at remarriage for divorced women was 31, whereas for widowed women it was 54.[99]

[94]Leslie A. Morgan, "Economic Change at Mid-Life Widowhood: A Longitudinal Analysis," *Journal of Marriage and the Family* 43 (November 1981):899–908.
[95]Morgan, "Economic Change," p. 906.
[96]National Center for Health Statistics, "Final Marriage Statistics, 1981," p. 9.
[97]National Center for Health Statistics, "Final Marriage Statistics, 1981," p. 9.
[98]National Center for Health Statistics, "Final Marriage Statistics, 1981," p. 8.
[99]National Center for Health Statistics, "Final Marriage Statistics, 1981," p. 9.

FIGURE 1.5

Trend in Rates of First Marriage, Divorce, and Remarriage

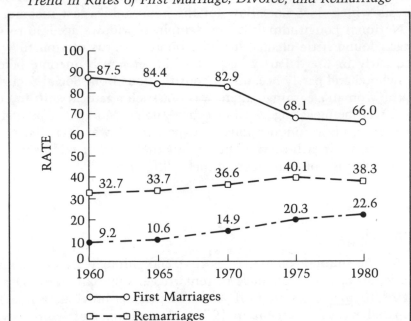

NOTE: First marriages per 1,000 never married women aged 14 and over (15 and over in 1980); remarriages per 1,000 divorced and widowed women aged 14 and over (15 and over in 1980); divorces per 1,000 married women aged 15 and over.

SOURCE: National Center for Health Statistics, "Advance Report of Final Marriage Statistics, 1981," *Monthly Vital Statistics Report*, vol. 32, no. 11, supplement (February 1984), table 4; and "Advance Report of Final Divorce Statistics," 1981," *Monthly Vital Statistics Report*, vol. 32, no. 9, supplement (2) (January 1984), table 10; *Vital Statistics of the United States, 1975*, vol. 3 (1979), table 1.7; *Vital Statistics of the United States, 1970*, vol. 3 (1974), table 1.20; *Vital Statistics of the United States, 1965*, vol. 3 (1968), table 1.7; and *Vital Statistics of the United States, 1960*, vol. 3 (1964), table I-M.

Women tend to remarry slightly sooner after divorce than after widowhood. Women who remarry after their first marriage ends in divorce do so within a median period of 3.2 years compared with 4.2 years for women who remarry after widowhood.[100] Typically, women remarry at a younger age than men, in part because they first marry

[100]U.S. Bureau of the Census, "Marriage, Divorce, Widowhood, and Remarriage," p. 14.

at a younger age.[101] Women who married at a young age the first time are the quickest to remarry.[102]

Black-White Differences in Remarriage

White women are more likely to remarry than Black women. Approximately 75 percent of White women remarried after divorce in the 1970s compared with 67 percent of Black women. The rates for Blacks and Whites were similar in the early 1960s, but Black remarriage rates are now lower than White remarriage rates for divorced women. Remarriage after widowhood has been similar by race and constant over time: About 10 percent of both Black and White widows remarried in the 1960s and 1970s.[103]

In a comparison of probabilities of break-ups in first and second marriages, McCarthy found that for Blacks second marriages were more likely to remain intact than first marriages. Among Whites, remarriages were more likely to end in divorce than first marriages. Blacks in remarriages, as well as first marriages, were less likely than Whites to obtain a divorce following a separation.[104]

Correlates of Remarriage

Remarriage is correlated with both age at divorce and educational attainment. The younger the age at divorce, the greater is the probability of remarriage; also women with less than a high school diploma remarry more often than women with some college.[105] Women with fewer children are most likely to remarry,[106] and women who are not on welfare are more likely to remarry than those who receive Aid to Families with Dependent Children.[107]

---

[101]U.S. Bureau of the Census, "Number, Timing, and Duration of Marriages and Divorces in the United States: June 1975," *Current Population Reports*, series P-20, no. 297 (Washington, DC: U.S. Government Printing Office, 1976), p. 8.

[102]Thornton and Rodgers, "Changing Patterns of Marriage."

[103]Thornton and Rodgers, "Changing Patterns of Marriage."

[104]James McCarthy, "Dissolution of First and Second Marriages."

[105]Sharon Price-Bonham and Jack Balswick, "The Noninstitutions: Divorce, Desertion, and Remarriage," *Journal of Marriage and the Family* 42 (November 1980):959–72.

[106]Graham Spanier and Paul C. Glick, "Paths to Remarriage," *Journal of Divorce* 3 (Spring 1980):283–98.

[107]Steven J. Bahr, "The Effects of Welfare on Marital Stability and Remarriage," *Journal of Marriage and the Family* 41 (August 1979):553–60.

Remarriage is also associated with a woman's short-term employment and her satisfaction with that employment. The more dissatisfied a woman is with her work, the more likely she is to remarry. Additionally, women in metropolitan areas are less likely to remarry than women living elsewhere (perhaps due to greater employment opportunities).[108] The stability of a woman's first marriage is influenced by the marital history of her husband: Women's first marriages are most unstable if their husbands were previously divorced. The stability of the second marriage for White women is inversely associated with the number of unwanted pregnancies and whether the woman worked before her first marriage. For Black women, remarriages are most stable if the husband was from a rural background.[109]

Mueller and Pope found that women generally marry a second husband of equal or higher status than their first husband.[110] This relationship holds regardless of presence of children or length of time between divorce and remarriage.

Consequences of Remarriage

Remarriage presents its own set of solutions and problems. Remarriage can be a solution to the loneliness and financial difficulties a woman often faces after divorce or widowhood. Yet remarriages can be beset by problems, so that divorced persons who remarry are likely to divorce again.[111]

One of the most common problems in remarriages results from combining separate families into "blended" or "reconstituted" new families. Since American society idealizes the nuclear family typical of first marriages, there are few behavioral guidelines for adults and children in second marriages.

In fact, the whole definition of "family" is altered. Does a wife's immediate family include her ex-husband, or just her children and

[108]Frank Mott and Sylvia F. Moore, "The Tempo of Remarriage Among Young American Women," *Journal of Marriage and the Family* 45 (May 1983):427–36.

[109]B. E. Aguirre and W. C. Parr, "Husbands' Marriage Order and the Stability of First and Second Marriages of White and Black Women," *Journal of Marriage and the Family* 44 (August 1982):605–20.

[110]Charles W. Mueller and Hallowell Pope, "Divorce and Female Remarriage Mobility: Data on Marriage Matches after Divorce for White Women," *Social Forces* 58 (March 1980): 726–38.

[111]U.S. Bureau of the Census, "Number, Timing, and Duration," p. 6; McCarthy, "Probability of Dissolution"; and Cherlin, "Effects of Children."

her new husband? Or does it include her husband's children as well? How many children from each spouse actually live with the newly remarried couple, and how many visit only on weekends or during the summer? The woman's definition of her family after she remarries may not even be the same as her child's definition of his family, since the child is more likely to still include the biological father (but perhaps not the father's new wife and children). Add the new baby of a remarried couple and the kinship possibilities multiply even further.

These differing definitions of family relationships present daily problems ranging from who disciplines whose children to who gets how much of a parent's or spouse's time and money. Sociologist Andrew Cherlin thinks that a lack of clear ways to deal with such relational problems is the main cause of higher divorce rates among remarried couples. Cherlin refers to remarriage as an "incomplete institution" lacking social support for the difficulties that inevitably arise.[112]

Summary

There have been major changes in marriage, divorce, and remarriage since 1960. Although lifetime singlehood may be increasing, the role of wife continues to be adopted by the vast majority of adult women. Marriage remains central to most women's lives. In this respect, young women today are making life choices similar to those of their mother's and grandmother's generations.

What has changed is the timing of entry into marriage and the extent of a woman's adult life that is spent in the married state. Young women today are postponing marriage longer than women of their mother's generation did. This delay gives them time to attend college and establish themselves in the workplace prior to marriage. One-half of women in their early 20s were still single in 1980 compared with fewer than one-third in 1960. Median age at first marriage is now later than the usual age at college graduation.

Young women continue to value "a happy marriage and family

[112]Andrew Cherlin, "Remarriage as an Incomplete Institution," *American Journal of Sociology* 84 (November 1978): 634–50; and Terence C. Halliday, "Comment: Remarriage: The More Complete Institution?" *American Journal of Sociology* 86 (November 1980):630–35.

life" but alternatives to marriage, such as cohabitation, have become more common and more socially acceptable. The divorce rate more than doubled between 1960 and 1981 and, although it has leveled off in recent years, it remains high by historical standards. It is estimated that one of two couples who marry today will eventually divorce. The likelihood of remarriage following divorce is high, but not as high for women as for men because of the demography of the marriage market. Remarriage is also much less common among Black women than among White women.

Women continue to outlive their husbands and greatly outnumber men at older ages. Over 50 percent of all elderly women are widowed compared with 13 percent of elderly men. While the proportion of elderly women who are widows has remained constant over time, the proportion of elderly men who are widowers has declined since 1960.

The significance of changes in marriage patterns becomes more apparent as we move to a discussion of women's changing economic roles in subsequent chapters. Decisions about marriage and children continue to influence women's educational and labor force plans. The woman who currently delays marriage until her later 20s or early 30s structures her adult life much differently than the woman, either her contemporary or of her mother's generation, who marries at age 20 and begins childbearing soon afterward.

The fact that women are spending an increasing number of years single prior to marriage, divorced or separated between marriages, and widowed after marriage helps place women's changed economic role in context. Women's family lives receive less media attention than changes in their labor force behavior but are tremendously important because marriage and family decisions can either facilitate or hinder women's educational and occupational progress. The single, divorced, or widowed woman finds herself in a much different economic situation than the married woman. And the economic well-being of women (more so than that of men) is conditioned by changes in marital status.

APPENDIX TABLE 1.A

Changes in the Marital Status of Women and Men (numbers in thousands)

Age and Marital Status	Women				Men			
	1950	1960	1970	1980	1950	1960	1970	1980
Total, 15 Years and Over	56,055	63,616	75,861	91,483	53,511	59,913	69,349	83,824
	100.0%	100.0%	100.0%	100.0%	100.0%	100.0%	100.0%	100.0%
Never Married	18.5	17.3	20.6	22.9	24.9	23.2	26.4	29.7
Married, Spouse Present	63.4	63.4	58.6	54.0	65.4	67.6	64.3	59.1
Separated	2.1	2.1	2.3	2.6	1.6	1.5	1.5	1.9
Spouse Absent	1.5	2.0	1.9	1.2	1.9	2.1	2.0	1.6
Widowed	12.0	12.4	12.7	12.3	4.2	3.5	3.1	2.5
Divorced	2.4	2.9	3.9	7.1	2.0	2.2	2.7	5.3
Total, 15–19 Years	5,322	6,589	9,485	10,409	5,323	6,699	9,718	10,639
	100.0%	100.0%	100.0%	100.0%	100.0%	100.0%	100.0%	100.0%
Never Married	82.9	83.9	88.1	91.2	96.7	96.1	95.9	97.2
Married, Spouse Present	15.0	13.3	9.2	7.0	2.5	2.9	3.2	1.9
Separated	0.7	0.6	0.5	0.5	0.2	0.1	0.2	0.2
Spouse Absent	0.9	1.8	1.5	0.9	0.5	0.8	0.6	0.6
Widowed	0.1	0.1	0.2	0.1	0.1	0.0	0.1	0.0
Divorced	0.3	0.3	0.3	0.4	0.1	0.1	0.1	0.1
Total, 20–24 Years	5,878	5,520	8,354	10,655	5,559	5,283	7,761	10,639
	100.0%	100.0%	100.0%	100.0%	100.0%	100.0%	100.0%	100.0%
Never Married	32.3	28.4	36.3	51.2	59.0	53.1	55.5	68.2
Married, Spouse Present	61.6	63.8	54.4	40.1	37.0	41.5	38.6	26.3
Separated	2.3	2.3	2.6	2.7	1.2	1.1	1.2	1.4
Spouse Absent	1.8	3.4	3.5	1.7	1.7	3.1	3.1	1.9
Widowed	0.4	0.3	0.7	0.2	0.2	0.1	0.2	0.1
Divorced	1.7	1.8	2.5	4.2	0.9	1.0	1.4	2.2

SOURCE: See Table 1.1.

APPENDIX TABLE 1.A (continued)

Changes in the Marital Status of Women and Men (numbers in thousands)

Age and Marital Status	Women				Men			
	1950	1960	1970	1980	1950	1960	1970	1980
Total, 25–29 Years	6,277	5,537	6,810	9,793	5,905	5,333	6,570	9,678
	100.0%	100.0%	100.0%	100.0%	100.0%	100.0%	100.0%	100.0%
Never Married	13.3	10.5	12.2	21.6	23.8	20.8	19.6	32.1
Married, Spouse Present	79.0	81.1	77.0	63.5	70.2	73.0	72.9	56.6
Separated	2.5	2.7	3.3	3.9	1.6	1.5	1.9	2.6
Spouse Absent	1.7	2.4	2.2	1.4	2.4	2.7	2.3	2.0
Widowed	0.9	0.7	1.1	0.5	0.3	0.2	0.3	0.1
Divorced	2.5	2.6	4.3	9.1	1.7	1.8	3.0	6.7
Total, 30–34 Years	5,897	6,111	5,869	8,954	5,562	5,840	5,608	8,756
	100.0%	100.0%	100.0%	100.0%	100.0%	100.0%	100.0%	100.0%
Never Married	9.3	6.9	7.4	10.6	13.2	11.9	10.7	14.9
Married, Spouse Present	82.2	83.9	80.6	72.2	80.5	81.6	81.6	71.8
Separated	2.5	2.9	3.5	4.0	1.7	1.7	1.9	2.8
Spouse Absent	1.4	2.0	2.1	1.1	2.2	2.3	2.1	1.6
Widowed	1.6	1.2	1.5	0.9	0.4	0.3	0.3	0.2
Divorced	3.0	3.1	5.0	11.2	2.1	2.2	3.3	8.7
Total, 35–39 Years	5,713	6,419	5,711	7,110	5,433	6,090	5,432	6,863
	100.0%	100.0%	100.0%	100.0%	100.0%	100.0%	100.0%	100.0%
Never Married	8.4	6.1	5.9	6.7	10.1	8.8	8.2	8.7
Married, Spouse Present	81.3	83.6	81.2	75.0	82.9	84.4	84.0	78.3
Separated	2.7	2.7	3.4	4.0	1.9	1.7	1.9	2.7
Spouse Absent	1.4	1.8	2.0	1.1	2.1	2.2	2.0	1.5
Widowed	2.7	2.2	2.2	1.6	0.7	0.5	0.5	0.3
Divorced	3.5	3.6	5.3	11.6	2.4	2.5	3.4	8.6

SOURCE: See Table 1.1.

APPENDIX TABLE 1.A (continued)

Changes in the Marital Status of Women and Men (numbers in thousands)

Age and Marital Status	Women				Men			
	1950	1960	1970	1980	1950	1960	1970	1980
Total, 40–44 Years	5,125	5,918	6,150	5,958	4,970	5,649	5,830	5,708
	100.0%	100.0%	100.0%	100.0%	100.0%	100.0%	100.0%	100.0%
Never Married	8.3	6.1	5.4	5.3	9.0	7.3	7.5	6.7
Married, Spouse Present	78.9	81.6	80.3	75.9	83.1	85.4	84.1	80.6
Separated	2.6	2.6	3.2	3.9	1.9	1.7	1.9	2.7
Spouse Absent	1.5	1.7	1.7	1.1	2.1	2.0	1.8	1.4
Widowed	5.0	4.0	3.7	2.8	1.2	0.8	0.8	0.5
Divorced	3.7	4.0	5.6	11.1	2.7	2.7	3.8	8.0
Total, 45–49 Years	4,553	5,554	6,255	5,679	4,444	5,375	5,809	5,346
	100.0%	100.0%	100.0%	100.0%	100.0%	100.0%	100.0%	100.0%
Never Married	7.9	6.5	5.3	4.7	8.7	7.2	6.6	6.0
Married, Spouse Present	75.7	78.2	78.8	75.8	81.9	84.7	84.7	81.8
Separated	2.6	2.5	2.8	3.4	2.1	1.8	1.9	2.4
Spouse Absent	1.6	1.7	1.6	1.0	2.2	1.9	1.7	1.4
Widowed	8.6	6.7	5.9	5.0	2.1	1.4	1.3	1.0
Divorced	3.6	4.3	5.5	10.1	2.9	3.0	3.8	7.5
Total, 50–54 Years	4,134	4,932	5,741	6,096	4,040	4,765	5,329	5,611
	100.0%	100.0%	100.0%	100.0%	100.0%	100.0%	100.0%	100.0%
Never Married	7.7	7.6	5.7	4.6	8.3	7.6	6.2	6.0
Married, Spouse Present	71.1	73.0	74.7	73.7	80.7	83.2	84.3	81.9
Separated	2.3	2.3	2.5	2.9	2.0	1.8	1.8	2.3
Spouse Absent	1.7	1.8	1.5	1.0	2.3	2.0	1.7	1.3
Widowed	13.9	11.1	10.0	8.7	3.7	2.3	2.1	1.8
Divorced	3.3	4.2	5.5	9.0	3.0	3.1	3.9	6.8

SOURCE: See Table 1.1.

43

APPENDIX TABLE 1.A (continued)

Changes in the Marital Status of Women and Men (numbers in thousands)

Age and Marital Status	Women				Men			
	1950	1960	1970	1980	1950	1960	1970	1980
Total, 55–59 Years	3,605	4,411	5,228	6,154	3,558	4,185	4,800	5,498
	100.0%	100.0%	100.0%	100.0%	100.0%	100.0%	100.0%	100.0%
Never Married	7.7	8.2	6.5	4.7	8.3	8.3	6.4	5.6
Married, Spouse Present	65.7	66.1	68.5	70.0	79.1	80.8	83.1	82.5
Separated	2.0	2.0	2.2	2.4	1.9	1.8	1.8	1.9
Spouse Absent	1.5	1.8	1.5	1.1	2.0	2.1	1.7	1.3
Widowed	20.5	17.9	16.1	14.2	5.9	3.8	3.2	2.8
Divorced	2.7	3.9	5.2	7.7	2.7	3.1	3.9	5.8
Total, 60–64 Years	3,028	3,727	4,599	5,440	2,983	3,384	4,059	4,695
	100.0%	100.0%	100.0%	100.0%	100.0%	100.0%	100.0%	100.0%
Never Married	8.2	7.7	7.2	5.2	8.6	7.7	6.6	5.2
Married, Spouse Present	56.9	58.1	59.7	62.7	75.4	79.1	81.0	82.2
Separated	1.7	1.6	1.9	1.9	1.9	1.7	1.7	1.7
Spouse Absent	1.5	1.7	1.5	1.1	2.0	2.2	1.9	1.3
Widowed	29.7	27.6	24.9	22.6	9.6	6.5	5.2	4.6
Divorced	2.1	3.3	4.8	6.5	2.5	3.0	3.6	5.0
Total, 65 Years and Over	6,523	8,898	11,658	15,236	5,734	7,309	8,433	10,263
	100.0%	100.0%	100.0%	100.0%	100.0%	100.0%	100.0%	100.0%
Never Married	8.9	8.5	8.1	6.7	8.4	7.7	7.5	5.5
Married, Spouse Present	33.2	34.7	33.9	35.0	62.1	67.0	68.3	72.5
Separated	1.0	1.0	1.0	1.0	1.7	1.5	1.5	1.3
Spouse Absent	1.5	1.7	1.6	1.4	1.9	2.4	2.6	2.4
Widowed	54.3	52.1	52.2	51.7	24.1	19.1	17.1	14.6
Divorced	1.1	2.0	3.2	4.2	1.9	2.3	3.0	3.6

SOURCE: See Table 1.1.

2

CHILDBEARING

A WOMAN may stop being a wife once she is divorced or widowed, but she never stops being a parent as long as her child lives. The anxiety sometimes associated with a first birth is the realization that it is an irreversible act. Unlike a spouse, a child cannot be divorced if things don't work out. Or as Alice Rossi put it, "We can have ex-spouses and ex-jobs but not ex-children."[1] Today women spend a smaller proportion of their lives at home with children than they did in the past, but the vast majority—nearly 90 percent—still become mothers by age 40.[2] Thus, motherhood, like marriage, determines a great deal of a woman's responsibilities and opportunities.

Although there is one biological father for every child born, there is not always a man present to assume the social role of fathering for every child. The recent rise in the number of births to unmarried mothers suggests that women are disproportionately shar-

[1]Alice Rossi, "Transition to Parenthood," *Journal of Marriage and the Family* 30 (February 1968):26–39.

[2]Suzanne M. Bianchi and Daphne Spain, "American Women: Three Decades of Change," *Special Demographic Analyses*, CDS-80–8, U.S. Bureau of the Census (Washington, DC: U.S. Government Printing Office, 1983).

ing the tasks of parenthood. The consequences of pregnancy (whether wanted or unwanted) are naturally greater for women than men. Teenage and out-of-wedlock births may not carry as much social stigma as they did in the past, but the results for women are still generally negative; they often translate into more pregnancy-related complications, lower educational attainment, and, ultimately, higher rates of poverty.[3]

Just as women now experience more variation in marital patterns, they also have more flexibility in fertility decisions than they did previously. The availability of contraception and legal abortion allows women to control their reproductive behavior in ways not possible twenty years ago.[4] One or two children typically require less time than three or four, and some women are choosing not to have children at all. Even one child makes a woman a full-time mother, but fewer children mean fewer years in this role, leaving more years in which other roles may be developed. For example, women without children at home are more likely to be employed full time than those with children.[5]

The greatest overall change in fertility over the past twenty years is that it has declined. However, the baby boom fertility of the 1950s and early 1960s was unusually high by historical standards, and American fertility is now in line with other industrialized nations and with the long-term historical trend toward lower fertility. This chapter focuses on a forty-year time span so that pre–baby boom baseline data can be established.

In addition to the decline in overall fertility, several other developments warrant attention. The timing of first births is being delayed, and women expect to have fewer children than they did in the past. Teenage fertility has declined, while out-of-wedlock fertility for Whites has risen, despite the increased availability of contraceptives and abortion. Birth rates have recently risen for women over 30. This chapter reviews racial differences and the correlates and consequences of the most significant fertility issues of the past four decades.

---

[3]Sandra L. Hofferth and Kristin A. Moore, "Early Childbearing and Later Economic Well-Being," *American Sociological Review* 44 (October 1979):784–815; and Linda J. Waite and Kristin A. Moore, "The Impact of an Early First Birth on Young Women's Educational Attainment," *Social Forces* 56 (March 1978):845–65.

[4]Charles F. Westoff and Norman B. Ryder, *The Contraceptive Revolution* (Princeton, NJ: Princeton University Press, 1977).

[5]Kristin A. Moore, Daphne Spain, and Suzanne M. Bianchi, "Working Wives and Mothers," *Marriage and Family Review* 7 (Fall–Winter 1984):77–98.

FIGURE 2.1

Trend in Total Fertility Rate of Black and White Women

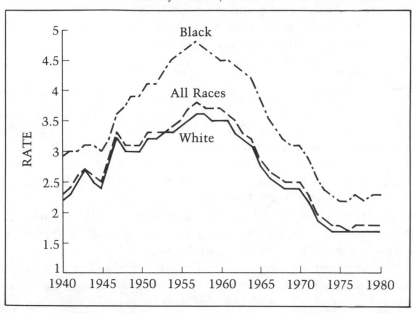

NOTE: Data for Blacks includes Blacks and other races; birth rates are live births per woman in specified group.

SOURCE: U.S. Bureau of the Census, *Historical Statistics of the United States: Colonial Times to 1970,* Bicentennial Edition (Washington, DC: U.S. Government Printing Office, 1975), series B11-19; National Center for Health Statistics, "Advance Report of Final Natality Statistics, 1981," *Monthly Vital Statistics Report,* vol. 32, no. 9, supplement (December 1983), table 4.

Fertility Trends

The great majority of women are mothers, but there have been variations over time in the number of children a woman bears. The measure often used to demonstrate the average number of children per woman is the Total Fertility Rate (TFR). The TFR reflects how many children a woman would bear over her lifetime, on average, if there were no changes in fertility rates over time.[6] Figure 2.1 shows changes in the TFR over time and by race.

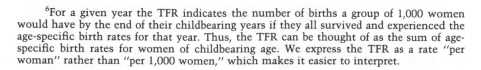

[6]For a given year the TFR indicates the number of births a group of 1,000 women would have by the end of their childbearing years if they all survived and experienced the age-specific birth rates for that year. Thus, the TFR can be thought of as the sum of age-specific birth rates for women of childbearing age. We express the TFR as a rate "per woman" rather than "per 1,000 women," which makes it easier to interpret.

The figure helps place the baby boom in demographic perspective. Women bore children at a rate of fewer than three births each during most of the 1940s and after 1965. Women had an average of 3.4 to 3.6 births during the baby boom, but that era was followed by a "baby bust" that has persisted for more than a decade. The TFR in 1980 was 1.8, well under the level (2.1) needed for natural replacement.

The Age-Specific Fertility Rate (ASFR) is used to determine the ages at which most childbearing occurs. As the name implies, the ASFR standardizes fertility data by age of the woman. It is calculated by dividing the number of live births per year (classified by mother's age) by the total number of women in that age category at the midpoint of the year. Because a woman's prime childbearing period occurs in her 20s, the ASFR for young women will be higher than the overall birth rate and the ASFR for older women will be considerably lower. Figure 2.2 shows the peaks and troughs of childbearing for American women between 1940 and 1980.

Not surprisingly, the highest fertility rates occur at ages 20 to 24 and 25 to 29. Fertility drops off rather sharply at ages 30 and over. Although more recent evidence indicates increased childbearing over age 30 (see this chapter's section on timing of fertility), about 80 percent of births still occur to women in their 20s.[7] The overall decline in the ASFR since 1960 reflects use of more effective contraceptives and an increasingly later age at first marriage.

Another measure which reflects a woman's individual reproductive history is the *number of children ever born*. This measure is most accurate only for women who have completed their childbearing years. However, it is often used for comparative purposes among younger women. The measure does not reflect true completed fertility for women still of reproductive age, and comparisons can be distorted by changes in the timing of births. The number of children ever born is calculated as a rate per 1,000 women, but can also be interpreted as a rate per woman, as in Table 2.1, which reports the number of children ever born to ever-married women still of childbearing age (those aged 15 to 44) and those normally past childbearing age (those aged 45 to 49).

Women aged 45 to 49 in 1940 were part of the birth cohort of 1891 to 1895 and experienced relatively high fertility. Women whose

[7]Martin O'Connell, "Countercyclical Fertility: A View from the Trough," unpublished manuscript, U.S. Bureau of the Census, Population Division, 1983.

FIGURE 2.2

Trend in Age-Specific Birth Rates

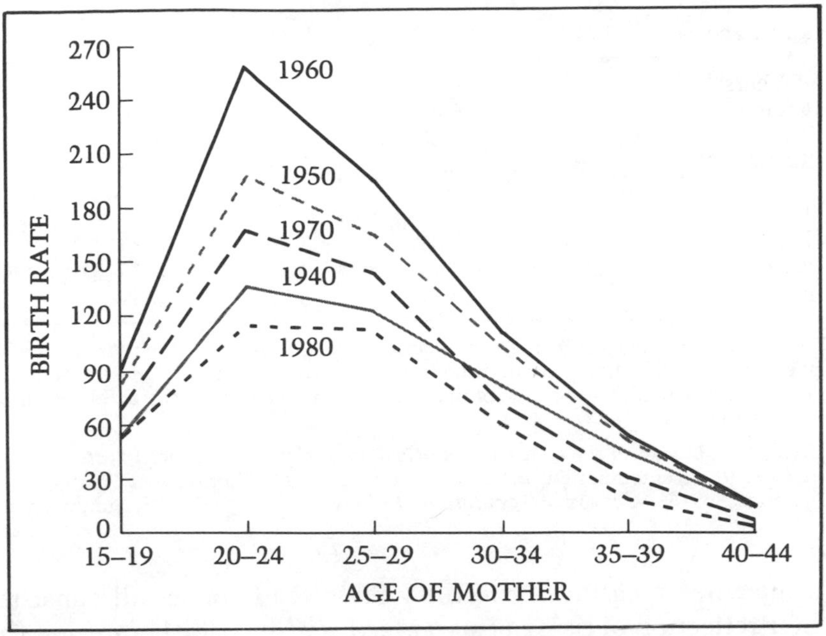

NOTE: Birth rates are live births per 1,000 women in specified age group.

SOURCE: U.S. Bureau of the Census, *Historical Statistics of the United States: Colonial Times to 1970,* Bicentennial Edition (Washington, DC: U.S. Government Printing Office, 1975), series B11-19; National Center for Health Statistics, "Advance Report of Final Natality Statistics, 1980," *Monthly Vital Statistics Report,* vol. 31, no. 8, supplement (November 1982), table 3.

reproductive years occurred during the Depression (1930 to 1935) were aged 45 to 49 in 1960, which is reflected by the low average of 2.4 children.[8] Those aged 45 to 49 in 1980 were born between 1931 and 1935, and because they reached childbearing age in 1951 to 1955 they contributed substantially to the baby boom; thus their completed fertility is higher than for other cohorts. We do not yet know the total number of children born to women born during the baby boom because they will all not reach the end of their reproductive years until the first decade of the twenty-first century.

[8]U.S. Bureau of the Census, "Fertility of American Women: June 1980," *Current Population Reports,* series P-20, no. 375 (Washington, DC: U.S. Government Printing Office, 1982), p. 5.

TABLE 2.1

Changes in the Number of Children Born to Married Women

Age and Race	1940	1950	1960	1970	1980
15–44 Years					
All Races	1.90	1.86	2.31	2.36	1.93
White	1.87	1.83	2.25	2.28	1.85
Black	2.10	2.09	2.81	2.98	2.46
45–49 Years					
All Races	3.00	2.49	2.40	2.85	3.23
White	2.97	2.46	2.35	2.79	3.11
Black	3.26	2.77	2.76	3.39	3.94

NOTE: Average number per woman; number of children includes all children ever born, irrespective of whether living at the time of the survey; married women include all who have ever been married, irrespective of marital status at the time of the child's birth or at the time of the survey.

SOURCE: U.S. Bureau of the Census, *Historical Statistics of the United States: Colonial Times to 1970*, Bicentennial Edition (Washington, DC: U.S. Government Printing Office, 1975), series B49–66; *Census of Population: 1980*, vol. 1, chap. D, U.S. Summary, table 270.

The three measures of fertility reviewed here are all consistent in their reflection of rising postwar fertility (the baby boom) and then declining fertility (the baby bust) in the late 1960s and 1970s. As Figure 2.3 demonstrates, the United States is similar to other industrialized countries in fertility levels.[9] Fertility rates in the United States, Canada, Australia, and Western Europe are much lower than rates in less developed countries, particularly African nations such as Kenya.

Black-White Differences in Fertility

One of the most important differences in American fertility is the variation by race of mother. Black fertility has always been higher than White fertility, although the trends have narrowed over time. The TFR shows that Black women averaged almost one birth more than White women in 1950 and 1960, but the decline in TFR between 1970 and 1980 was greater for Blacks than Whites. (See Figure 2.1.) The number of children ever born shows a similar pattern. At every date and for both age groups of ever-married women, Blacks averaged more children ever born than Whites. (See Table 2.1.)

[9]United Nations, *Demographic Indicators of Countries: Estimates and Projections as Assessed in 1980* (New York: United Nations, 1982).

FIGURE 2.3
Total Fertility Rates for Selected Countries

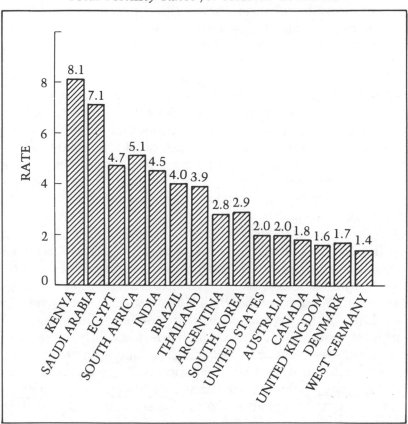

NOTE: Births per woman; medium variant projections.
SOURCE: United Nations, *Demographic Indicators of Countries: Estimates and Projections as Assessed in 1980* (New York: United Nations, 1982).

Blacks and Whites experienced peak fertility during the baby boom, as reflected by the highest average number of children born to women aged 45 to 49 in 1980. A racially similar low occurred for women aged 45 to 49 in 1960, whose childbearing took place during the Depression.[10]

Age-Specific Fertility Rates are consistently higher for Blacks than Whites, with the exception of the 25-to-29-year age category. In both 1940 and 1980, Black fertility was lower than White fertility for

[10]Readers interested in historic trends in Black fertility are referred to Reynolds Farley, *Growth of the Black Population: A Study of Demographic Trends* (Chicago: Markham, 1970).

women aged 25 to 29. Part of this difference may be attributable to higher fertility rates among Blacks at younger and older ages. Teenage births, for example, are almost three times greater for Blacks than Whites (see this chapter's section on teenage and out-of-wedlock fertility for more detail). Fertility at ages over 30 is also higher for Blacks.

There has never been any question that Black fertility is higher than White fertility. The questions arise when it comes to explaining this phenomenon. One demographic cause for higher Black fertility is the different age structures of the Black and White populations. The Black population had a median age of 24.9 in 1980 versus 31.3 for the White population, and a younger population means a higher proportion of women in their prime childbearing ages.[11] But aside from purely age-related distinctions, there are other explanations offered for the existing differentials.

Two competing theories of the persistence of racial differences in fertility have not been resolved. One is the "social characteristics" hypothesis.[12] This hypothesis attributes racial differences in fertility to intervening socioeconomic variables. For example, fertility is higher among low-income and poorly educated women, and Blacks are more likely than Whites to be poor and less well educated. The assumption behind this approach is that fertility differences will disappear when socioeconomic discrepancies are eliminated.

In competition with this explanation is the "minority group status" hypothesis,[13] which asserts that race has an independent effect on fertility regardless of intervening socioeconomic considerations. Some current research lends support to the independent effects of race. Black women have an earlier age at first birth than White

[11]John Reid, "Black America in the 1980s," *Population Bulletin*, vol. 37, no. 4 (Washington, DC: Population Reference Bureau, December 1982).

[12]Donald Bogue, *Principles of Demography* (New York: Wiley, 1969); Reynolds Farley, "Recent Changes in Negro Fertility," *Demography* 3 (1966):188–203; and Ralph Thomlinson, *Population Dynamics* (New York: Random House, 1965).

[13]Frank D. Bean and John P. Marcum, "Differential Fertility and the Minority Group Status Hypothesis: An Assessment and Review," in Frank D. Bean and W. Parker Frisbie, eds., *The Demography of Racial and Ethnic Groups* (New York: Academic Press, 1978), pp. 189–211; Calvin Goldscheider and Peter Uhlenberg, "Minority Group Status and Fertility," *American Journal of Sociology* 74 (January 1969):361–72; Robert Kennedy, "Minority Group Status and Fertility: The Irish," *American Sociological Review* 38 (February 1973):85–96; and Craig St. John, "Race Differences in Age at First Birth and the Pace of Subsequent Fertility: Implications for the Minority Group Status Hypothesis," *Demography* 19 (August 1982):301–14.

women, and the pace of subsequent fertility is faster for Blacks than Whites.[14]

However, there is evidence that college-educated Black women have completed fertility similar to White women.[15] These findings suggest some support for the social characteristics hypothesis and point out the difficulties in arriving at satisfactory explanations. We know, for example, that Blacks have an earlier age at first birth because of higher premarital and teenage fertility. But is it because there are few alternatives to achieving adulthood for Black girls, and the Black community supports early motherhood, as Rainwater proposed in line with the minority group hypothesis?[16] Or is it because young Black fertility is mediated through low income and lower educational attainment, as the social characteristics hypothesis suggests?

Causes and Correlates of Declining Fertility

The search for explanations of racial differences in fertility remains unresolved. So also the debate continues on why and when fertility rises or falls. The two major contending explanations for changes in fertility rates are the Easterlin and the Butz and Ward hypotheses. Easterlin proposed that fertility moves in predictable cycles depending on the income and employment opportunities of cohorts (generations) of men.[17] According to this theory, lifestyle aspirations are formed at an early age based on the income of one's parents. As cohorts reach adulthood and enter the labor force, their own income will match, exceed, or fall below that needed to sustain their desired standard of living. If their "relative income" is greater than anticipated, they will have more children; if it is less than hoped, they will have fewer children. Coupled with this theory is Easterlin's proposition of a negative relationship between cohort size and success of the cohort in the labor market: Small cohorts will do well financially while larger cohorts will suffer from increased competition for fewer jobs.[18] For example, the small birth cohorts of the

[14]St. John, "Race Differences," p. 312.

[15]Craig St. John and Harold Grasmick, "Decomposing the Black/White Fertility Differential," *Social Science Quarterly* 66 (March 1985):132–46.

[16]Lee Rainwater, *Behind Ghetto Walls* (Chicago: Aldine, 1970).

[17]Richard Easterlin, "Relative Economic Status and the American Fertility Swing," in Eleanor Sheldon, ed., *Family Economic Behavior* (Philadelphia: Lippincott, 1973), pp. 170–223.

[18]Richard Easterlin, *Births and Fortune* (New York: Basic Books, 1980).

1930s experienced favorable labor market conditions in the 1950s and responded by increasing their fertility (which produced the baby boom). But the large baby boom cohort entering the labor force during the 1970s suffered adverse labor market conditions and responded by reducing fertility (thus the "birth dearth").

There is conflicting support for Easterlin's model. It implies a cohort theory of fertility change (that is, that preferences are formed early and do not change over the life cycle), yet changes in fertility are quite sensitive to period effects (the fertility rates of all age groups move in the same direction at the same time).[19] It is also the case that generational cycles smooth out over time and lose their importance as determinants of fertility.[20]

Some studies have found little validity in the Easterlin hypothesis,[21] while others verify its accuracy.[22] Much of the discord comes from applying aggregate data to an individual behavior model and from using different definitions of "relative income." Easterlin's biggest oversight is his emphasis on the income and employment opportunities of men which ignores the role of women in the childbearing decision-making process, as well as the importance of recent changes in women's labor force participation and perceived opportunity costs to childbearing.

The Butz and Ward model perhaps overcompensates for Easterlin's exclusion of women in the childbearing decision. Their theory is that three factors affect the timing of fertility decisions: the proportion of women in the labor force, women's earnings, and men's earnings.[23] While increases in the husband's income may increase the demand for children, the wife's wages will have the opposite effect. Increases in women's wages serve to depress fertility by increas-

[19]Robert Kleinbaum, "Forecasting U.S. Age Specific Fertility Rates," unpublished manuscript, Population Studies Center, University of Michigan, 1983.

[20]D. P. Smith, "A Reconsideration of Easterlin Cycles," *Population Studies* 35 (July 1981):247–64.

[21]Thomas W. Pullum, "Separating Age, Period, and Cohort Effects in White U.S. Fertility, 1920 to 1970," *Social Science Research* 9 (September 1980):225–44; and Arland Thornton, "Fertility Change after the Baby Boom: The Role of Economic Stress, Female Employment, and Education," final report to the National Institute of Child Health and Human Development (November 1976).

[22]Barbara Devaney, "An Analysis of Variations in U.S. Fertility and Female Labor Force Participation Trends," *Demography* 20 (May 1983):147–62; and Ronald D. Lee, "Demographic Forecasting and the Easterlin Hypothesis," *Population and Development Review* 2 (September-December 1976):459–68.

[23]William Butz and Michael Ward, "The Emergence of Countercyclical U.S. Fertility," *American Economic Review* 69 (June 1979):318–27.

ing the cost of the wife's foregone wages. By considering the earnings of both men and women, Butz and Ward account for the postwar upswing in fertility with the rising incomes of men, while the decline in the 1970s can be explained by increases in women's wages and labor force participation.

The Butz and Ward countercyclical theory has predicted fertility swings fairly well, but at least one recent development casts doubt on its relevance for the future. O'Connell points out that the Butz and Ward model is based on the assumption that trade-offs between fertility and employment are made in the context of married-couple households. Yet the percentage of currently married women aged 20 to 24 dropped from 64 to 39 percent between 1960 and 1982; among women aged 25 to 29, those currently married with a spouse present declined from 82 to 62 percent.[24] Given these significant decreases in the proportion of women under 30 who are married, the hypothesized relationship between female employment and fertility may not apply since so many women are outside the married-couple household on which the theory is based. Of course, delayed marriage, like lower fertility, might be predicted by higher earnings opportunities for women. In this case, the large numbers of employed, unmarried women would support the Butz and Ward hypothesis.

Delayed age at first marriage is not the only reason fewer women in their prime childbearing years are not currently married; another reason is the higher incidence of divorce and separation. Marital dissolution reduces fertility by taking women out of socially acceptable unions for childbearing.[25] Time spent between marriages is usually time lost for reproduction for most women. Remarriage appears to allow White women to recoup lost childbearing opportunities by starting a new family, but remarriage for Blacks tends to lower their completed fertility.[26] The currently high divorce rate combined with a later age at marriage may mean that the Butz and Ward model will become increasingly less applicable in predicting future fertility.

[24]O'Connell, "Countercyclical Fertility," pp. 1, 8.

[25]Kingsley Davis and Judith Blake, "Social Structure and Fertility: An Analytic Framework," *Economic Development and Cultural Change* 4 (1955–56):211–35; Helen P. Koo and Barbara K. Janowitz, "Interrelationships between Fertility and Marital Dissolution: Results of a Simultaneous Logit Model," *Demography* 20 (May 1983):129–46; and R. G. Potter and F. E. Kobrin, "Some Effects of Spouse Separation on Fertility," *Demography* 19 (February 1982):79–95.

[26]Arland Thornton, "Marital Dissolution, Remarriage and Childbearing," *Demography* 15 (August 1978):361–80.

Changing Birth Expectations

Theoretical explanations of fertility swings may account for changes on the aggregate level, but there are correlates of the fertility decline that operate more directly on the individual level. For example, preferences and expectations are for smaller families now than they were in the past, and those intentions are achieved by individual women. Data on birth expectations have been gathered since the first Growth of American Families Survey in 1955.[27] The intent was to help demographers develop population projections based on the number of children a woman said that she expected. National Fertility Studies begun in 1965 and the June supplements to the Census Bureau's Current Population Survey (CPS) beginning in 1971 have provided continuous data on birth expectations.

Birth expectations have declined over the past two decades for a variety of reasons. As more women have entered the labor force, they have scaled down their expectations for large families. More effective methods of contraception have reduced the likelihood of an unplanned pregnancy and thus women have more control over their desired family size. By marrying later, women are also postponing childbearing and not anticipating as many years at risk of pregnancy.[28]

The most important group in the analysis of birth expectations are women aged 18 to 24, because these women are just beginning their reproductive years. Table 2.2 shows the decline over time in birth expectations for this group.

By 1982, birth expectations were for 2.1 children among both White and Black wives aged 18 to 24 compared with expectations for over three children each in the 1960s. Preferences for the two-child

[27]Ronald Freedman, P. K. Whelpton, and Angus Campbell, *Family Planning, Sterility, and Population Growth* (New York: McGraw-Hill, 1959).
[28]Lolagene C. Coombs, "Reproductive Goals and Achieved Fertility: A Fifteen Year Perspective," *Demography*, 16 (November 1979):523–34; Ronald Freedman, Deborah S. Freedman, and Arland D. Thornton, "Changes in Fertility Expectations and Preferences between 1962 and 1977: Their Relation to Final Parity," *Demography* 17 (November 1980):365–78; Che-Fu Lee and Mohammad M. Kahn, "Factors Related to the Intention to Have Additional Children in the United States: A Reanalysis of Data from the 1965 and 1970 National Fertility Studies," *Demography* 15 (August 1978):337–44; Arland Thornton, Ronald Freedman, and Deborah S. Freedman, "Further Reflections on Changes in Fertility Expectations and Preferences," *Demography* 21 (August 1984):423–29; S. Philip Morgan, "Intention and Uncertainty at Later Stages of Childbearing: The United States, 1965 and 1970," *Demography* 18 (August 1981):267–86; and Martin O'Connell and Carolyn C. Rogers, "Assessing Cohort Birth Expectations Data from the Current Population Survey, 1971–1981," *Demography* 20 (August 1983):369–84.

TABLE 2.2

Changing Birth Expectations of Young Married Women

Year	All Races	White	Black
1955	—	3.2	—
1960	3.1	3.0	—
1965	3.1	3.1	3.4
1971	2.4	2.4	2.6
1976	2.1	2.1	2.3
1982	2.1	2.1	2.1

NOTE: Lifetime births expected by currently married women aged 18 to 24.

SOURCE: U.S. Bureau of the Census, "Perspectives on American Fertility," *Current Population Reports*, series P-23, no. 70 (Washington DC: U.S. Government Printing Office, 1978), table 3–1; "Fertility of American Women: June 1983," *Current Population Reports*, series P-20, no. 395 (Washington, DC: U.S. Government Printing Office, 1983), table 1.

family have increased while preferences for larger families have declined. In 1983, one-half of wives expected a total of two lifetime births compared with only one-quarter in 1960. Preferences for four children declined from 37 percent in 1960 to just 7 percent in 1983. Expectations of childlessness have remained stable at about 4 to 5 percent.[29]

The underlying assumption in using birth expectations is that women know how many children they want. Yet a variety of factors can operate to produce indecision: marital status and age, current and future economic conditions, or present family size. Among White wives in the 1970 National Fertility Study, 10 percent expressed uncertainty about future fertility plans.[30] CPS figures show that 12 percent of wives aged 18 to 34 were uncertain of birth expectations in 1971, although that proportion had declined to 9 percent by 1983.[31]

Birth expectations can change over time depending on the number of children a woman already has. For example, the response of a childless woman in her late 20s will be different from the response of a woman who already has one or two children. Among currently

[29]U.S. Bureau of the Census, "Perspectives on American Fertility," *Current Population Reports*, series P-23, no. 70 (Washington, DC: U.S. Government Printing Office, 1978), table 3.3; and U.S. Bureau of the Census, "Fertility of American Women: June 1983," *Current Population Reports*, series P-20, no. 395 (Washington, DC: U.S. Government Printing Office, 1983), table 7.

[30]S. Philip Morgan, "Parity-Specific Fertility Intentions and Uncertainty: The U.S., 1970 to 1976," *Demography* 19 (August 1982):315–34.

[31]U.S. Bureau of the Census, "Fertility 1983," p. 6.

married women aged 25 to 29 in 1983, one-half of those with no children expected two future births. Among women aged 25 to 29 with one child, only one-fifth expected two future births, and among those with two children, only one-twentieth expected two future births.[32]

Just how good are stated birth expectations in predicting future fertility? At least one study found them to be consistent with future aggregate fertility,[33] but data from both the National Fertility Surveys and the June Current Population Surveys indicate that reproductive intentions tend to overestimate short-range fertility rates.[34] O'Connell and Rogers found that birth expectations of married women are very good predictors of completed fertility. The failure of recent expectations to predict the fertility decline of the 1970s may have been due to the childbearing of women who were unmarried at the beginning of the decade. The authors suggest that birth expectations can be useful predictors of completed cohort fertility if adjustments are made for the proportion married within each birth cohort.[35] Still another theory is that lowered fertility precedes lowered expectations, so that norms change in response to changes in behavior.[36]

It is generally accepted now that the ideal family size for Americans is two children, although preferences may vary somewhat depending on the sex of children already born.[37] Blake attributed the decline in ideal family size to Americans' greater awareness of population problems and predicted that it might be a temporary response.[38] However, a two-child norm appears to be still operative ten years after Blake's prediction. Perhaps part of its persistence is the availability of contraception and abortion, which allows women to achieve their reproductive goals more easily than they could in the past.

[32]U.S. Bureau of the Census, "Fertility 1983," p. 21.

[33]Ronald D. Lee, "Target Fertility, Contraception, and Aggregate Rates: Toward A Formal Synthesis," *Demography* 14 (November 1977):455–79.

[34]Martin O'Connell and Maurice Moore, "New Evidence on the Value of Birth Expectations," *Demography* 14 (August 1977):255–64; and Charles F. Westoff and Norman B. Ryder, "The Predictive Validity of Reproductive Intentions," *Demography* 14 (November 1977):431–54.

[35]O'Connell and Rogers, "Assessing Cohort Birth Expectations," p. 1.

[36]Easterlin, "Relative Economic Status."

[37]Douglas M. Sloane and Che-Fu Lee, "Sex of Previous Children and Intentions for Further Births in the United States, 1965–1976," *Demography* 20 (August 1983):353–67.

[38]Judith Blake, "Can We Believe Recent Data on Birth Expectations in the United States?" *Demography* 11 (February 1974):25–44.

Contraception and Abortion

Contraception and abortion have made it easier to prevent unwanted pregnancies and to plan the timing of wanted births.[39] Between 1965 and 1982, the percentage of unwanted births to currently married women declined from 20 to 7 percent; the percentage of births mistimed fell from 45 to 22 percent.[40] The proportion of currently married women aged 15 to 44 who used contraception increased from 63 to 68 percent between 1965 and 1982; the increase was from 64 to 69 percent among White wives and from 56 to 61 percent among Black wives.[41] Since women not using contraception include those pregnant, those trying to get pregnant, and those contraceptively sterile at the time of the interview, an estimated 95 percent of women exposed to the "risk" of childbearing were actually practicing contraception in 1982.[42]

The increase in contraceptive use between 1965 and 1982 is not especially large because American women had been relying on contraception for some time. The biggest change involved effectiveness of the methods used. More effective forms of contraception such as the pill, the intrauterine device (IUD), and sterilization were not widely available until the 1970s. As an example of differences in effectiveness, the rhythm method has a failure rate of 19 percent compared with a failure rate of only 2.5 percent for the pill.[43] In other words, 19 percent of wives using the rhythm method had an unintended pregnancy within the first year of contraceptive use compared with less than 3 percent of wives using the pill. As Figure 2.4 demonstrates, two-thirds of all contraceptors in 1965 relied on traditional methods of birth control (primarily the condom). By 1982 about two-thirds of all contracepting wives were using more effective methods.

[39]Robert H. Weller and Frank B. Hobbs, "Unwanted and Mistimed Births in the United States: 1968–1973," *Family Planning Perspectives* 10 (May-June 1978):168–72; and Charles F. Westoff, "The Decline of Unplanned Births in the United States," *Science* 191 (January 9, 1976):38–41.

[40]William F. Pratt, William D. Mosher, Christine A. Bachrach, and Marjorie C. Horn, "Understanding U.S. Fertility: Findings from the National Survey of Family Growth, Cycle III," *Population Bulletin*, vol. 39, no. 5 (Washington, DC: Population Reference Bureau, December 1984), table 14.

[41]National Center for Health Statistics, "Trends in Contraceptive Practice: United States, 1965–76," *Vital and Health Statistics*, series 23, no. 10 (Washington, DC: U.S. Government Printing Office, 1982), pp. 25, 26; and National Center for Health Statistics, "Use of Contraception in the United States, 1982," *Vital and Health Statistics*, series 23, no. 102 (Washington, DC: U.S. Government Printing Office, 1984), p. 3.

[42]National Center for Health Statistics, "Use of Contraception," p. 3.

[43]Pratt et al., "Understanding U.S. Fertility," table 5.

FIGURE 2.4

Trend in Contraceptive Use Among Married Women

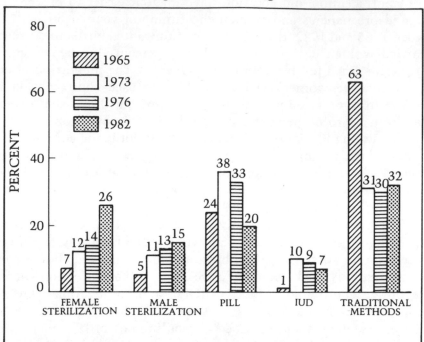

Note: Traditional methods include diaphragm, condom, foam, periodic abstinence, withdrawal, douche, other; base for percentages is all currently married women aged 15 to 44 who report using contraception.

SOURCE: National Center for Health Statistics, "Trends in Contraceptive Practice: United States, 1965–76," *Vital and Health Statistics*, series 23, no. 10 (Washington, DC: U.S. Department of Health and Human Services, 1982), table 7; William F. Pratt, William D. Mosher, Christine A. Bachrach, and Marjorie C. Horn, "Understanding U.S. Fertility: Findings from the National Survey of Family Growth, Cycle III," *Population Bulletin*, vol. 39, no. 5 (Washington DC: Population Reference Bureau, 1984), table 8.

Female sterilization outranked oral contraception as the leading form of birth control for the first time in 1982. The pill enjoyed a high point of popularity in the 1970s when nearly one-third of all contracepting women were using it, but showed a sharp decline by 1982. Greater knowledge of the health risks associated with pill use, especially for smokers and women over 35, probably contributed to the decline in the pill's popularity and to the increase in the choice of sterilization by both men and women.

Couples who choose sterilization are primarily older couples who expect no more children, while those on the pill are younger and plan to have more children. Increasingly, couples are choosing sterilization rather than continued pill use in later years. In 1982, 62 percent of couples intending to have no more children were contraceptively sterile (male or female) compared with 18 percent in 1965. Among contracepting couples intending one or more future births, the leading form of birth control has consistently been the pill (38 percent in 1965; 61 percent in 1973; and 45 percent in 1982).[44]

Currently married Black women are slightly less likely to be using contraception than White women (61 versus 69 percent in 1982). The proportion of Black women who are currently married and not using contraception has been nearly twice the White proportion since 1965. Among users of contraception, about one-third of currently married Black women were sterilized compared with one-quarter of White women in 1982. (Black men, however, are much less likely to have vasectomies than White men: 4 versus 16 percent). Other racial differences include higher use of the pill among Blacks and lower use of condoms.[45]

The contraceptive choices of unmarried women differ from those of wives. In 1982 sexually active single (that is, never-married) women were about twice as likely as married women to risk an unintended pregnancy by not using any form of contraception. When they do use some form of birth control, half choose the pill compared with only 20 percent of wives. About 50 percent of women who are widowed, divorced, or separated use contraception (versus 68 percent of wives and 35 percent of singles) and about 30 percent use the pill.[46]

Although the Catholic Church specifically forbids the use of contraception (other than the rhythm method), reported contraceptive use differs little by religion. In 1982, 52 percent of Catholic women and 55 percent of Protestant women aged 15 to 44 used some method of contraception. Among contracepting Catholics, 6 percent used the rhythm method compared with 3 percent of Protestants.

---

[44]Pratt et al., "Understanding U.S. Fertility," table 8.
[45]Pratt et al., "Understanding U.S. Fertility," table 8; and National Center for Health Statistics, "Trends," pp. 25–26.
[46]Pratt et al., "Understanding U.S. Fertility," table 7.

Approximately 28 percent of contracepting Catholics and 30 percent of Protestants used the pill.[47]

Liberalized abortion laws first went into effect in the United States in 1967 and abortion became legal nationwide in 1973. Between 1973 and 1980 the number of abortions performed annually rose from 745,000 to 1.3 million. The ratio of abortions to live births has increased from about 22 abortions per 100 live births in the early 1970s to a high of 42 in the late 1970s; the ratio in 1980 was 36 abortions per 100 live births.[48] In other words, there was about one legal abortion for every three live births in 1980.

Women who obtain abortions are most often young, White, and unmarried. In 1980 about 65 percent of women who obtained abortions were under 25, 70 percent were White, and 75 percent were unmarried.[49] In 1982, 40 percent of all women (regardless of marital status) said they would consider having an abortion if faced with an unwanted pregnancy (48 percent of Black women compared with 40 percent of White women). About one-third of married women say

---

[47]Pratt et al., "Understanding U.S. Fertility," table 7. Although both Catholic and Protestant fertility followed the same postwar decline, there is debate over whether the Catholic–non-Catholic differential in fertility has converged. Jones and Westoff announced "the end of 'Catholic' fertility" in 1979, yet a replication of their work by Mosher and Hendershot found a continued fertility differential by religion. Using 1976 data from the National Survey of Family Growth, Mosher and Hendershot found a fertility decline among both Catholics and Protestants between 1966 and 1975, a faster decline among Catholic couples, and convergence between Catholic and non-Catholic fertility. However, they also found a larger religious difference in Total Marital Fertility Rates than did Jones and Westoff and attribute the difference mainly to measurement techniques. A variety of other studies support Mosher and Hendershot's results, especially in the greater likelihood of Protestants to remain voluntarily childless. In general, most studies support convergence of fertility over time, but not a complete disappearance of differences by religion. See Elise Jones and Charles F. Westoff, "The End of 'Catholic' Fertility," *Demography* 16 (May 1979):209–18; William D. Mosher and Gerry E. Hendershot, "Religion and Fertility: A Replication," *Demography* 21 (May 1984):185–91; William D. Mosher and Gerry E. Hendershot, "Religious Affiliation and the Fertility of Married Couples, *Journal of Marriage and the Family* 46 (August 1984):671–78; Susan G. Janssen and Robert Hauser, "Religion, Socialization, and Fertility," *Demography* 18 (November 1981):511–28; Nan Johnson, "Religious Differentials in Reproduction: The Effects of Sectarian Education," *Demography* 19 (November 1982):495–509; Dudley L. Poston, Jr. and Kathryn B. Kramer, "Patterns of Childlessness Among Catholics and Non-Catholics in the United States," *Texas Population Research Center Papers*, no. 6.006 (Austin: University of Texas, 1984); and Georges Sabagh and David Lopez, "Religiosity and Fertility: The Case of Chicanos," *Social Forces* 59 (December 1980):431–39.

[48]U.S. Department of Health and Human Services, Center for Disease Control, "Abortion Surveillance 1979–1980" (Atlanta: U.S. Department of Health and Human Services, 1983), p. 1.

[49]U.S. Department of Health and Human Services, "Abortion Surveillance," p. 1.

they would consider an abortion compared with about one-half of unmarried women.[50]

Attitudes toward abortion became much more liberal immediately after it was legalized, but recent studies indicate a shift back to more conservative views. The woman's health and possible deformity of the child are still acceptable reasons for abortion to a majority of survey respondents, but not wanting a child for personal or financial reasons is less favorably perceived.[51]

Estimates are that approximately 18 percent of American women aged 18 to 44 in 1981 had obtained a legal abortion since 1967. If current rates of abortion continue, about 40 percent of women will have had at least one abortion by age 45.[52]

Timing of Fertility

The heightened ability to control fertility has resulted in pronounced changes for women in the timing of births. The most significant of these changes is delayed childbearing.

The timing of a first birth is important to a woman because it involves such a big change in lifestyle and life chances.[53] In addition to presenting health risks for the mother and child, very young childbearing can conflict with a woman's educational and career goals, which may be realized more easily by a childless woman than by a mother. Until very recently, for example, a teenage pregnancy was grounds for the mother's expulsion from high school (although not the father's). A high school graduate with college or job aspirations might find that childbearing in the teens or early 20s presents barriers to future economic achievement. The timing of a first birth also

---

[50]Jacqueline D. Forrest and Stanley K. Henshaw, "What U.S. Women Think and Do About Contraception," *Family Planning Perspectives* 15 (July-August 1983):157–66.

[51]Judith Blake and Jorge H. Del Pinal, "Negativism, Equivocation, and Wobbly Assent: Public 'Support' for the Prochoice Platform on Abortion," *Demography* 18 (August 1981): 309–20; and Helen R. Ebaugh and C. Allen Haney, "Shifts in Abortion Attitudes: 1972–1978," *Journal of Marriage and the Family* 42 (August 1980):491–500.

[52]Forrest and Henshaw, "What U.S. Women Think," p. 160.

[53]Steven D. McLaughlin and Michael Micklin, "The Timing of the First Birth and Changes in Personal Efficacy," *Journal of Marriage and the Family* 45 (February 1983):47–56; Harriet B. Presser, "The Timing of the First Birth, Female Roles and Black Fertility," *Milbank Memorial Fund Quarterly* 49 (July 1971):329–61.

has implications for subsequent childbearing and completed family size.[54]

The general decline in fertility during the past two decades has been accompanied by a delay in the timing of childbearing as well. Median age at first birth was 21.4 between 1960 and 1964 and had risen to 22.3 by 1975–79.[55] Growing proportions of women born since the late 1930s have been postponing their first birth.[56] Seventy percent of women born between 1935 and 1939 (mothers of the baby boom children) had their first births by age 25. This proportion fell to 60 percent for women born ten years later and to 53 percent for women in the 1950–54 birth cohort (that is, those currently in their early 30s).[57]

Delayed childbearing is a result of both delayed marriage and the postponement of children within marriage. The proportion of women who have had their first birth within the first year of marriage has declined over time. Two-fifths of women who first married in the early 1960s had a child within one year compared with only one-third of women who first married in the early 1970s. Among the earlier marriage cohort, 30 percent had their second child within three years of marriage but only 17 percent of the later marriage cohort had borne their second child within three years. That is, the median interval between births has increased. The median interval between first and second births was 30 months in 1945–49; it declined to 26 months during the baby boom years of 1960–64, and then lengthened to 36 months by 1975–79.[58]

Although a woman is biologically capable of having children until the onset of menopause, most childbearing ceases long before then. For women who had completed their childbearing years by 1980, 95 percent had had their last child by age 39, 82 percent by age 35, and 53 percent by age 30. Even among women with five or more children, nearly two-thirds had completed childbearing by age 35.[59]

---

[54]U.S. Bureau of the Census, "Perspectives"; and U.S. Bureau of the Census, "Childspacing among Birth Cohorts of American Women: 1905 to 1959," *Current Population Reports*, series P-20, no. 385 (Washington, DC: U.S. Government Printing Office, 1984), pp. 6–9.

[55]U.S. Bureau of the Census, "Fertility of American Women: June 1979," *Current Population Reports*, series P-20, no. 358 (Washington, DC: U.S. Government Printing Office, 1980), table A.

[56]Jane R. Wilkie, "The Trend Toward Delayed Parenthood," *Journal of Marriage and the Family* 43 (August 1981):583–92.

[57]U.S. Bureau of the Census, "Childspacing among Birth Cohorts," p. 1.

[58]U.S. Bureau of the Census, "Childspacing among Birth Cohorts," p. 1.

[59]U.S. Bureau of the Census, "Childspacing among Birth Cohorts," p. 4.

On a cohort basis, the median age of the mother at birth of the last child has declined while median age at the birth of the first child has remained approximately stable over the long run, thus compressing the number of childbearing years into a shorter time frame. For example, among women born between 1880 and 1889, median age at first birth was 23.0 and at last birth was 32.9, a difference of 9.9 years. For women born between 1920 and 1929, median age at first birth was 22.7 and at last birth was 31.5, a difference of 8.8 years.[60] The decline in the age at last birth is due mainly to the smaller number of children borne to each woman, since the interval between births is increasing again.

One of the clearest indicators of delayed childbearing is the change in the percentage of currently childless women by age. Table 2.3 shows differences in childlessness by race and age from 1940 to 1980.

Proportions childless among ever-married women under 30 increased steadily after the peak of the baby boom. For those aged 20 to 24, the proportion childless rose from 24 to 42 percent between 1960 and 1980; for those aged 25 to 29, from 13 to 27 percent. While fertility has been declining for younger women, it has recently risen for older women. Between 1980 and 1982 the fertility rate for women aged 30 to 34 increased by 13 percent.[61] These data suggest that currently childless women in their 20s may be delaying childbearing until their 30s rather than foregoing motherhood altogether.

Statistics for 1940 and 1950 help place the current increase in childlessness in perspective. Proportions childless among ever-married women under 30 were almost as high in 1940 as in 1980. For women aged 25 to 29 proportions childless in 1940 were *greater* than in 1980. A decade of economic depression as well as marital disruptions associated with World War II help account for such high rates of childlessness in 1940. Slight declines in childlessness by 1950 reflect the very beginning of the baby boom, but war-related fertility disruptions are still apparent.

Regardless of fluctuations in timing of births, the table shows little support for an increase in lifetime childlessness among married women. The proportion childless for ever-married women aged 15 to

[60]U.S. Bureau of the Census, "Perspectives," p. 20.
[61]U.S. Bureau of the Census, "Fertility of American Women: June 1982 (Advance Report), *Current Population Reports*, series P-20, no. 379 (Washington, DC: U.S. Government Printing Office, 1983), table A.

TABLE 2.3

Changes in the Percentage of Ever-Married Women Who Remain Childless

Race and Year	Total	Age					
		15–19	20–24	25–29	30–34	35–39	40–44
ALL RACES							
1940	26.5%	54.6%	39.9%	30.1%	23.3%	19.9%	17.4%
1950	22.8	52.8	33.3	21.1	17.3	19.1	20.0
1960	15.0	43.6	24.2	12.6	10.4	11.1	14.1
1970	16.4	50.9	35.7	15.8	8.3	7.3	8.6
1980	20.2	52.5	41.9	27.3	14.4	8.8	7.1
WHITE							
1940	25.9	56.4	40.3	29.7	22.3	18.9	16.7
1950	21.8	55.4	34.0	20.1	15.8	17.5	18.9
1960	14.6	46.0	25.0	12.3	9.7	10.2	13.0
1970	16.7	53.7	37.5	16.1	8.1	6.9	8.1
1980	21.2	54.4	44.5	29.2	15.0	8.9	6.9
BLACK							
1940	32.8	46.6	38.7	35.1	31.0	28.8	25.8
1950	30.8	38.0	28.9	30.0	30.8	32.3	30.1
1960	18.7	25.3	17.0	14.2	15.8	20.0	24.7
1970	13.8	32.2	20.7	12.6	9.4	9.8	13.0
1980	13.3	40.2	24.4	15.3	10.3	8.7	8.5

SOURCE: U.S. Bureau of the Census, *Historical Statistics of the United States: Colonial Times to 1970,* Bicentennial Edition (Washington, DC: U.S. Government Printing Office, 1975), series B49–66; *Census of Population: 1980,* vol. 1, chap. D, U.S. Summary, table 270.

44 has increased since 1960, but among women aged 40 to 44 (who can be assumed to have completed their childbearing years), childlessness declined steadily from 20 percent in 1950 to 7 percent in 1980. Further support for delayed (versus no) childbearing is provided by birth expectations of currently childless wives: In 1983, 46 percent of 30-to-34-year-old childless wives expected to remain childless, a significant decline from the 68 percent in 1976 and 74 percent in 1971 who said they expected no children.[62] Although more women are remaining childless into their 30s, fewer of them intend to remain childless throughout life than was true a decade ago.

We do not yet know what the levels of childlessness will ultimately be for women now in their 20s and 30s. Despite their inten-

[62]U.S. Bureau of the Census, "Fertility 1983," p. 20; and U.S. Bureau of the Census, "Fertility 1982 (Advance Report)," p. 4.

tions to eventually have children, women who are currently delaying marriage and motherhood may end up having no children either because they subsequently find they cannot have children or because their desire for children changes the longer they delay. Repeated temporary postponements beyond the period of childbearing is one of the most common reasons for voluntary childlessness.[63] Some researchers are projecting very high levels of childlessness for women born during the 1950s. Bloom, for example, anticipates a rise in childlessness to about 25 percent for recent White cohorts and 20 percent for non-White cohorts; other researchers have made similarly high estimates of future childlessness.[64]

Related to the issue of childlessness is that of the only-child family. Although even one child makes a woman a full-time mother, the demands on a mother's time and the number of years spent in childrearing are fewer for one child than for two or more. Lifetime birth expectations for only one child increased from 7 percent in 1960 to 13 percent in 1983 among wives aged 18 to 34.[65] The prevalence of one-child families may continue to increase as more women postpone childbearing and enter the labor force. The rising cost of raising children may also influence family size preferences.

The proportion of currently married women aged 30 to 34 with one child who expected no future births was 62 percent in 1983.[66] Masnick reports that the levels of expected single-child parenthood are 10 to 12 percent for White women and 15 to 20 percent for Black women.[67] The higher rate of only-children among Black women may be a result of higher labor force participation rates and the constraints of lower socioeconomic status coupled with higher divorce and separation rates. Masnick predicts that the proportion of women

[63]J. E. Veevers, "Voluntarily Childless Wives: An Exploratory Study," *Sociology and Social Research* 57 (April 1973):356–65.

[64]David Bloom, "What's Happening to the Age at First Birth in the United States? A Study of Recent Cohorts," *Demography* 19 (August 1982):351–70; David Bloom and James Trussell, "What Are the Determinants of Delayed Childbearing and Permanent Childlessness in the United States?" *Demography* 21 (November 1984):591–612; George Masnick and Mary Jo Bane, *The Nation's Families: 1960–1990* (Boston: Auburn House, 1980); and Charles F. Westoff, "Some Speculations on the Future of Marriage and Fertility," *Family Planning Perspectives* 10 (March-April 1978):79–83.

[65]U.S. Bureau of the Census, "Perspectives," table 3–3; and U.S. Bureau of the Census, "Fertility 1983," table 7.

[66]U.S. Bureau of the Census, "Fertility 1983," p. 21.

[67]George S. Masnick, "The Continuity of Birth Expectations Data with Historical Trends in Cohort Parity Distributions: Implications for Fertility in the 1980's," in Gerry Hendershot and Paul Placek, eds., *Predicting Fertility: Demographic Studies of Birth Expectations* (Lexington, MA: Heath, 1981).

who have only one child will reach an all-time high with the baby boom cohort: "Women born in the late 1950s are expected to set new records with regard to the proportion having only one child, with about 25 percent settling into this parity category by the end of their reproductive ages."[68]

Black-White Differences in Timing of Fertility

Although historically Blacks have had higher fertility than Whites, paradoxically they also have had higher rates of childlessness. From 1940 until 1970 childlessness among women nearing the end of their childbearing years (those aged 40 to 44) was much greater for Blacks than Whites (see Table 2.3). By 1980 the proportion childless among older women was only slightly higher for Black women. Reasons offered for the high proportions childless among Black women born in the early part of the century include subfecundity (resulting from poor nutrition and health), greater instability of marriages, and underregistration of first births.[69]

Delayed childbearing is more characteristic of White women than Black women.[70] Blacks start childbearing earlier than Whites, which is one reason for larger completed Black family size. Proportionately twice as many Black women as White women born during the baby boom had a first birth by age 20: 41 percent versus 19 percent.[71]

Black women are also more likely to have a birth within the first year of marriage than White women, although the likelihood has decreased over time for both races. Two-thirds of Black women who first married between 1960 and 1964 had a child within twelve months compared with two-fifths of White women. One decade later 62 percent of Black women and 30 percent of White women had a first birth within twelve months of marriage.[72] The percentage point

[68]George S. Masnick, "Appendix B: Parity Projections," final report prepared for the U.S. Department of Housing and Urban Development, 1985, p. 6.
[69]Bloom, "What's Happening," p. 365; Joseph A. McFalls, Jr. "Frustrated Fertility: A Population Paradox," *Population Bulletin*, vol. 34, no. 2 (Washington, DC: Population Reference Bureau, 1979), p. 37; and U.S. Bureau of the Census, "Childspacing among Birth Cohorts," p. 3.
[70]Bloom, "What's Happening," p. 1.
[71]U.S. Bureau of the Census, "Childspacing among Birth Cohorts," table A.
[72]U.S. Bureau of the Census, "Trends in Childspacing: June 1975," *Current Population Reports*, series P-20, no. 315 (Washington, DC: U.S. Government Printing Office, 1978), table D.

TABLE 2.4

Median Number of Months Between Births, Selected Periods

Birth Interval	1945–49		1955–59		1965–69		1975–79	
	White	Black	White	Black	White	Black	White	Black
First and Second	30.9	23.9	28.2	23.4	29.6	26.4	35.7	39.1
Second and Third	31.9	24.2	31.9	25.6	34.9	28.7	40.1	37.2
Third and Fourth	29.5	23.7	30.5	24.1	35.2	27.0	42.2	28.2

SOURCE: U.S. Bureau of the Census, "Childspacing Among Birth Cohorts of American Women: 1905 to 1959," *Current Population Reports*, series P-20, no. 385 (Washington, DC: U.S. Government Printing Office, 1984), table 10.

decline for White women was thus greater than that for Black women.

The median interval between first marriage and first birth was 4.1 months for Black women in the early 1960s and had lengthened to 8.5 months by the early 1970s. For White women the median interval between first marriage and first birth was 13.6 months in the early 1960s and 18.6 months one decade later.[73] These statistics indicate a greater incidence of premaritally conceived births for Blacks than Whites (see the next section on teenage and out-of-wedlock fertility).

Traditionally the average interval between births has been much shorter for Black women than White women, as Table 2.4 demonstrates. At every date and for every interval except that between first and second births in 1975–79, Blacks experienced shorter intervals than Whites between births at all parities. Until the 1970s Blacks averaged about two years between births compared with about 2.5 years for Whites. By the end of the 1970s, however, both Blacks and Whites were waiting three or more years on average between births.

Not only do Black women begin having children at an earlier age than White women, but they also spend more years bearing children. For women born between 1930 and 1939, median age for Blacks was 20.6 for the first birth and 31.0 years for the last birth, a difference of 10.4 years. White women born during the same period had a later age at first birth (22.1) and a younger age at last birth (29.5), for a childbearing span of only 7.4 years.[74]

[73]U.S. Bureau of the Census, "Perspectives," table 2–3.
[74]U.S. Bureau of the Census, "Childspacing among Birth Cohorts," table B.

Causes and Correlates of Delayed Childbearing

Why are women delaying childbearing longer now than they did in the past? Later age at marriage and greater frequency of divorce remove women from the traditional context of childbearing (that is, marriage) for longer periods of time than was true in the past. Access to contraception and abortion also allows women to time the frequency of their pregnancies, both inside and outside of marriage.

Ward and Butz argue that current fertility delays are due to higher labor force participation and wage rates for women, causing them to postpone childbearing until the opportunity costs are lower.[75] Easterlin's explanation is that poor employment options for young men have influenced the timing of births.[76] Others believe that normative changes have occurred which reduce the importance of childbearing as women's roles expand to make motherhood a choice rather than an obligation.[77]

Each of these broad explanations has some merit. Yet it is also possible to look at individual correlates to discover which women are most likely to delay childbearing or forego it entirely. For example, one of the clearest relationships is between educational attainment and the timing of childbearing. Numerous studies have shown that more highly educated women postpone first births longer than less educated women.[78] Women who remain childless are also likely to have higher educational attainment than women with children.[79]

Education operates to delay or prevent childbearing in several ways. The first is that time spent in school (college or post-graduate

---

[75]Michael Ward and William Butz, "Completed Fertility and Its Timing," *Journal of Political Economy* 88 (October 1980):917–40.

[76]Easterlin, "Relative Economic Status."

[77]Norman B. Ryder, "The Future of American Fertility," *Social Problems* 26 (February 1979):359–70; and Charles F. Westoff, "Marriage and Fertility in the Developed Countries," *Scientific American* 239 (June 1978):51–57.

[78]Bloom and Trussell, "What Are the Determinants"; Ronald R. Rindfuss, Larry L. Bumpass, and Craig St. John, "Education and Fertility: Implications for the Roles Women Occupy," *American Sociological Review* 45 (June 1980):431–47; and Ronald R. Rindfuss, S. Philip Morgan, and C. Gray Swicegood, "The Transition to Motherhood: The Intersection of Structural and Temporal Dimensions," *American Sociological Review* 49 (June 1984):359–72.

[79]David E. Bloom and Ann R. Pebley, "Voluntary Childlessness: A Review of the Evidence and Implications," *Population Research and Policy Review* 1 (October 1982):203–24; G. F. Dejong and R. R. Sell, "Changes in Childlessness in the United States: A Demographic Path Analysis," *Population Studies* 31 (March 1977):129–41; and P. Neal Ritchey and C. Shannon Stokes, "Correlates of Childlessness and Expectations to Remain Childless," *Social Forces* 52 (March 1974):349–56.

training) is ordinarily time spent outside a reproductive union. In other words, a woman who wants a college or professional degree will often not jeopardize that goal by having children while still in school. It may also be that women who pursue higher education are a self-selected group with little interest in childbearing or that traditional values and attitudes toward children change while a woman is in school. One theory is that well-educated women respond most strongly to the prevailing socioeconomic climate and therefore are most likely to postpone fertility when economic conditions are difficult.[80] Regardless of the cause, rising educational attainment for women means proportionately more women may delay childbearing in the future.

Another factor associated with delayed childbearing is labor force participation. Women who work outside the home delay family formation longer and are also more likely to remain childless than women who are not employed.[81] Women who plan to work also plan smaller families, and one way to accomplish that goal is to delay the birth of the first child.[82]

A wife in the labor force helps the family's asset accumulation, and delayed childbearing eases the financial burden during the early years of marriage when couples are often trying to buy their first home. Highly educated women with professional aspirations may delay motherhood because they view childbearing as an interruption in their careers. Repeated postponement of the first birth for work-related reasons may eventually result in childlessness.[83] For example, professional and managerial occupations have disproportionately high numbers of childless women, while unskilled and agricultural occupations have disproportionately fewer childless women.[84]

The biological inability to bear children plays a fairly minor role in delayed and foregone childbearing. Infertility is defined as the inability to conceive after a year of intercourse without contraception. Among all currently married women aged 15 to 44, 14 percent were

[80]Rindfuss, Morgan, and Swicegood, "The Transition to Motherhood."

[81]Bloom and Trussell, "What Are the Determinants"; Elise Jones, "Ways in Which Childlessness Affects Women's Employment: Evidence from the U.S. 1975 National Fertility Study," *Population Studies* 36 (March 1982):5–14; and Jane R. Wilkie, "Delayed Parenthood."

[82]Linda J. Waite and Ross Stolzenberg, "Intended Childbearing and Labor Force Participation of Young Women: Insights from Nonrecursive Models," *American Sociological Review* 41 (April 1976):235–52.

[83]Veevers, "Voluntarily Childless."

[84]Bloom and Pebley, "Voluntary Childlessness"; and Wilkie, "Delayed Parenthood."

identified as infertile in 1982, up only slightly from 13 percent in 1965. The incidence of infertility does rise with age, however: from about 10 percent of couples in the 20-to-29-year age range to 27 percent of couples in the 40-to-44-year age range.[85] Some studies have found an increase in the incidence of infertility over time, possibly due to a rise in diseases such as Pelvic Inflammatory Disease which causes sterility in women. There is, however, no strong relationship between postponed births and infertility.[86]

Rindfuss and Bumpass suggest that age also works in a normative capacity to limit childbearing: there are norms about the "proper" timing of children, and older couples who have a first or additional baby may find themselves socially out of step with their peers.[87]

Consequences of Delayed Childbearing

Women who delay childbearing have smaller families than women who have an early first birth.[88] The most obvious biological reason is that women who start having children in their late 20s, whether due to later marriage or successful contraception, are at reproductive risk for fewer years than women who have their first

[85]Pratt et al., "Understanding U.S. Fertility," table 11; and William D. Mosher and Christine A. Bachrach, "Childlessness in the United States: Estimates from the National Survey of Family Growth," *Journal of Family Issues* 3 (December 1982):517–44; and William D. Mosher, "Fecundity and Infertility in the United States, 1965–1982," paper presented at the annual meeting of the Population Association of America, Minneapolis, May 3–5, 1984.

[86]John C. Barrett, "Effects of Various Factors on Selection for Family Planning Status and Natural Fecundability: A Simulation Study," *Demography* 15 (February 1978):87–98; John Bongaarts, "A Method for the Estimation of Fecundability," *Demography* 12 (November 1975):645–60; Jane Menken, "Seasonal Migration and Seasonal Variation in Fecundability: Effects on Birth Rates and Birth Intervals," *Demography* 16 (February 1979):103–20; Jane Menken "Age and Fertility: How Late Can You Wait?" *Demography* 22 (November 1985):469–83; and William B. Mosher, "Infertility Trends Among U.S. Couples: 1965–1976," *Family Planning Perspectives* 14 (January-February 1982):22–27.

[87]Ronald R. Rindfuss and Larry L. Bumpass, "Age and the Sociology of Fertility: How Old Is Too Old?" in Karl E. Taeuber, Larry L. Bumpass, and James A. Sweet, eds., *Social Demography* (New York: Academic Press, 1978), pp. 43–55.

[88]Larry L. Bumpass, Ronald R. Rindfuss, and Richard B. Janosik, "Age and Marital Status at First Birth and the Pace of Subsequent Fertility," *Demography* 15 (February 1978):75–86; Margaret M. Marini, "Measuring the Effects of the Timing of Marriage and First Births," *Journal of Marriage and the Family* 43 (February 1981):19–26; Margaret M. Marini, "Effects of the Timing of Marriage and First Birth on Fertility," *Journal of Marriage and the Family* 43 (February 1981):27–48; Margaret M. Marini and P. J. Hodsdon, "Effects of the Timing of Marriage and First Birth of the Spacing of Subsequent Births," *Demography* 18 (November 1981):529–48; and Amy Ong Tsui, "The Family Formation Process Among U.S. Marriage Cohorts," *Demography* 19 (February 1982):1–27.

child at age 22. Since most childbearing occurs in a seven to ten year time frame, however, women in their late 20s or 30s are still capable of bearing several children. Yet they do not have as many children as younger childbearers, which indicates the operation of other factors.

We have already mentioned the role of later age at marriage in delaying childbearing—the older the age at first marriage and the longer the first birth interval, the smaller the number of children.[89] Young mothers have fewer educational, lifestyle, and labor force options and may have less knowledge of contraception; early childbearers are also less successful in achieving family planning goals.[90] Early motherhood, reinforced by rapid subsequent fertility, limits other life options for women which might compete with childbearing.[91]

It is not clear whether completion of a certain level of education affects the timing of first births or whether the effects of an early or unplanned first birth affect educational attainment. However, women with less formal schooling tend to have higher fertility than those with more than a high school diploma. For recent cohorts it appears that women who did not complete high school may have failed to do so because of an early birth.[92]

A young mother without educational credentials may also have difficulty finding suitable employment, which in turn leads to lower income. In addition to having less education, for example, early childbearers work more hours than older mothers. Lower education is correlated with lower earnings among women and other household members (usually the husband). Since early childbearers tend to have larger families, limited resources must be distributed among more family members, and the incidence of poverty is greater.[93]

Very late childbearing may be advantageous for women. Hofferth found that women who had their first child at age 30 or later are significantly better off financially than either women who have children in their 20s or women without children.[94] Also, women aged 60 or older with only one or two children were better off finan-

[89]Marini, "Measuring the Effects," p. 26; and Marini, "Effects of the Timing."

[90]Barbara Vaughn, James Trussell, Jane Menken, and Louise Jones, "Contraceptive Failure Among Married Women in the U.S.: 1970–1973," *Family Planning Perspectives* 9 (November-December 1977):251–58; and Wilkie, "Delayed Parenthood."

[91]Bumpass, Rindfuss, and Janosik, "Age and Marital Status," p. 83.

[92]U.S. Bureau of the Census, "Childspacing among Birth Cohorts," p. 9.

[93]Hofferth and Moore, "Early Childbearing."

[94]Sandra Hofferth, "Some Long Term Economic Consequences for Women of Delayed Childbearing and Reduced Family Size," *Demography* 21 (May 1984):141–55.

cially than those with a larger family or with no children. Hofferth concludes that "late childbearing coupled with small family size appears associated with higher incomes and living standards of women."[95] This would complement the theory that a reduction in the childbearing time span can significantly minimize interruptions in a woman's educational or working career and thus increase her long-run economic assets. Another interpretation might be that women with the greatest financial advantages delay childbearing. Like most issues surrounding fertility, the causality of the relationship is unclear.

There can also be disadvantages to later childbearing. Health risks to both mother and baby increase with older women, but there are social issues to consider as well. Women who wait until their 30s to have children will be entering their 50s with teenagers. Since earnings peak when most couples are in their 50s, the greatest psychological and financial demands on older parents may arise just when most people are planning retirement. Ironically, the freedom gained in the 20s by delayed childbearing must be paid for in later years when the financial picture may be even less predictable.[96]

Teenage and Out-of-Wedlock Fertility

The most adverse consequences of early childbearing accrue to women who have teenage or out-of-wedlock births. Out-of-wedlock fertility has been increasing while marital fertility has declined, despite the wider availability of contraception and abortion.

The proportion of births classified as out of wedlock in any given year depends on the birth rate of married women as well as the actual number of out-of-wedlock births. Over the past two decades, the combination of the decrease in marital births and the increase in out-of-wedlock births has resulted in a higher proportion of all births being classified as out of wedlock.

In 1982 almost one birth in five was to an unmarried mother. The rising age at first marriage has contributed to this increase in nonmarital fertility by increasing the number of women "at risk" of bearing a child out of wedlock. However, this is only part of the

[95]Hofferth, "Long-Term Economic Consequences," p. 21.
[96]Arland Thornton and Deborah Freedman, "The Changing American Family," *Population Bulletin*, vol. 38, no. 4 (Washington, DC: Population Reference Bureau, 1983), p. 15.

TABLE 2.5

Changes in the Birth Rates of Unmarried Women

Race and Year	Total	Age 15–19	20–24	25–29	30–34	35–39	40–44
ALL RACES							
1940	7.1	7.4	9.5	7.2	5.1	3.4	1.2
1950	14.1	12.6	21.3	19.9	13.3	7.2	2.0
1960	21.6	15.3	39.7	45.1	27.8	14.1	3.6
1970	26.4	22.4	38.4	37.1	27.0	13.3	3.6
1980	29.4	27.6	40.9	34.0	21.1	9.7	2.6
1982	30.0	28.9	41.4	35.1	21.9	10.0	2.7
WHITE							
1940	3.6	3.3	5.7	4.0	2.5	1.2	
1950	6.1	5.1	10.0	8.7	5.9	2.0	
1960	9.2	6.6	18.2	18.2	10.8	3.9	
1970	13.8	10.9	22.5	21.1	14.2	4.4	
1980	17.6	16.2	24.4	20.7	13.6	6.8	1.8
1982	18.8	17.7	25.7	22.2	14.7	7.1	2.0
BLACK AND OTHER							
1940	35.6	42.5	46.1	32.5	23.4	9.3	
1950	71.2	68.5	105.4	94.2	63.5	20.0	
1960	98.3	76.5	166.5	171.8	104.0	35.6	
1970	89.9	90.8	120.9	93.7	69.9	21.6	
1980	77.2	81.7	106.6	79.1	46.9	19.2	5.6
1982	73.9	79.2	102.1	78.9	44.4	20.0	5.4

NOTE: Number of births per 1,000 unmarried women.

SOURCE: U.S. Bureau of the Census, *Historical Statistics of the United States: Colonial Times to 1970,* Bicentennial Edition (Washington, DC: U.S. Government Printing Office, 1975), series B28–35; National Center for Health Statistics, "Advance Report of Final Natality Statistics, 1982," *Monthly Vital Statistics Report,* vol. 33, no. 6, supplement (September 1984), table 18.

explanation because the number of out-of-wedlock births has increased more rapidly than has the number of single women.[97]

Although teenage fertility in general has been decreasing—in 1960 there were 89 births per 1,000 women aged 15 to 19 but that rate had dropped to 53 per 1,000 by 1982[98]—teenage fertility outside of marriage has been rising (see Table 2.5). Among women aged 15

[97]U.S. Bureau of the Census, "Perspectives," table 5–1 and p. 39; and National Center for Health Statistics, "Advance Report of Final Natality Statistics, 1982," *Monthly Vital Statistics Report,* vol. 32, no. 9, supplement (Washington, DC: U.S. Government Printing Office, 1984), table 16 and p. 6.

[98]U.S. Bureau of the Census, *Historical Statistics of the United States, Colonial Times to 1970,* Bicentennial Edition, pt. 1 (Washington, DC: U.S. Government Printing Office, 1975), series B11–19; and National Center for Health Statistics, "Final Natality Statistics, 1982," table 3.

to 19 the number of births to unmarried women rose steadily from 7 per 1,000 in 1940 to 29 per 1,000 in 1982. Cohort data from the 1980 CPS reveal a similar increase: Whereas for cohorts born before 1940, only about 19 percent of births by age 20 occurred out of wedlock, the corresponding percentages were 27 and 39 percent for the 1945–49 and 1955–59 cohorts, respectively.[99]

Some premarital conceptions are "legitimated" by marriage before the birth occurs. About 6 to 7 percent of young women who married in the 1940s were pregnant at the time of their marriage. By the 1970s 13 to 14 percent of young women were pregnant when they married. The increase is even more pronounced for young teenagers. Among women aged 14 to 17 nearly one-third of those who married in the late 1970s were already pregnant compared with fewer than one-tenth of those married during the 1940s. Older teenagers have the next highest rate of premarital fertility: 18 percent of 18- and 19-year-olds who married in the late 1970s were already pregnant compared with 9 percent of 20- and to 21-year-olds and 4 percent of 22-to-24-year-olds.[100]

Black-White Differences in Teenage and Out-of-Wedlock Fertility

Racial differences in teenage and out-of-wedlock fertility are especially pronounced. Teenage fertility among Blacks historically has been approximately twice as high as that among Whites. Black (and other race) women aged 15 to 19 experienced their highest birth rate during the 1950s, reaching a peak of 173 births per 1,000 in 1957; rates of White teenagers also peaked that year at 85 births per 1,000. By 1982 rates had declined to 97 for Black teens and to 45 for White teens.[101]

Racial differences remained sizable, however, particularly among younger teens. In 1982 the birth rate for Black women aged 15 to 17 was nearly three times the White rate (71 per 1,000 versus 25 per 1,000); among women aged 18 and 19 the Black rate was twice the White rate (133 per 1,000 versus 71 per 1,000).[102]

[99]U.S. Bureau of the Census, "Perspectives," p. 39; and U.S. Bureau of the Census, "Childspacing among Birth Cohorts," table C.

[100]U.S. Bureau of the Census, "Childspacing among Birth Cohorts," table 8.

[101]U.S. Bureau of the Census, *Historical Statistics*, series B11–19; and National Center for Health Statistics, "Final Natality Statistics, 1982," table 3.

[102]National Center for Health Statistics, "Final Natality Statistics, 1982," table 3.

TABLE 2.6

Percentage of Births That Occurred Outside of Marriage, 1980

Age	All Races	White	Black
All Ages	18.4%	11.0%	55.2%
Under 15 Years	88.7	75.4	98.5
15–19 Years	47.6	33.0	85.1
20–24 Years	19.3	11.5	56.0
25–29 Years	9.0	5.0	36.2
30 Years and Over	8.0	4.9	28.9

SOURCE: National Center for Health Statistics, "Advance Report of Final Natality Statistics, 1980," *Monthly Vital Statistics Report*, vol. 31, no. 8, supplement (November 1982), tables 2 and 15.

Much of the racial difference in overall fertility among teenagers can be attributed to extreme differences in birth rates outside of marriage (see Table 2.5). Out-of-wedlock birth rates for Blacks aged 15 to 19 historically have been approximately ten times greater than those for Whites. In 1940, for example, when White teenage nonmarital childbearing was at its lowest (3 births per 1,000), Black and other race out-of-wedlock births was 42 per 1,000. Among Black and other race teenagers out-of-wedlock fertility rates rose between 1940 and 1970 but declined by 1980, whereas among White teenagers out-of-wedlock birth rates have risen steadily since 1940. Despite the decline in the 1970s, rates for Blacks remain much higher than for Whites. In 1980 the out-of-wedlock birth rate was 82 among Blacks and other races aged 15 to 19 compared with 16 among Whites. By 1982 the White teenage out-of-wedlock birth rate had risen to 18, and the rate for Blacks and other races had declined to 79. (See Table 2.5.)

At older ages out-of-wedlock birth rates are still rising for White women, while Black rates reached a peak in the 1960s and have declined since. Although rates have converged, Black out-of-wedlock fertility rates remain considerably higher than those of Whites.

One of the best indicators of racial differences in out-of-wedlock fertility is the proportion of all births that occur to unmarried women. As Table 2.6 demonstrates, more than one in two Black children are born out of wedlock compared with about one in ten White children.

Differences are particularly striking among teenagers. Eighty-five percent of births to Black teens aged 15 to 19 occur outside of marriage compared with 33 percent of births to White teens. Racial differences persist among women into their 20s: 48 percent of Black births are out of wedlock versus 8 percent of White births.

Among Black women aged 14 to 29 who first married between 1975 and 1979, 12 percent were pregnant at the time of marriage. This was not much different from White women, 13 percent of whom were pregnant when they married. However, significantly more Black than White women already had a child before they married: 44 percent versus 7 percent.[103] This means that more than 50 percent of all Black marriages start out with children present or on the way compared with about 20 percent of White marriages.

Why are there such large differences in White and Black out-of-wedlock fertility? One explanation is that the vital statistics registration system may underreport White out-of-wedlock first births.[104] Another possible reason is that the Black community may be more accepting and supportive of children born out of wedlock and thus the social stigma is not as great as for Whites.[105]

Recent research suggests that Black teenagers are more likely than White teenagers to believe that children ensure marital success, personal security, and social approval. Moore and Waite found, however, that a teenage first birth for Blacks actually increased marital instability.[106] Black teens were also more likely than White teens to think that couples should have as many children as they wanted.[107]

The family environment of Blacks has been explored as a reason for higher Black nonmarital fertility. Black girls who grow up in homes with only one parent, with a large number of siblings, and with a sister who has had a teenage pregnancy experience higher rates of sexual intercourse and pregnancy than Black girls in two-parent, smaller families. Teens from upper class homes, who reside in good neighborhoods, and whose parents exert strict control over dating have lower fertility.[108]

[103]U.S. Bureau of the Census, "Childspacing among Birth Cohorts," table 8.
[104]Martin O'Connell, "Comparative Estimates of Teenage Illegitimacy in the United States, 1940–44 to 1970–74," *Demography* 17 (February 1980):13–24.
[105]Robert Staples, "Towards a Sociology of the Black Family: A Theoretical and Methodological Assessment," *Journal of Marriage and the Family* 33 (February 1971):119–38; and Martin O'Connell, "Comparative Estimates."
[106]Kristin A. Moore and Linda J. Waite, "Marital Dissolution, Early Motherhood and Early Marriage," *Social Forces* 60 (September 1981):20–40.
[107]Kenrick Thompson, "A Comparison of Black and White Adolescents' Beliefs about Having Children," *Journal of Marriage and the Family* 42 (February 1980):133–40.
[108]Dennis P. Hogan and Evelyn M. Kitagawa, "The Impact of Social Status, Family Structure, and Neighborhood on the Fertility of Black Adolescents," *American Journal of Sociology* 90 (January 1985):825–55.

Black teens are more likely than White teens to use contraception: In 1982 about 40 percent of never-married Black women aged 15 to 19 were using some type of contraception compared with 25 percent of White women. This seeming inconsistency with higher fertility rates among Blacks is due to higher levels of sexual activity among Black teens and hence a higher risk of pregnancy. Sixty percent of White teens in 1982 reported they had never had sexual intercourse compared with 40 percent of Black teens.[109]

Causes and Correlates of Teenage and Out-of-Wedlock Fertility

One of the clearest correlates of increased out-of-wedlock fertility is increased sexual activity. The number of unmarried teens and older women engaging in nonmarital intercourse has increased significantly over the past two decades.[110] Estimates for the early 1980s are that about 50 percent of all teens and 70 percent of single women in their twenties are sexually active.[111]

Black teenage girls are more likely to have premarital intercourse than White girls and are more likely to begin sexual activity at an earlier age. Black teens are more likely to use contraception and less likely to marry before a birth than White teens.[112] These relationships are influenced by differences in socioeconomic status between the two groups and it is hard to disentangle the direct effects of race.

The increase in the proportion of children born out of wedlock is due in part to the increase in the average age at marriage. The later a woman marries, the longer she is at risk of a pregnancy prior to marriage. Older teens who might have lived at home in the 1950s

---

[109]National Center for Health Statistics, "Use of Contraception, 1982," p. 4.

[110]Catherine S. Chilman, "Social and Psychological Research Concerning Adolescent Childbearing: 1970–1980," *Journal of Marriage and the Family* 42 (November 1980):793–806; William F. Pratt and Gerry E. Hendershot, "The Use of Family Planning Services by Sexually Active Teenage Women," paper presented at the annual meeting of the Population Association of America, Minneapolis, May 3–5, 1984; Koray Tanfer and Marjorie C. Horn, "Contraceptive Use, Pregnancy and Fertility Patterns Among Single American Women in Their 20s," *Family Planning Perspectives* 17 (January-February 1985):10–19.

[111]Pratt and Hendershot, "The Use of Family Planning."

[112]Dennis P. Hogan, Nan M. Astone, and Evelyn M. Kitagawa, "The Impact of Social Status, Family Structure, and Neighborhood on Contraceptive Use Among Black Adolescents," unpublished manuscript, Population Research Center, University of Chicago, April 1984; and John Kantner and Melvin Zelnik, "Sexual Experiences of Young Unmarried Women in the U.S.," *Family Planning Perspectives* 4 (October 1972):9–17.

are now more likely to live independently (see chapter 3). Some of the causes of increased sexual activity among teens may include less restrictive parental control and more permissive sexual norms in society.

Although use of contraceptives has increased, it has not kept pace with the level of sexual activity. Zelnik and Kantner found that only 40 percent of sexually active teenage women "always" used contraception and 20 percent said they never used contraception.[113] Women whose attitudes toward premarital sex are similar to their parents' attitudes tend to be less sexually active or to use contraception more. Teens who are influenced most by their peers are more sexually active, use contraception less consistently, and have higher levels of premarital pregnancy than teens influenced by their parents.[114]

Young girls (under 18) of minority or low socioeconomic status are least likely to use contraceptives effectively or consistently. A misunderstanding of biology, complicated by lack of access to confidential family planning services, also hinders effective contraceptive use. Finally, the irregular sexual activity characteristic of teenagers may leave some girls contraceptively unprepared for sexual encounters.[115] This list is not exhaustive, and no one factor completely determines teenage sexual activity, but a combination of demographic, social, and psychological variables interact to determine different levels of activity.

Between 1972 and 1975 the abortion rate rose for all teenagers and nearly doubled for girls under 15.[116] There were actually more abortions than live births for girls under 15 between 1974 and 1976. National data for 1973–77 showed that teenage abortion rates were higher for Blacks than for Whites.[117]

[113]Melvin Zelnik and John Kantner, "First Pregnancies to Women Aged 15–19: 1971–1976," *Family Planning Perspectives* 10 (January-February 1978):10–20.

[114]Farida Shah and Melvin Zelnik, "Parent and Peer Influence on Sexual Behavior, Contraceptive Use, and Pregnancy Experience of Young Women," *Journal of Marriage and the Family* 43 (May 1981):339–48.

[115]Larry Freshnock and Phillips Cutright, "Models of Illegitimacy: United States, 1969," *Demography* 16 (February 1979):37–48; and Chilman, "Social and Psychological Research."

[116]Wendy Baldwin, "Adolescent Pregnancy and Childbearing—Growing Concerns for Americans," *Population Bulletin*, vol. 31, no. 2 (Washington, DC: Population Reference Bureau, 1980).

[117]Jacqueline D. Forrest, Ellen Sullivan, and Christopher Tietze, "Abortions in the United States 1977–1979," *Family Planning Perspectives* 11 (November-December 1979):329–41.

Certain demographic variables repeatedly appear associated with high rates of out-of-wedlock childbearing. Women who are less educated, poor, and not in the labor force have higher rates of nonmarital pregnancy than better educated, wealthier women who work.[118] As mentioned earlier, part of the reason that women with lower educational attainment have more out-of-wedlock births is that they may have dropped out of school due to an early birth. The highest rates of birth before marriage in 1970 involved women with an elementary school education or less; the highest rates of births shortly after marriage involved women who had dropped out of high school.[119]

Consequences of Teenage and Out-of-Wedlock Fertility

"For many young women, the experience of a premarital pregnancy defines their life options with a vengeance: such women reach their early twenties already enmeshed in the responsibilities of caring for a family above average in size."[120] While this may be a particularly severe analysis of the outcome of early pregnancies, there is general agreement that teenage motherhood has few, if any, economic benefits.

Teenage pregnancies, particularly out-of-wedlock ones, present special problems for the individual as well as society. The young mother may suffer from a lowered sense of self-esteem, be less likely to continue her education, and therefore have fewer occupational choices, and, ultimately, be less self-sufficient.[121] Teenage mothers have more births in their lifetime and more unintended births than women who delay childbearing.

From society's standpoint, the cycle of early parenthood and higher fertility is likely to be perpetuated among children of teenage parents.[122] Some studies have shown developmental problems and lower academic achievement for children of teenagers.[123]

[118]U.S. Bureau of the Census, "Premarital Fertility," *Current Population Reports*, series P-23, no. 63 (Washington, DC: U.S. Government Printing Office, 1976), pp. 23 and 33; and U.S. Bureau of the Census, "Perspectives," table 5–5.

[119]U.S. Bureau of the Census, "Premarital Fertility," p. 23.

[120]Bumpass, Rindfuss, and Janosik, "Age and Marital Status," p. 83.

[121]McLaughlin and Micklin, "The Timing of the First Birth."

[122]Josefina J. Card, "Long-Term Consequences for Children of Teenage Parents," *Demography* 18 (May 1981):137–56.

[123]Wendy Baldwin and Virginia S. Cain, "The Children of Teenage Parents," *Family Planning Perspectives* 12 (January-February 1980):34–43; and Card, "Long-Term Consequences."

The earlier childbearing occurs, the greater the likelihood of poverty later in life.[124] Premarital pregnancy has a direct effect on the number of children born, an effect which is mediated through a shortened first birth interval.[125] Age at first marriage and premarital pregnancy also interact to shorten the length of the second birth interval, which helps to explain larger completed family size among women with a premarital pregnancy.[126]

Moore and Waite found that teenage parenthood did not increase the risk of later divorce or separation as much as teenage marriage.[127] However, girls who get pregnant may feel that they have to get married. Evidence supporting this outcome is presented by Marini, who also found that premarital pregnancy has a negative effect on both the marital and parental satisfaction of women but has no effect on men.[128] Marini suggests that this discrepancy between men's and women's satisfaction is due to the woman's greater need to marry (for financial or emotional security), which might mean that the decision to marry is less voluntary for women than men. A premarital pregnancy may also force a woman into the motherhood role before she is adequately prepared.

In sum, the adverse effects of young parenthood include lower educational attainment, larger family size, and greater dependency on welfare. Ironically, sometimes the consequences of early childbearing are less severe if the mother does *not* marry immediately, since marital stability appears to be more dependent on age at marriage than age at first birth. Perhaps the most important effect is that early childbearing makes personal and social development and financial security more difficult for the young mother to achieve.

Summary

The fertility of American women has declined substantially since the baby boom years. From a high of 3.8 average births per woman in 1957, the Total Fertility Rate dropped to 1.8 by 1980. This level is below that needed for natural replacement of the population.

[124]Hofferth and Moore, "Early Childbearing."
[125]Marini, "Measuring the Effects"; and Marini and Hodson, "Effects of the Timing of Marriage."
[126]Marini and Hodsdon, "Effects of the Timing."
[127]Moore and Waite, "Marital Dissolution."
[128]Marini, "Effects of the Number and Spacing."

Black fertility has traditionally been higher than White fertility, with Blacks averaging about one birth more per woman than Whites.

Lowered birth expectations have accompanied the actual decline in fertility. Most women expected about three lifetime births in the 1960s compared with about two births today. The proportion of women anticipating smaller (two-child) families has doubled over time, while the proportion expecting larger families of four or more children has declined. Birth expectations are fairly good indicators of the eventual fertility of married women, although 9 percent of women report uncertainty about future fertility plans.

The majority of currently married women use some form of contraception, a practice that has not changed much since the 1960s. What has changed is the effectiveness of the methods used. Two-thirds of all contraceptors in 1965 used less effective methods such as the condom or rhythm method, but by 1983 two-thirds of contraceptors were using the more effective pill, intrauterine device, or sterilization.

Partly because of the ability to control fertility through contraception, women have been delaying childbearing. In 1983, approximately 25 percent of ever-married women aged 25 to 29 were still childless, compared with just 13 percent in 1960. This rate of childlessness approaches that recorded in 1940, a level temporarily high due to the Depression. Statistics up to 1983 reflect no greater trend toward lifetime childlessness, but projections are that women in the baby boom cohort may finish their childbearing years with an all-time high level of childlessness.

The rate of teenage childbearing has declined over time in line with overall fertility trends. However, the rate of births to unmarried women has increased significantly since 1940. The birth rate for unmarried teens rose from 7 to 29 per 1,000 between 1940 and 1982; the birth rate for unmarried women in their early 20s rose from 10 to 41. Teenage childbearing, whether to unmarried or married women, generally has negative economic consequences for the woman.

Reductions in fertility mean that women have more opportunities to pursue alternatives to the mothering role. Later chapters on education, labor force participation, and earnings summarize changes for women that have accompanied this decline in fertility.

3

LIVING ARRANGEMENTS

THE FAMILY and household living arrangements of women are an important area of attention for two reasons. First, changes in household living arrangements have been extreme during the past four decades. Second, family life cycles and household living arrangements are intimately tied to women's economic and social-psychological well-being. The course of women's family lives differs in important ways from that of men's. And women's family experiences are not uniform: Racial subgroups of women structure their lives differently.

We have seen that the majority of women continue to marry and have children. Like women of their mother's and grandmother's generations, most women today assume the roles of wife and mother for at least part of their adult lives. However, the amount of time women spend in the "wife" role has declined in recent years. Research shows that women born about 1930 will spend more of their adult lives married than women born earlier or later.[1] Estimates are

[1]Robert Schoen, William L. Urton, Karen Woodrow, and John Baj, "Marriage and Divorce in Twentieth Century American Cohorts," *Demography* 22 (February 1985):101-14.

that the average time spent in first marriages has declined by ten or eleven years over the last three decades.[2] Women have come to spend an increasing number of years single prior to marriage or divorced between marriages. White women, but not Black women, are spending an increasing number of years in second and third marriages.

As was shown in chapter 1, median age at first marriage was unusually low for those born during the Depression, but has since returned to the higher levels which characterized the late nineteenth and early twentieth centuries. The proportion who remain single until their late 20s or early 30s has increased dramatically among recent cohorts of women, and it is possible that the proportion of young women today who remain single throughout life may even surpass the high levels of the early part of the century.[3] For many women this lengthening of years prior to first marriage means that their first independent residence is not shared with a husband. Rather, young adults increasingly live alone, with friends, or with a member of the opposite sex for a period prior to marriage.

The family *life cycle* of an increasing proportion of women is interrupted by divorce. That is, many women do not have an unbroken string of years living with a spouse until the "empty nest"

---

[2]Thomas J. Espenshade, "Marriage Trends in America: Estimates, Implications, and Underlying Causes," *Population and Development Review* 11 (June 1985): tables 2 and 3. Obviously, synthetic cohort estimates must be viewed with a certain degree of caution since they do not represent the actual experience of a single cohort but rather the cumulative experience of several cohorts at a point in time. Nevertheless, these period estimates are valuable for assessing recent change in marital and family living arrangements, although the full extent of change will not be known until young women today actually pass through their adult years. Espenshade estimates that White women in the late 1970s were spending an average of 24 years, or 31 percent of their adult lives, in their first marriage compared with 34 or 35 years, or 47 percent of adult lives, during the 1950s. Among Black women, about 13 years on average were spent in first marriages in the late 1970s, down from 24 years in the early 1950s. These estimates imply that only 17 percent of the adult lives of Black women were spent in first marriages in 1975–80 compared with the 31 percent for White women and 37 percent for Black women in the early 1950s.

[3]Espenshade, "Marriage Trends in America"; Arland Thornton and Willard Rodgers, "Changing Patterns of Marriage and Divorce in the United States," final report to the National Institute of Child Health and Human Development (Ann Arbor: Institute for Social Research, 1983); and U.S. Bureau of the Census, "Marital Status and Living Arrangements: March 1982," *Current Population Reports*, series P-20, no. 380 (Washington, DC: U.S. Government Printing Office, 1983), pp. 1–2.

phase[4]—not because of early death of a spouse, as in the past, but because of marital dissolution. Ross and Sawhill view these periods as transitional since the majority of those who divorce do remarry, but such interruptions place an increasing number of women in the role of sole economic provider for themselves and their children during periods of their adult lives.[5] Not only divorce, but out-of-wedlock childbearing, which is particularly high among teenagers, places more women outside the traditional married couple framework.

Finally, life expectancy continues to advance, but the sex differential in mortality remains about seven years at birth and four and one-half years at age 65. Even women who may have moved from their parental home directly into a residence with a husband, with no disruption of that marital arrangement due to divorce, are likely to survive their husband and spend several years at the end of their life in which they must either live with relatives or live alone. The character of their lives, their needs, and their problems differ according to this choice in living arrangements.

We turn our attention in this chapter to a description of trends in living arrangements and to differences between men and women and subgroup variations in these trends. Our aim is to better understand the causes and consequences of recent changes in women's family lives.

Changing Distribution of Households

The vast majority of Americans live in households; a relatively small minority reside in institutions or other group quarters.

[4]Glick's analysis of cohorts of women born between 1880 and 1950 has been important in illustrating such changes as the increased number of years couples spend alone together after their children leave home, that is, the "empty nest" phase. See Paul C. Glick, "The Family Cycle," *American Sociological Review* 12 (April 1947):164–74; Paul C. Glick, *American Families* (New York: Wiley, 1957); Paul C. Glick, "Updating the Life Cycle of the Family," *Journal of Marriage and the Family* 39 (February 1977):5–13; Paul C. Glick and Robert Parke, "New Approaches in Studying the Life Cycle of the Family," *Demography* 2 (1965):187–202; Arthur J. Norton, "The Family Life Cycle Updated: Components and Uses," in Robert F. Winch and Graham B. Spanier, eds., *Selected Studies in Marriage and the Family* (New York: Holt, Rinehart, & Winston, 1974), pp. 162–67; Arthur J. Norton, "Family Life Cycle: 1980," *Journal of Marriage and the Family* 45 (May 1983):267–76; and Paul C. Glick and Arthur J. Norton, "Marrying, Divorcing, and Living Together in the U.S. Today," *Population Bulletin*, vol. 32, no. 5 (Washington, DC: Population Reference Bureau, 1977).

[5]Heather L. Ross and Isabel V. Sawhill, *Time of Transition: The Growth of Families Headed by Women* (Washington, DC: Urban Institute, 1975).

Throughout U.S. history, from 1790 to the present, the rate of household formation has exceeded the rate of population increase, and the average size of households has declined with each succeeding census.[6] Despite rising income and presumably greater ability to buy privacy, there was not a great increase in persons living apart from families during the early part of the century; but an income threshold may have been reached during the 1940s.[7] Since that time there has been an increased propensity for people to live alone. And partly because of the increased joint survival of couples, there has also been an increase in two-person households. In 1980 over one-half of all households were one- and two-person units.[8]

Changes in marriage and divorce, childbearing, and life expectancy have altered the age composition of the population and the structure of American households in recent decades. Economic variables such as the price of housing and the income to afford one's own separate residence, as well as changes in preferences to live independently, have interacted with these demographic factors to affect living arrangements. An important consequence of recent changes is that an increased proportion of all households are maintained by women.

The distribution of households by type (family/nonfamily) and sex of householder is shown in Table 3.1 for each census date from 1940 through 1980. In censuses prior to 1980 one person in each household was designated as the head, and the relationship of all other persons to this household head was ascertained. In 1980 the Census Bureau discontinued use of the term "household head" and moved to the reference person, or householder, concept. That is, in each household, a person in whose name the housing unit was owned or rented was designated as the householder, and the relationship of all other persons to this householder was determined.[9]

---

[6]Suzanne M. Bianchi, "Changing Concepts of Households and Families in the Census and CPS," *Proceedings of the Social Statistics Section* (Washington, DC: American Statistical Association, 1982), figure 1.

[7]Thomas K. Burch, Kauser Thomas, and Marilyn McQuillan, "Changing Household Headship in the United States, 1900 to 1970: A Preliminary Test of the Income Threshold Hypothesis," paper presented at the annual meeting of the Population Association of America, Pittsburgh, April 1983.

[8]Bianchi, "Changing Concepts"; and James A. Sweet, "Components of Change in the Number of Households, 1970–80," *Demography* 21 (May 1984):129–40.

[9]For a comparison of pre- and post-1980 terminology, see U.S. Bureau of the Census, "Household and Family Characteristics: March 1980," *Current Population Reports*, series P-20, no. 366 (Washington, DC: U.S. Government Printing Office, 1981), table E.

TABLE 3.1

Changing Distribution of Households (numbers in thousands)

Household Type	1940	1950	1960	1970	1980	Percent Change			
						1940–50	1950–60	1960–70	1970–80
Total Households	35,087	42,251	52,809	63,573	80,389	20.4%	25.0%	20.4%	26.5%
	100.0%	100.0%	100.0%	100.0%	100.0%				
Family Households	90.0	88.1	85.0	80.5	73.3	17.9	20.5	14.0	15.1
Married Couple	75.8	77.0	74.7	69.2	60.1	22.4	21.2	11.5	9.9
Female Householder	9.9	8.0	7.8	8.7	10.5	–2.5	22.6	33.2	52.5
Male Householder	4.3	3.1	2.4	2.6	2.6	–13.7	–3.2	28.0	29.3
Nonfamily Households	10.0	11.9	15.0	20.0	26.8	43.3	58.5	56.6	73.0
Female Householder	5.4	7.1	9.4	12.3	15.3	59.4	65.4	56.7	57.9
Male Householder	4.6	4.4	5.6	7.3	11.4	16.4	58.1	56.4	98.5

NOTE: 1940 data obtained from 1950 and 1960 census publications.

SOURCE: U.S. Bureau of the Census, *Census of Population: 1950*, vol. 4, Special Reports, pt. 2, Chap. A, "General Characteristics of Families," tables D, E, 1, and 4; *Census of Population: 1960*, vol. 2, Subject Reports, "Families," PC(2)-4A, tables 1 and 4; *Census of Population: 1970*, vol. 2, Subject Reports, "Family Composition," PC(2)4A, table 1; *Census of Population; 1980*, vol. 1, chap. B, U.S. Summary, table 46.

Current census definitions rely on this relationship information to distinguish between family households (households of two or more persons in which the householder and at least one other person are related by blood, marriage, or adoption) and nonfamily households (households in which the householder lives either alone or with nonrelatives). Family households can be further subdivided into three categories. If the householder is married and living with his or her spouse, the family is referred to as a husband-wife or married couple family. If, on the other hand, the householder is not living with a spouse but with some other relative—for example, a child, parent, sibling—the household is referred to as a male-maintained or female-maintained family household, depending on the sex of the householder.[10] Nonfamily households are also divided into those maintained by a female and those maintained by a male.

Within the subgroup of households which include families, only persons related to the householder are considered family members. Not all families include children: Under the census definition, for example, two adult sisters living together would be considered a family.

During the 1940s and 1950s, as the age at first marriage declined, single family housing became more plentiful, and income rose, there was a swelling in the number of husband-wife households. Young adults were increasingly able to marry, buy homes, and establish residential independence from relatives.[11] Although the number of husband-wife households increased in subsequent decades, growth was much slower than the overall rate of household formation. Whereas 83 percent of the net growth in households in the 1940s was in husband-wife families, these households accounted for only 26 percent of the overall increase in the 1970s.

By 1980 a minority of all households included a husband-wife couple living with their own children. The proportion of all households maintained by a married couple declined from a high of 77

[10]In censuses prior to 1980, these would have been referred to as "female-headed" and "other male-headed" families. Before 1980 "male-headed" families often included "husband-wife" as well as "other male-headed" families because the husband was always designated as the head in husband-wife families. This practice has been discontinued, and, in this monograph, the term "male-maintained" family never includes married couples, only male family householders who are not living with a spouse.

[11]Frances E. Kobrin, "Household Headship and Its Changes in the United States, 1940–1960, 1970," *Journal of the American Statistical Association* 68 (December 1973):793–800; and John Modell, "Normative Aspects of American Marriage Timing Since World War II," *Journal of Family History* 5 (Summer 1980): 210–34.

percent in 1950 to 60 percent in 1980. Only about 50 percent of these married couple units had dependent children in them, and hence only about 30 percent of all households in 1980 housed the "typical" nuclear family. Furthermore, as divorce rates have risen, a declining proportion of these households include a couple in which both partners are in a first marriage.

As the percentage growth in husband-wife households has declined, other types of households have been increasing. The proportion of residences (family or nonfamily) maintained by a woman increased from 15 to 26 percent between 1940 and 1980. During the 1970s, a decade of accelerated growth in families maintained by women and continued rapid expansion of nonfamily units, 44 percent of the increase in households was accounted for by female householders, whereas married couples accounted for only 26 percent and male householders 30 percent of additional households.

The number of families maintained by a woman actually declined during the 1940s but increased—at an increasing rate—in each decade after 1950. During the 1970s the number of female-maintained families increased from 5.5 to 8.1 million, a 52 percent increase, and these households accounted for 11 percent of all households by 1980. Male-maintained families, by comparison, increased from 1.6 to 2.1 million, a 29 percent increase, and accounted for just under 3 percent of all households. The probability that there are dependent children in the household remains much higher in families maintained by a woman. In 1983, 60 percent of female-maintained families included children compared with 37 percent of male-maintained families.[12]

Nonfamily households, in particular those maintained by women, have also increased dramatically. Between 1940 and 1980 nonfamily residences increased from 10 to 27 percent of all households and, in 1980, 57 percent of these households were maintained by women. Much of the increase for women is accounted for by the increase in older women who live alone. Among men, living alone or with nonrelatives is most common during young adult years. Hence, the increase in male nonfamily units accelerated during the 1970s as the large number of unmarried young adult males born during the 1950s came of age. One difference between men and women

---

[12]U.S. Bureau of the Census, "Household and Family Characteristics: March 1983," *Current Population Reports*, series P-20, no. 388 (Washington, DC: U.S. Government Printing Office, 1984), table A.

is that men have a longer period of nonfamily living prior to marriage, whereas women have a much higher probability of residing alone during their later years because women tend to outlive the men they marry.

From the perspective of individual women, these changes in the composition of households mean that a declining proportion of adult women are found to be living with a spouse at any given point in time. Table 3.2 shows the change in household living arrangements of Black and White women and men. The majority of White women were married and living with a spouse, but this proportion declined from 70 percent in 1960 to 62 percent in 1980. Among Black women just over one-half were living with a spouse in 1960 compared with a little more than one-third in 1980. Trends are parallel for White and Black men, but a higher proportion of men are living in husband-wife households.

Black women are much more likely than White women to be managing a family household without the assistance of a spouse. Also, the increase in families maintained by women has been greater among Blacks than Whites. Consequently, in 1980, 8 percent of White women were maintaining families without a spouse present compared with 25 percent of Black women. Whereas 5 percent of White women were single-parent householders—that is, the family they were maintaining included dependent children under the age of 18—17 percent of Black women were in this single-parent householder role.

Changing Propensities to Live Independently

Trends in marital status, reviewed in chapter 1, showed that the proportion of the population who were married and living with a spouse increased between 1940 and 1960 but has declined since that time. As the proportion of the population who are currently married changes, the proportion of adults who might conceivably maintain their own household changes. One would expect more female householders in 1980 than in 1950 merely because of changes in marital status; that is, since the proportion of women who are not currently married has increased, the population "at risk" of maintaining a household other than a husband-wife family has increased. There could be no change in propensity to form independent households

TABLE 3.2

Changes in Household Living Arrangements of White and Black Women and Men

Sex and Household Status	All Races			White			Black		
	1960	1970	1980	1960	1970	1980	1960	1970	1980
WOMEN									
Total, 18 Years and Over	100.0%	100.0%	100.0%	100.0%	100.0%	100.0%	100.0%	100.0%	100.0%
Wife	68.0	64.3	58.7	69.8	66.4	61.7	52.2	46.4	36.9
Family Householder	7.1	8.4	10.0	6.3	7.0	8.0	14.9	19.9	24.9
(Single Parent)	(3.2)	(4.6)	(6.0)	(2.7)	(3.5)	(4.5)	(7.0)	(13.5)	(17.0)
Nonfamily Householder	8.7	11.5	15.0	8.7	11.7	15.5	8.7	10.8	13.8
(Living Alone)	(7.8)	(10.6)	(13.5)	(7.9)	(10.8)	(14.0)	(7.3)	(9.8)	(12.4)
Other	16.2	15.9	16.2	15.3	15.0	14.8	24.3	22.8	24.3
MEN									
Total, 18 Years and Over	100.0%	100.0%	100.0%	100.0%	100.0%	100.0%	100.0%	100.0%	100.0%
Husband	75.1	73.1	66.2	76.7	74.7	68.6	61.4	58.9	48.8
Family Householder	2.5	2.6	2.7	2.4	2.4	2.4	3.2	4.3	4.7
(Single Parent)	(0.6)	(0.9)	(1.0)	(0.5)	(0.8)	(0.9)	(1.0)	(1.9)	(2.1)
Nonfamily Householder	5.5	7.8	12.0	5.2	7.4	11.7	7.9	10.9	14.7
(Living Alone)	(4.8)	(6.6)	(9.5)	(4.6)	(6.3)	(9.3)	(6.4)	(9.4)	(12.4)
Other	16.9	16.5	19.1	15.7	15.4	17.3	27.5	25.9	31.9

SOURCE: 1960, 1970, and 1980 Census 1/1,000 Public Use Microdata Sample files.

and still we might see increases in households other than married couple families. In order to focus on changing propensities of living independently, we calculate the likelihood of maintaining one's own household for males and females aged 20 and over who are not currently married and living with a spouse. Appendix Table 3.A (which appears at the end of this chapter) shows the percentage of unmarried men and women who are householders for five-year age groups, and Figure 3.1 displays the trend for somewhat more aggregated age groupings.[13]

As can be seen in Figure 3.1, there is no question that unmarried men and women of all ages have become more likely to form independent households. At the youngest ages the propensity to live independently increased throughout the 1940-80 period. At older ages the proportion of unmarried adults who maintained their own separate household did not begin to rise until the 1950s.

The likelihood that an unmarried person will maintain an independent residence generally increases with age and then drops off at ages over 65. The propensity to maintain an independent household is relatively low for 20-to-24-year-olds, a group which is often either living in group quarters, such as college dormitories or military barracks, or which still lives with parents, other relatives, or friends. However, even at these young adult ages the propensity to live independently has increased.[14]

Focusing on slightly older ages, women in their late 20s or early 30s who were unmarried in 1940 had a less than one in five chance of establishing an independent household. By 1980, 61 percent of

[13]Kobrin provides a detailed picture of changes in both family and nonfamily headship among men and women for the 1940–60 period. She uses the now discontinued census procedure of designating males as heads of all husband-wife households. Her at-risk population is the total population and husbands are included in the count of male heads. We find it more useful to think of married couples as cohouseholders and focus only on those not currently married as at risk of maintaining independent households (other than husband-wife households). See Frances E. Kobrin, "Components of Change in United States Household Headship" (unpublished dissertation, University of Pennsylvania, 1971); Frances E. Kobrin, "Household Headship;" and Frances E. Kobrin, "The Fall of Household Size and the Rise of the Primary Individual," *Demography* 13 (February 1976): 127–38.

[14]A change in the way college students were enumerated between the 1940 and 1950 censuses partly explains the increase in this decade. In the census of 1940 students away at college were enumerated as they are in the Current Population Survey, that is, as if they were living in the home of their parents. In the 1950–80 censuses, college students were enumerated at their residence on the date of enumeration. Hence, students away at school were counted among the group quarters population if living in college dormitories and among the population in nonfamily households if residing alone or with roommates in off-campus housing.

FIGURE 3.1

Trend in Percentage of Unmarried Men and Women
Who Maintain Households

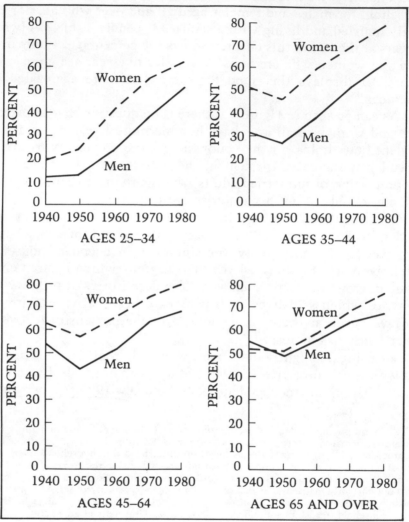

NOTE: Unmarried includes never married, widowed, divorced, and separated.

SOURCE: See Appendix Table 3.A.

women in this age group maintained their own separate residences. At the other end of the age spectrum, women over age 65 in 1940 were only slightly more likely to manage a household than to live in the home of friends or relatives; that is, 52 percent were householders and 48 percent resided in someone else's household. In 1980 almost four out of five unmarried women maintained an independent residence during their older years—a very significant change.

The propensity to form an independent household is (and has been historically) higher for unmarried women than for unmarried men. In 1980, for example, rates were 10 to 15 percentage points higher for women than for men at most ages. Also, the number of unmarried women over age 30 who are maintaining households exceeds the number of men by an ever-increasing amount because of women's greater propensity to live independently, their lower remarriage rate, and their greater longevity. At ages 65 and over, for example, the population "at risk" in 1980 was 9.1 million unmarried women, of whom 7 million were maintaining their own household, compared with 2.7 million unmarried men, 1.8 million of whom were managing their own household. Numerically the most important change in women's living arrangements is this large increase in independent living among older women.

Living Arrangements of the Elderly

The increase in elderly women who live alone has been an important trend, accounting for a significant share of the increase in female householders in the post–World War II period. Living alone in old age is much more a "female" phenomenon than a "male" one because of women's greater life expectancy. Whether the greater tendency to maintain an independent household among older women remains once other variables that might differ by sex are controlled, such as economic status and kin availability, has not been definitively answered.

Women are supposedly more family oriented than men, which should differentially predispose them to reside with kin in old age. However, married couple households are typically managed by women; thus, during the years prior to old age, women develop greater ability, and perhaps desire, to maintain their own independent residence than men. The first argument leads to the expectation that men will live independently in old age more often than women, other things equal; the latter that women have the higher probability of living alone. Because of the numerical dominance of women among the unmarried elderly, many multivariate studies focus solely on women. Of those that focus on both sexes, Kobrin finds that women are *more* likely than men to live with relatives, other things equal,[15] and Bishop finds no significant sex differences.[16]

What are some of the factors which might explain the large increase in elderly women who live alone in recent decades? Some studies emphasize changes in norms, tastes, or preferences, either on the part of the elderly or their grown children with whom they might live, or both. Kobrin, for example, argues that there has been a normative shift away from including nonnuclear kin, such as grandparents, in households.[17] Beresford and Rivlin emphasize the increased "taste" or desire for privacy among the elderly.[18] Bishop reports that social-psychological studies indicate that older persons express strong preferences for maintaining independent households.[19] However, changing tastes or preferences are not independent of changing ability to afford independent living. Income data are readily available but data on preferences are not, and much research has focused on the importance of income in explaining living arrangement changes.

Beresford and Rivlin were among the first to suggest the importance of income in enabling the elderly to afford separate living, to "consume privacy."[20] Numerous studies find that independent living among the elderly increases as income increases.[21] Women's living

---

[15]Frances E. Kobrin, "Family Extension and the Elderly: Economic, Demographic, and Family Cycle Factors," *Journal of Gerontology* 36 (May 1981):370–77.

[16]Christine E. Bishop, "The Demand for Independent Living by the Elderly: Effects of Income and Disability," unpublished manuscript, 1983.

[17]Kobrin, "Rise of the Primary Individual."

[18]John C. Beresford and Alice M. Rivlin, "Privacy, Poverty, and Old Age," *Demography* 3 (1966):247–58.

[19]Bishop, "Demand for Independent Living."

[20]Beresford and Rivlin, "Privacy, Poverty."

[21]Bishop, "Demand for Independent Living"; Albert Chevan and J. Henry Korson, "The Widowed Who Live Alone: An Examination of Social and Demographic Factors," *Social Forces* 51 (September 1972):45–53; Saul Schwartz, Sheldon Danziger, and Eugene Smolensky, "The Choice of Living Arrangements by the Elderly" (Washington, DC: Brookings Institution, 1983); Beth J. Soldo and Patience Lauriat, "Living Arrangements Among the Elderly in the United States: A Loglinear Approach," *Journal of Comparative Family Studies* 7 (Summer 1976):351–66; Beth J. Soldo, Michael Sharma, and Richard T. Campbell, "The Effects of Functional Health Status and Demographic Characteristics on the Living Arrangement of Older Unmarried Women," revision of a paper presented at the 1981 annual meeting of the Population Association of America, 1983.

arrangements may be more responsive than men's to changes in income. Michael, Fuchs, and Scott argue that an income threshold was reached during the 1940s and that the increase in retirement income since that time has been the overwhelming cause of the increase in living alone among elderly women.[22] However, this argument about change over time in the behavior of individuals is based on an empirical analysis of aggregate, cross-sectional data for states in 1970. Preliminary attempts to model change over time by Burch and colleagues and cross-sectional, micro-level analysis by Pampel do not support the income threshold argument.[23] Recent evidence on the interrelationship of living arrangements, income, and a third variable, kin availability, also casts doubt on the simple economic interpretation of changes in independent living among elderly women.[24]

The "kin availability" explanation, primarily a demographic argument, is that mortality and fertility have interacted to decrease the number of relatives with whom older persons might live should they prefer living with others.[25] As life expectancy has increased, the "supply" of older widowed parents has grown, but the long-term downward trend in fertility has resulted in each elderly person today having fewer sons, daughters, nieces, or nephews—that is, fewer relatives with whom he or she might live. Wolf argues that kin availability is an important constraint on the living arrangement choices of the elderly.[26] One problem in researching this topic is that not many data sets have information on living kin. It is known that the probability of living with kin declined sharply between 1962 and 1975,[27] but that the probability of living alone remains lower for those with at least one living child.[28] Bishop estimates that the net

[22]Robert Michael, Victor R. Fuchs, and Sharon R. Scott, "Changes in the Propensity to Live Alone: 1950–1976," *Demography* 17 (February 1980):39–56.

[23]Burch et al., "Changing Household Headship"; and Fred C. Pampel, "Changes in the Propensity to Live Alone: Evidence from Consecutive Cross-Sectional Surveys, 1960–1976," *Demography* 20 (November 1983):433–48.

[24]Douglas A. Wolf, "Kinship and the Living Arrangements of Older Americans," final report to the National Institute of Child Health and Human Development (Washington, DC: Urban Institute, January 1983) and Douglas A. Wolf, "Kin Availability and the Living Arrangements of Older Women," *Social Science Research* 13 (March 1984):72–89.

[25]Kobrin, "Rise of the Primary Individual."

[26]Wolf, "Kinship."

[27]Ethel Shanas, "A National Survey of the Aged," final report to the Administration on Aging, U.S. Department of Health, Education, and Welfare, 1978; and Ethel Shanas, Peter Townsend, Dorothy Wedderburn, Henning Friis, Paul Milhoj, and Jan Stehouwer, *Old People in Three Industrial Societies* (New York: Atherton Press, 1968).

[28]Chevan and Korson, "Living Arrangements of Widows"; Christine A. Bachrach, "Childlessness and Social Isolation Among the Elderly," *Journal of Marriage and the Family* 42 (August 1980): 627–36; and Wolf, "Kinship."

effect of having at least one adult child is to decrease the probability of living alone by 25 percent for women and 17 percent for men.[29]

The extensive geographic mobility of the population also separates the elderly from their grown children.[30] Proximity of living children and other relatives is generally not available in the data sets which include information on living relatives and hence has not been throughly studied.

Another factor not always available in data used to study living arrangements of the elderly is health or disability status. Age is sometimes used as a proxy but is not highly correlated with independent living among the elderly.[31] Studies find, as might be expected, that living alone declines with increased disability.[32] Bishop's findings suggest that as income rises, disability becomes less a deterrent to independent living, but Soldo, Sharma, and Campbell find no disability-income interaction.[33]

Various studies have tested whether marital status affects probabilities of residing alone. Findings are contradictory. For example, Soldo, Sharma, and Campbell report no differences among never-married, divorced, or widowed women; Kobrin finds that the divorced are more likely to live with others than the never married; and Bishop finds that the never married more likely to live with others than the widowed, divorced, or separated.[34] Each of these studies is multivariate, reporting net effects of marital status; but data sets, other independent factors, and estimation techniques differ, which may explain the conflicting findings.

Finally, a few studies have investigated racial differences: Propensities differ by race with Black elderly women less likely to live alone than White women. Soldo and Lauriat find race effects overshadowed by income effects,[35] but two recent multivariate (logit) studies of living arrangements among the elderly find Black women

[29]Bishop, "Demand for Independent Living."

[30]This variable is of some importance, though much less so than income, in the Michael et al. analysis. See Michael et al., "Propensity to Live Alone."

[31]Bishop, "Demand for Independent Living."

[32]Thomas Tissue, "Low Income Widows and Other Aged Singles," *Social Security Bulletin* 42 (December 1979):3–10; and Thomas Tissue and John L. McCoy, "Income and Living Arrangements Among Poor Aged Singles," *Social Security Bulletin* 44 (April 1981):3–13.

[33]Bishop, "Demand for Independent Living"; Soldo, Sharma, and Campbell, "Effects of Functional Health Status."

[34]Soldo, Sharma, and Campbell, "Effects of Functional Health Status"; Kobrin, "Family Extension"; and Bishop, "Demand for Independent Living."

[35]Soldo and Lauriat, "Living Arrangements."

more prone to live with others, net of controls for income and kin availability.[36]

Changes in Nonfamily Living in the 1970s

Kobrin has shown that the number of "primary individuals," the name formerly used by the Census Bureau to refer to nonfamily householders, increased dramatically between 1950 and 1974.[37] Two-thirds of the increase for women was among those over 65. For men, on the other hand, over half of the growth was among those under 35.

During the 1970s, growth in nonfamily living among women was not as concentrated within the older age groups as it was in previous decades, although the number of elderly women who lived alone continued to increase. Because of the large size of the baby boom cohorts reaching adulthood in the 1970s and because these cohorts postponed marriage, women under 30 accounted for over 30 percent of the growth in nonfamily householders during the 1970s compared with 18 percent of the growth during the 1960s. Among men, householders under age 30 represented 50 percent of the growth during the 1970s. An additional 19 percent was accounted for by those aged 30 to 35. (See Table 3.3.)

At least three separate components contributed to the growth in nonfamily living during the 1970s. First, as indicated in Figure 3.1, there was an increase in the propensity to form independent households among the unmarried population. Second, there were shifts in the proportion of the population in the unmarried state, particularly at young ages. Hence, even if there had been no change in propensity to maintain households among young adults, there would have been more unmarried young adults "at risk" of maintaining their own household in 1980 than in 1970. This factor alone would have led to an increase in the number of householders. Finally, the population continued to grow throughout the 1970s, and the growth was disproportionately large among young adults in the prime household-forming ages and among the elderly. Even if there were no change in marital patterns or in the propensity to form independent households,

---

[36]Bishop, "Demand for Independent Living"; and Wolf, "Kin Availability."
[37]Kobrin, "Rise of the Primary Individual"; and Kobrin, "Components of Change."

TABLE 3.3

Changes in the Number of Nonfamily Householders (numbers in thousands)

Sex and Age	1960	1970	1980	Change in Number		Percentage Distribution of Change in Number	
				1960–70	1970–80	1960–70	1970–80
FEMALE HOUSEHOLDER	5,002	7,842	12,337	2,840	4,495	100.0%	100.0%
Under 25 Years	176	521	1,207	345	686	12.1	15.3
25–29 Years	116	283	1,014	167	731	5.9	16.3
30–34 Years	126	163	631	37	468	1.3	10.4
35–44 Years	372	371	647	−1	276	0.0	6.1
45–54 Years	726	855	993	129	138	4.5	3.1
55–64 Years	1,222	1,730	2,063	508	333	17.9	7.4
65–74 Years	1,440	2,254	3,041	814	787	28.7	17.5
75 Years and Over	824	1,665	2,737	841	1,072	29.6	23.8
MALE HOUSEHOLDER	2,995	4,627	8,941	1,632	4,314	100.0%	100.0%
Under 25 Years	190	575	1,591	385	1,016	23.6	23.6
25–29 Years	200	471	1,625	271	1,154	16.6	26.8
30–34 Years	203	307	1,140	104	833	6.4	19.3
35–44 Years	412	572	1,170	160	598	9.8	13.9
45–54 Years	490	655	932	165	277	10.1	6.4
55–64 Years	570	744	956	174	212	10.7	4.9
65–74 Years	575	728	849	153	121	9.4	2.8
75 Years and Over	355	575	678	220	103	13.5	2.4

SOURCE: U.S. Bureau of the Census, *Census of Population: 1960*, vol. 1, pt. 1, U.S. Summary, table 181; *Census of Population: 1970*, vol. 1, pt. 1, U.S. Summary, section 2, table 204; *Census of Population: 1980*, vol. 1, pt. 1, U.S. Summary, chap. D, table 265.

population increase alone would have resulted in an increase in the number of nonfamily householders.

Kobrin has decomposed the 1950–74 increase in primary individuals (nonfamily householders) into the three components (propensity, marital status, population growth) and finds the increase in propensity to live independently to be the factor of most significance.[38] Using a somewhat different decomposition technique, we find that between 1970 and 1980 increased propensity to form independent households was the most significant factor among young adults, but population increase rivaled the propensity factor in accounting for the increase in elderly women who live alone.[39]

Nonfamily Living Among Young Adults

We have reviewed the various factors contributing to changed living arrangements among elderly women, but have not discussed the motivating forces among young women. Much of the research on young adults has focused not on their living arrangements, but on changes in statuses that mark the transition to adulthood: finishing school, entering the work force, getting married, and having children.[40] In the midst of all these transitions, children establish residential independence from their parents. Marriage is a transition which almost always results in separate household formation. At midcentury, young adults were establishing independent households at young ages because they were marrying early.[41] But as marriage is delayed, establishing an independent residence increasingly precedes

[38]Kobrin, "Rise of the Primary Individual."

[39]The decomposition was computed using the five-year age groups shown in Appendix Table 3.1. For a discussion of the logarithmic technique used, see James F. O'Connor, "A Logarithmic Technique for Decomposing Change," *Social Methods and Research* 6 (August 1977):91–102.

[40]Dennis P. Hogan, "The Variable Order of Events in the Life Course," *American Sociological Review* 43 (August 1978):573–86; Dennis P. Hogan, "The Transition to Adulthood as a Career Contingency," *American Sociological Review* 45 (April 1980):261–75; Margaret M. Marini, "The Transition to Adulthood: Sex Differences in Educational Attainment and Age at Marriage," *American Sociological Review* 43 (August 1978):483–507; Margaret M. Marini, "The Order of Events in the Transition to Adulthood," *Sociology of Education* 57 (April 1984):63–84; and James A. Sweet, "Changes in the Allocation of Time of Young Women Among Schooling, Marriage, Work, and Childrearing: 1960–1976," Working Paper no. 79–15 (Madison: Center for Demography and Ecology, University of Wisconsin, 1979).

[41]Halliman Winsborough, "Statistical Histories of the Life Cycle of Birth Cohorts: The Transition from Schoolboy to Adult Male," in Karl E. Taeuber, Larry L. Bumpass, and James A. Sweet, eds., *Social Demography* (New York: Academic Press, 1978), pp. 231–60.

marriage; young women move in with friends or partners of the opposite sex or live alone prior to marriage. The geographic mobility which often accompanies college attendance and job seeking results in more young adults who do not live in the same place as their parents. This also encourages the trend toward nonfamily living.[42] As more young adults pursue higher education, more leave home after high school. Sweet has shown that during the 1960s education was a factor in the greater number of young adult years spent living independently of the parental home.[43] Increased college enrollment during the 1970s provides a better explanation for the greater propensity to live independently among women than among men. As we shall see in the next chapter, women's college enrollment rates increased throughout the 1970s whereas men's tapered off after the Vietnam War ended.

As with the question of what motivates independent living on the part of the elderly, some emphasize changes in norms, tastes, or preferences of young adults to live alone or with nonrelatives while others emphasize income. Michael, Fuchs, and Scott, for example, suggest that young adults, particularly young women whose labor force participation rates have increased over time, have become better able to afford to live independently of others than they were in the past.[44] An alternative explanation is that those who reached adulthood during the 1970s, the older brothers and sisters in large baby boom families, were squeezed out of the parental household at early ages by the presence of younger siblings.[45] Young adults were eager to leave crowded households and parents and younger siblings were happy to have more space and privacy.

Unmarried women and men in their late teens and early 20s remain more likely to live with their parents than to establish sepa-

---

[42]Frances K. Goldscheider and Julie DaVanzo, "Living Arrangements and the Transition to Adulthood," *Demography* 22 (November 1985):545–63.

[43]Sweet shows that the propensity of young adults to move away to attend college did not increase during the 1960s. If anything, with the expansion of community colleges, a higher proportion were attending school while living at home in 1970 than in 1960. But so many more young adults went to college at the end of the decade than at the beginning that both the number living at home and moving away to attend college increased. James A. Sweet, "Recent Trends in the Household and Family Status of Young Adults," Working Paper no. 78–9 (Madison: Center for Demography and Ecology, University of Wisconsin, 1978).

[44]Michael, Fuchs, and Scott, "Propensity to Live Alone."

[45]George S. Masnick and John R. Pitken, "The Baby Boom and the Squeeze on Multigenerational Households," Working Paper no. W83-6 (Cambridge, MA: Joint Center for Urban Studies, Harvard University and Massachusetts Institute of Technology, 1983).

rate households. In 1980, only 28 percent of unmarried women 20 to 24 years of age and 23 percent of unmarried men of the same age maintained an independent household, for example. (See Appendix Table 3.A at the end of this chapter.) However, propensities to live independently were considerably higher for this age group and for those in their late 20s in 1980 than they had been in previous decades. And because the number of men and women in these age groups was so large, the impact they had on changes in household structure was substantial during the 1970s.

Families Maintained by Women

Although the growth in families maintained by women has not been as substantial as the increase in living alone among young adults and elderly women, it is of much importance because these families have high rates of poverty. With families maintained by a woman, there is the additional concern about the economic and social-psychological well-being of children raised by only one parent. Much more attention has been given to families maintained by a woman than to families maintained by a man because it is much more common for mothers to raise children alone. In 1983, for example, over 90 percent of children in one-parent situations lived with their mother.[46]

As noted earlier, census definitions of family require only that two related persons be living together. Two sisters living together constitute a family under this definition, and statistics on female-maintained families usually are not restricted to parent-child households. Because the growth of families *with children* is of much more interest than the growth of other types of families, most of our discussion focuses on families which include children under the age of 18.

As shown in Table 3.4, the number of female householders with children more than doubled between 1960 and 1980, with more of that growth occurring in the 1970s than in the 1960s. Female family householders as a group were younger in 1980 than in 1960 or 1970, and the majority were either divorced or separated. The number of

[46]U.S. Bureau of the Census, "Marital Status and Living Arrangements: March 1983," *Current Population Reports*, series P-20, no. 389 (Washington, DC: U.S. Government Printing Office, 1983), table 4.

TABLE 3.4

Changing Distribution of Female Family Householders with Children (numbers in thousands)

Age and Marital Status	Number			Percentage Distribution			1960–80 Change	
	1960	1970	1980	1960	1970	1980	Number	Percent
Total, 15 Years and Over	1,892	3,017	4,932	100.0%	100.0%	100.0%	1,915	101.2%
Under 35 Years	666	1,274	2,515	35.2	42.2	51.0	1,241	186.3
35–44 Years	679	978	1,576	35.9	32.4	32.0	598	88.1
45–64 Years	531	743	824	28.1	24.6	16.7	81	15.3
65 Years and Over	16	22	17	0.8	0.7	0.3	−5	−31.3
Total, All Statuses	1,892	3,017	4,932	100.0%	100.0%	100.0%	1,915	101.2
Separated	454	767	1,047	24.0	25.4	21.2	280	61.7
Spouse Absent	253	251	171	13.4	8.3	3.5	−80	−31.6
Widowed	606	748	593	32.0	24.8	12.0	−155	−25.6
Divorced	496	991	2,295	26.2	32.8	46.5	1,304	262.9
Never Married	83	260	826	4.4	8.6	16.7	566	681.9

SOURCE: U.S. Bureau of the Census, *Census of Population: 1960*, vol. 2. "Families," PC(2)-4A, tables 5 and 6; *Census of Population: 1970*, vol. 2. 2, "Family Composition," PC(2)-4A, tables 6 and 8; *Census of Population: 1980*, vol. 1, chap. D, U.S. Summary, tables 267 and 268.

widows (or married women whose spouse was absent for reasons other than marital discord) who were family householders actually declined between 1960 and 1980.

Perhaps the most noteworthy change shown in Table 3.4 is the large increase in female householders who have never been married. Between 1960 and 1980 the number of never-married female family householders with children grew from less than 100,000 to over 800,000. Never-married women now account for 17 percent of female-maintained families with children compared with only 4 percent in 1960.

What factors underlie the growth in female-maintained families with children? Several existing studies investigate components of the increase in families maintained by women.[47] First, the increase is in part due to a change in living arrangements, that is, an increased tendency for women to form an independent household after a divorce rather than move in with relatives.[48] The first two rows of Table 3.5 show changes in the living arrangements of never-married and previously married mothers living with their own children.

---

[47]For a comprehensive study of 1960–70 changes in the family headship of women, see Ross and Sawhill, *Time of Transition;* Rosemary S. Cooney, "Demographic Components of Growth in White, Black, and Puerto Rican Female-Headed Families: Comparison of the Cutright and Ross/Sawhill Methodologies," *Social Science Research* 8 (June 1979):144–158; and Phillips Cutright, "Components of Change in the Number of Female Family Heads Aged 15–44: United States, 1940–70," *Journal of Marriage and the Family* 36 (November 1974):714–21.

[48]Cutright, in his examination of the 1940–1970 period, emphasizes the importance of the living arrangements factor in the increase in family headship (Cutright's terminology) on the part of women between the ages of 14 and 44. In their decomposition of 1960–70 growth in Black and White female-maintained families, Ross and Sawhill stress increased marital disruption as the important factor in the increase in female-maintained families with children. Cooney, in her attempt to resolve the inconsistencies between Cutright and Ross and Sawhill, suggests that the focus on the different time periods is the major reason that the two studies differ for Whites. If one takes a longer time frame, living arrangement propensities are the major factor, but during the 1960s, increased marital disruption was particularly important. These are not the major components of change for Blacks and Puerto Ricans, however. For these two groups, increases in the presence of children and population growth are more important. All of these studies have their limitations. Cooney's study is not a national study: Only data for the mid-Atlantic region are used. Cutright uses children ever born rather than the presence of children to estimate the number of women at risk of maintaining a family with dependent children. The Ross and Sawhill methodology for decomposing change is somewhat unusual and when applied to the decade of the 1970s results in attributing much of the change to the interaction component. Because each decomposition results in different emphasis, we have taken the posture of showing changes in each of the components but stopping short of assessing the relative importance of the factors. We have defined the "children" components in line with Ross and Sawhill, that is, as presence of children, rather than as Cutright does, that is, as children ever born. In some ways the Cutright definition is more appealing because it is more in line with the demographic notion of the "at risk" population. But as Cooney notes, the children ever born variable is inadequate without additional information on age and current living arrangements of those children.

TABLE 3.5

Changes in Families Maintained by Women with Children (numbers in thousands)

	Whites			Blacks		
	1960	1970	1980	1960	1970	1980
LIVING ARRANGEMENTS						
Percentage of Never-Married Mothers who Maintain Own Household	81.3%	61.1%	65.7%	78.1%	60.6%	70.5%
Percentage of Formerly Married Mothers who Maintain Own Household	82.2	87.7	91.4	80.0	89.1	91.9
CHILDREN						
Percentage of Women in Disrupted Marital Statuses with Children Under 18 Years	15.3	17.1	18.3	27.5	34.0	34.8
Percentage of Never-Married Women with Children Under 18 Years	0.3	0.9	2.1	4.8	11.9	21.6
MARITAL DISRUPTION						
Percentage of Ever-Married Women in Disrupted Marital Statuses	19.6	22.3	26.7	33.1	38.0	46.0
Divorced	3.4	4.8	8.7	4.6	7.1	13.8
Separated	1.6	1.9	2.2	10.7	12.5	13.0
Widowed	14.6	15.7	15.9	17.8	18.6	19.2
POPULATION AT RISK						
Percentage of Women Currently Unmarried	34.6	39.3	42.2	47.9	55.9	64.4
Never Married	18.6	21.8	21.2	22.0	28.7	34.1
In Disrupted Statuses	16.0	17.5	21.0	25.9	27.2	30.3
Total Women	58,040	68,873	77,346	6,873	8,122	10,219
Total Female Family Householders with Children	1,191	1,891	2,945	448	840	1,522

NOTE: Married women with an absent spouse are excluded from the count of women in disrupted statuses and the count of female householders. Data for 1960 are for nonwhites.

SOURCE: U.S. Bureau of the Census, *Census of Population: 1960*, "Families," Subject Report, PC(2)-4A, tables 6 and 21; and "Marital Status," PC(2)-4E, table 1; *Census of Population: 1970*, "Family Composition," PC(2)-4a, tables 20 and 25, and "Marital Status," PC(2)-4c, table 1; *Census of Population: 1980*, vol. 1, chap. D, U.S. Summary, tables 264 and 267.

Among both races, the propensity to form an independent household increased for previously married (that is, currently divorced, widowed, or separated) women. Never-married mothers, on the other hand, became less likely to maintain a separate household between 1960 and 1970. After 1970, however, the propensity to live independently increased, particularly among Black never-married women.

A second component of the growth in the number of female-maintained families is the greater probability that a child is present when a separation, divorce, or death of a father occurs. As noted in chapter 1, divorce is replacing death as the major component of marital disruption. Since divorce occurs earlier in the life cycle, it more often involves marriages with children than does disruption that results at later stages of the life cycle from the death of a spouse. Ross and Sawhill suggest that the presence of children was an important factor in explaining the increase in families maintained by a woman in the 1960s.[49] The percentage of formerly married women who had dependent children increased from 15 to 17 percent among Whites and from 28 to 34 percent among Blacks between 1960 and 1970. During the 1970s, however, the proportion of formerly married women with children increased only slightly.

A third, related component of the growth in female-maintained families is the change in the probability that a never-married woman will be raising a child born out of wedlock. This out-of-wedlock component, Ross and Sawhill find, is a more important factor for Blacks than for Whites.[50] The fourth row of Table 3.5 confirms this for the 1970s as well as the 1960s. Among both races the probability that a never-married woman is living with an own child under 18 has risen, but the level for Blacks is much higher and the increase is much steeper. In 1980, 15 percent of never-married Black women were raising children compared with 1 percent of White women. The increased proportion of female-maintained families with a never married householder, noted earlier in Table 3.4, is heavily dominated by Black women.

Apart from whether or not a marital disruption involves children, the sheer increase in disruptions is a fourth component of the increase in families maintained by women. As Table 3.5 shows, the percentage of ever-married women who are currently separated, di-

[49]Ross and Sawhill, *Time of Transition*.
[50]Ross and Sawhill, *Time of Transition*.

vorced, or widowed has increased from 20 to 27 percent among Whites and from 33 to 46 percent among Blacks. The increase in divorce is most important, but among Blacks there has also been an increase in the percentage of women who are separated or widowed. The result of marital status changes, both the increased proportion of women whose marriages have dissolved and, among Blacks, the sizable increase in the proportion of women who have never married, has been to alter the proportion of women who are not currently married. In 1960, 35 percent of White women and 48 percent of Black women above the age of 14 were unmarried. By 1980, these percentages had risen to 42 and 64 percent, respectively. Had there been no change in propensity to form independent households, in the presence of children when a divorce occurred, or in out-of-wedlock childbearing, the number of female-maintained families would still have increased because the increase in divorce and the delay in first marriage placed more women "at risk" of rearing children outside marriage in 1980 than in 1970. Ross and Sawhill have shown that increased marital disruption was also an important component of the increase during the 1960s.[51]

Finally, apart from all changes in living arrangements, children, and marital disruption, the mere increase in the number of women has resulted in some increase in the number of female householders with children. It is interesting to note, however, that growth in female householders far surpassed that which might be accounted for by mere population increase. During the 1960s the number of women aged 14 and over increased by less than 20 percent, whereas female-maintained families with children grew by 54 percent among Whites and 72 percent among Blacks. During the 1970s the increase in female family householders with children was 55 percent for Whites and 81 percent for Blacks—much higher than the population increase of 12 percent among White women and 26 percent among Black women. (See Table 3.5.)

Summary

Women are spending more of their adult lives outside the traditional husband-wife, nuclear family. There have been sizable in-

---

[51]Ross and Sawhill, *Time of Transition.*

creases in independent, nonfamily living among unmarried young adults and elderly women. And although residing with a spouse remains the most common living arrangement of women in their 30s and 40s, a growing proportion are raising a family alone.

As we shall discuss in the next two chapters, more young women are enrolling in college and entering the work force than was true in the past. These nonfamily transitions of finishing school and starting a job, along with the family transitions of marriage and children, have typically marked the passage to adulthood. What is unique about young women of recent cohorts is that a relatively high proportion have delayed family transitions and entered adulthood by assuming nonfamily adult roles, whereas women of their mothers' generation made the transition to adulthood by marrying and having children. Accompanying this "nonfamily" transition to adulthood has been the increased propensity of young women to live independently prior to marriage—either residing alone, with friends, or with a partner of the opposite sex.

When we examine trends in living arrangements that have characterized the entire post–World War II period, we find that the most significant change has been the increase in elderly women who live alone following the death of a spouse. Except during the 1970s, when growth in nonfamily households managed by young women was extensive, the growth in nonfamily households maintained by women has been dominated by older women. Living alone in old age is very much a "female" phenomenon because women live longer and are less likely to remarry than men.

In 1950 unmarried (usually widowed) women over age 65 were as likely to live with others as maintain an independent household. Today almost four of five such women live independently. The very dramatic shift reflects changes in preferences, available kin with whom an elderly woman might live, health, and economic ability to afford to live separately from adult children or other relatives.

As divorce rates have risen, growth in the number of families maintained by women has accelerated. An increasing number of women either choose or are forced to "go it alone" during mid-life, sometimes for an extended number of years. This trend is apparent among both Black and White women, but has been more substantial among Blacks. Also, a sizable percentage of Black families are maintained by a woman who has never married.

The increase in families with children which are managed by

women is of concern because, as we shall document in later chapters, the economic well-being of these households is often marginal. Increasingly, women do not live as wives for an unbroken string of years as they raise their children. Family life courses of women have become less predictable. These changes in family roles have made women's economic roles increasingly important. It is to changes in women's participation in education and the world of paid employment that we now turn.

APPENDIX TABLE 3.A

Changes in Percentage of Unmarried Women and Men Who Maintain Independent Households

Sex and Age	1940	1950	1960	1970	1980
TOTAL UNMARRIED WOMEN	39.0%	41.6%	53.5%	60.5%	65.1%
20–24 Years	3.5	6.4	14.3	21.4	27.6
25–29 Years	13.3	18.2	33.7	49.6	55.1
30–34 Years	28.2	30.0	46.7	60.6	69.6
35–39 Years	45.9	40.5	54.9	65.8	76.6
40–44 Years	57.7	48.5	60.8	68.9	78.9
45–49 Years	64.2	55.2	63.7	71.6	79.5
50–54 Years	64.8	57.6	64.6	72.8	79.5
55–59 Years	63.9	58.3	64.6	74.1	80.5
60–64 Years	60.3	56.4	65.9	74.9	81.1
65–69 Years	57.9	55.8	65.4	75.1	81.7
70–74 Years	54.3	55.2	62.2	73.8	81.2
75 Years and Over	44.4	44.1	52.1	62.5	72.7
TOTAL UNMARRIED MEN	24.9	25.5	35.0	43.1	47.6
20–24 Years	3.3	3.8	7.6	14.5	22.9
25–29 Years	8.7	10.2	18.9	33.6	45.1
30–34 Years	17.1	16.5	27.5	41.7	55.3
35–39 Years	27.1	23.4	33.8	47.4	59.9
40–44 Years	36.9	30.4	40.2	52.7	62.4
45–49 Years	46.0	36.9	46.0	58.6	65.1
50–54 Years	52.8	41.7	49.9	61.4	67.2
55–59 Years	57.6	46.1	52.7	65.3	69.1
60–64 Years	59.8	48.7	57.5	67.8	71.0
65–69 Years	60.5	51.1	59.6	68.6	72.1
70–74 Years	57.1	51.4	59.3	68.6	71.7
75 Years and Over	48.3	44.8	51.6	59.7	64.3

NOTE: Persons aged 20 and over who were never married, widowed, divorced or separated.

SOURCE: U.S. Bureau of the Census, *Census of Population: 1950*, vol. 2, pt. 1, U.S. Summary, tables 104 and 105; *Census of Population: 1940*, vol. 4, pt. 1, U.S. Summary, tables 6 and 11; *Census of Population: 1960*, vol. 1, pt. 1, U.S. Summary, tables 176 and 181; *Census of Population: 1970*, vol. 1, pt. 1, U.S. Summary, section 2, tables 203 and 204; *Census of Population: 1980*, vol. 1, pt. 1, U.S. Summary, chap. D, tables 264 and 265.

4

EDUCATION

"OH, HOW immensely important is the preparation of the Daughters of the land to be good mothers." Thus spoke Mary Lyon, founder of Mount Holyoke College, in justifying the creation of her school for women in the nineteenth century.[1] At the opening of Rutgers Female College in 1867, the Reverend Dr. Todd expressed a similar sentiment: "The glory of woman is in her home. . . . I want her educated to feel that the highest glory of woman is the paradise of home. . . ."[2]

Attitudes like these are not expressed in print very often anymore. Most Americans now believe that women and men should have equal access to higher education for the intellectual and employment opportunities it provides. Yet as recently as 1960 only 6 percent of adult American women had a college degree compared with 10 percent of adult men. By 1980, 13 percent of women and 20 percent of men 25 years old and over had college degrees. Enrollment rates for women of college age equaled those of men in 1980 for the first time in American history, and half of all bachelor's degrees

[1] Joellen Watson, "Higher Education for Women in the United States: A Historical Perspective," *Educational Studies* 8 (Summer 1977):133–46.
[2] Watson, "Higher Education," p. 134.

went to women. During the 1970s, in particular, women made striking gains relative to men in postsecondary enrollment and attainment. The increased enrollment of women in colleges and universities was accompanied by a revision of the beliefs about the value of advanced education for women. No longer is a college education viewed merely as a means of making women better homemakers and mothers.

Higher education has many inherent values. In addition to imparting a certain body of specialized knowledge, college attendance is often an intermediate step in the transition from childhood to adulthood. A college degree is becoming increasingly necessary in the American economy, making it important for women to continue improving their educational attainment in order to compete in the job market. Higher education can also mean higher income, and the relative improvement in educational attainment for women has the potential to reduce the wage difference between men and women.

Despite equal enrollment rates, the content of postsecondary education has remained different for women and men. A higher proportion of women major in education, the humanities, and health sciences, while proportionately more men major in physical sciences and engineering.[3] Census data cannot tell us why men and women decide to major in certain subjects. Economists within the human capital tradition argue that it is largely a matter of choice, whereas sociologists attribute it to sex role socialization and institutional barriers. Both explanations have merit. As definitions of women's "proper" role expand to include a variety of life choices, early childhood socialization may become less rigid and young girls will less often be steered into traditionally female courses in school. This greater freedom, in turn, means that more fields of study are open to young women by the time they reach college. Tracking at the lower

---

[3]Title IX of the 1972 Civil Rights Act was intended to create opportunities for women who want to enter traditionally male fields. Title IX specifically forbade sex discrimination in schools that receive federal assistance. Until 1984 this was interpreted to mean *every* department and program of a college was prevented from discriminating on the basis of sex if *any* department or program received federal aid. This interpretation facilitated the growth in women's enrollment, participation in sports, and admission to professional schools. In March 1984, as this book was being written, the Supreme Court reinterpreted the scope of Title IX. Only departments or programs that directly receive federal aid now have to comply with antidiscriminatory legislation. Programs not directly receiving aid are no longer subject to federal regulation. Advocates of women's rights immediately began lobbying for legislation to overturn the decision.

levels undoubtedly persists, but the days when girls were counseled away from taking math and science courses are disappearing.

In addition to women and men majoring in different fields of study, women are less likely than men to seek professional and doctoral degrees (although the proportion of higher degrees awarded to women has increased greatly in the last decade). Why does this differential exist? Earlier marriage and childbearing are two explanations, although their importance in determining educational attainment may be declining. Women tend to marry about two years younger than men, which means that their schooling is more often curtailed. The educational attainment of single women is closer to that of men than to that of married women, for example.[4] The early arrival of children is also negatively related to educational attainment, although there is disagreement on the causality of the relationship.

The increased educational attainment of women has coincided with delays in marriage and childbearing and more independent lifestyles among young adult women. Schooling decisions link family roles of women (discussed in the preceding three chapters) to the work roles of women (the focus of the next two chapters). Women who finish schooling with a high school diploma and marry and have children in their early 20s tend to have less career-oriented lives than women who earn advanced degrees, establish themselves in a career track, and then combine careers with family responsibilities in their 30s. Each life pattern has its advantages and disadvantages, although the first is the more traditional and remains the more typical path for women to follow. But a growing minority of women are choosing the second life course. This chapter reviews changes in educational attainment and school enrollment, the proportion of degrees granted to women, and sex differences in fields of study—changes which are pivotal to understanding women's changing family and economic roles.[5]

---

[4]U.S. Bureau of the Census, "A Statistical Portrait of Women in the United States: 1978," *Current Population Reports, Special Studies,* series P-23, no. 100 (Washington, DC: U.S. Government Printing Office, 1980), p. 36.

[5]Three major data sources are used in this chapter. The 1960, 1970, and 1980 Censuses of Population provide information on years of school completed by adults. The October school enrollment supplements to the Current Population Survey, spanning the last two decades, are used to track changes in college enrollment. And the *Digest of Education Statistics,* an annual compilation of education statistics issued by the National Center for Education Statistics, is used to analyze the trend in degrees conferred on women.

Educational Attainment

The average educational attainment of the population has increased over time, as shown in Table 4.1. The proportion of the population who complete high school has increased sharply. In 1960 approximately two-fifths of men and women 25 years and over were high school graduates, and by 1980 approximately two-thirds of both sexes had earned at least a high school diploma. The percentage of adult women with at least a college degree more than doubled between 1960 and 1980, from 6 to 13 percent, whereas for men the increase was from 10 to 20 percent. Although women have gained in educational attainment in absolute terms, the gap between the proportion of women and men who complete college has actually widened over time (from 4 to 7 percentage points).

Improvements in educational attainment have been particularly pronounced for Blacks. In 1960, 65 percent of all adult Black men and 58 percent of Black women had an elementary school education or less. By 1980 about 26 percent of Black women and men had an elementary school education or less. The proportion of Blacks with a

TABLE 4.1

Changes in Educational Attainment of Black and White Women and Men Aged 25 and Over (percentage completing)

Years of School and Race	Women			Men		
	1960	1970	1980	1960	1970	1980
ELEMENTARY (8 Years or Fewer)						
Total, All Races	37.5%	26.9%	17.3%	41.2%	27.2%	17.8%
White	35.4	25.3	15.6	39.0	27.4	16.4
Black	58.0	41.3	25.6	64.5	47.9	27.4
HIGH SCHOOL (12 Years or More)						
Total, All Races	43.0	52.9	66.4	40.0	52.0	67.9
White	45.1	55.2	68.9	42.1	54.2	70.2
Black	22.0	32.3	51.1	18.3	29.9	51.1
COLLEGE (16 Years or More)						
Total, All Races	5.8	7.9	12.9	9.6	13.5	20.4
White	6.0	8.3	13.5	10.3	14.4	21.8
Black	3.6	4.6	7.7	3.0	4.2	3.3

SOURCE: 1960, 1970, and 1980 Census 1/1,000 Public Use Microdata Sample.

high school diploma increased from 22 percent for women and 18 percent for men in 1960 to about 51 percent for both women and men in 1980. The proportion of Black women and men with four or more years of college more than doubled between 1960 and 1980.

The rising level of educational attainment for Blacks and Whites is due in part to the aging of the population. That is, as older generations with less formal education have been replaced by younger generations with more education, the overall level of attainment has risen. Table 4.2 shows educational attainment for ten-year age groups in 1960, 1970, and 1980. In 1960, 19 percent of

TABLE 4.2

Changes in Educational Attainment of Women and Men
in Selected Age Groups (percentage completing)

	Women			Men		
	1960	1970	1980	1960	1970	1980
ELEMENTARY (8 Years or Fewer)						
Total, 25 and Over	37.5%	26.9%	17.3%	41.2%	27.2%	17.8%
25–34 Years	16.9	9.7	4.8	21.5	11.2	5.1
35–44 Years	24.7	14.8	8.1	28.3	18.2	10.0
45–54 Years	39.3	23.6	14.8	43.0	25.5	17.4
55–64 Years	54.3	36.8	21.8	58.5	42.0	24.2
65–74 Years	65.6	50.7	34.8	70.9	58.4	39.5
75 Years and Over	70.1	60.1	50.0	75.8	67.6	57.0
HIGH SCHOOL (12 Years or More)						
Total, 25 Years and Over	43.0	52.9	66.4	40.0	52.0	67.9
25–34 Years	60.2	71.3	84.5	57.1	72.4	85.3
35–44 Years	53.1	62.6	76.9	50.7	61.0	77.5
45–54 Years	40.1	54.4	66.3	36.0	53.3	65.6
55–64 Years	29.1	42.2	57.6	25.5	37.6	57.1
65–74 Years	21.3	32.0	44.0	17.6	26.2	41.7
75 Years and Over	18.5	25.8	34.3	15.1	21.0	29.3
COLLEGE (16 Years or More)						
Total, 25 Years and Over	5.8	7.9	12.9	9.6	13.5	20.4
25–34 Years	7.4	12.3	20.7	14.4	19.2	26.1
35–44 Years	6.3	8.4	14.8	11.4	17.6	24.8
45–54 Years	6.0	6.9	10.0	8.4	12.5	19.7
55–64 Years	5.0	6.9	8.3	6.3	9.1	14.7
65–74 Years	3.1	5.4	7.6	4.7	6.7	10.6
75 Years and Over	2.8	4.1	5.7	3.5	5.5	8.1

SOURCE: 1960, 1970, and 1980 Census 1/1,000 Public Use Microdata Sample.

women and 15 percent of men aged 75 and over had a high school education; by 1980, 34 percent of elderly women and 29 percent of elderly men had completed high school. By comparison, women and men in the youngest age group had high school completion rates of approximately 85 percent in 1980. Thus, the proportion of the population with a minimum of formal education has gradually declined.

Currently, almost 85 percent of the population graduates from high school, but among young adults the proportion of men with college or graduate training exceeds that of women. In 1980, 26 percent of men aged 25 to 34 had earned at least a bachelor's degree compared with 21 percent of young women. As we shall see, most of this attainment differential arises from the fact that women remain less likely than men to earn graduate or professional degrees. Women's undergraduate enrollment rates have actually equaled and surpassed those of men in recent years.

College Enrollment

There has been great progress in college enrollment and completion rates for women relative to men in the last two decades. One of the most significant aspects of the delay in first marriage is that more women have the opportunity to enter and finish college before marriage. The median age of first marriage for women had risen to almost 23 years by 1983.[6] Since college graduation typically occurs at age 21 or 22, over half of all young women are currently waiting until after this age to marry.

Women's college enrollment rates have increased since the late 1950s, but rates for men (which increased between 1949 and 1969) declined in the 1970s. College enrollment rates for women more than doubled between 1960, when 12 percent of women aged 18 to 24 were enrolled, and 1981, when 25 percent of women in this age group were enrolled. In 1960, 20 percent of men aged 18 to 24 were enrolled and rates reached a peak of 29 percent about 1970. By 1981

[6]U.S. Bureau of the Census, "Marital Status and Living Arrangements: March 1983," *Current Population Reports*, series P-20, no. 389 (Washington, DC: U.S. Government Printing Office, 1984), table A.

the enrollment rate of college-age males stood at 25 percent—the same as that for females.[7]

Figure 4.1 shows college enrollment trends disaggregated by age for the 1965–81 period. At ages 18 and 19 women's rates actually surpass those of men, in part because more men are still in high school at these ages. By the time most college students are in their junior and senior years, the rates for women and men are very similar. At the older ages of 22 to 24, when a sizable percentage of those enrolled are in professional and graduate degree programs, women's enrollment in 1981 lagged behind that of males by about 5 percentage points. Yet even for this age group, the trend lines show that enrollment rates of women have become much more similar to those of men during the last two decades.

The increase in college enrollment for women has also been impressive at older ages. The number of women aged 25 to 34 enrolled in college rose by 79 percent between 1974 to 1981, while the number of men enrolled at that age rose only slightly. The number of women 35 years old and over enrolled in college rose by 72 percent during that period, while the number of men enrolled was unchanged. By 1981 students of "traditional" college age (age 21 and under) were no longer the majority of all college students.[8]

From 1972 to 1981 total college enrollment grew by 33 percent. Male enrollment rose by 12 percent while female enrollment rose by 63 percent. In 1979 for the first time female college students out-

[7]Enrollment rates for males are calculated using the total population as the base. Typically, the civilian population is used, but this tends to distort college enrollment trends for males because of the large fluctuations in the male civilian population during and after the Vietnam War. Using the civilian population as the base for calculating enrollment rates results in a much larger increase in the 1960s and a much greater decline in the 1970s for males than does using the total population. That is, enrollment of those aged 18 to 24 increased from 24 percent in 1960 to 36 percent in 1969 and then declined to 27 percent in 1981.

This is not to say that all of the changes in college enrollment of young adult males resulted from the fluctuations in the civilian population. There was an increase in enrollment rates in the 1960s and a subsequent decline in the 1970s. College attendance qualified as a draft deferment in the 1960s, causing part of the rise in enrollment, and the elimination of the draft in the 1970s may have reduced enrollment rates slightly. The expiration of GI benefits probably also contributed to the decline in enrollment among men. U.S. Bureau of the Census, "Educational Attainment in the United States: March 1981 and 1980," *Current Population Reports*, series P-20, no. 390 (Washington, DC: U.S. Government Printing Office, 1984), p. 2.

[8]U.S. Bureau of the Census, "School Enrollment—Social Economic Characteristics of Students: October 1981 (Advance Report)," *Current Population Reports*, series P-20, no. 373 (Washington, DC: U.S. Government Printing Office, 1983).

FIGURE 4.1

Trend in Percentage of Women and Men Enrolled in College

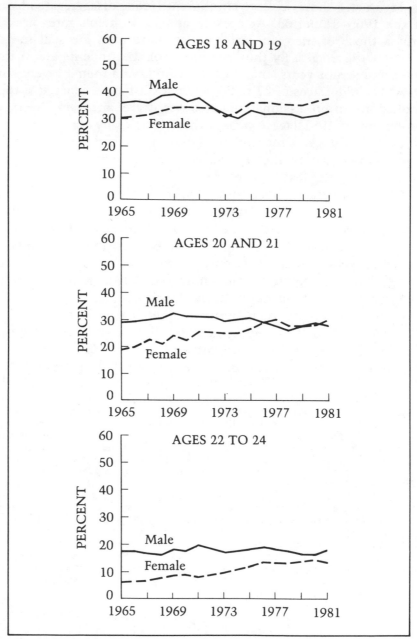

SOURCE: U.S. Bureau of the Census, "School Enrollment—Social and Economic Characteristics of Students: October 1981 and 1980," *Current Population Reports*, series P-20, no. 400 (Washington, DC: U.S. Government Printing Office, 1981), table A.3.

numbered male students. Part of the growth in women's enrollment was due to increases in part-time attendance and enrollment in two-year colleges. In 1981, one-third of female undergraduates aged 14 to 34 were enrolled in two-year colleges, and more than one-quarter were going to school part-time. However, women's increased enrollment cannot be completely attributed to higher part-time attendance. More than half of the increase in the last decade was in full-time enrollment.[9]

Women's gains in college enrollment are especially pronounced when examined as a proportion of total enrollment. Since 1960 the proportion of college students who are female has risen from about one-third to one-half. The actual number of women aged 14 to 34 who were enrolled increased from 1.2 million in 1960 to 5.2 million in 1980. Changes for women past the traditional age for attending college are particularly striking. For all ages 22 and over, the proportion of female students enrolled more than doubled. Within the age group 30 to 34, for example, the proportion female increased from one-quarter of all those enrolled to over one-half.[10] As enrollment increases, completion rates for women may also rise, eventually leading to convergence with men in attainment of college degrees and, perhaps, advanced degrees.

Field of Study

As educational enrollment and attainment rates for women have increased, new fields of study have become more open to women. Business provides the most striking example. Only 8 percent of all bachelor's degrees in business went to women in 1965, but by 1980 that proportion had jumped to 34 percent. The proportion of MBAs awarded to women rose from 3 to 22 percent during the same period (see Table 4.3).

Other traditionally male fields showed comparable changes. In architecture, 8 percent of bachelor's degrees went to women in 1965 compared with 28 percent in 1980. Engineering degrees were rare for

[9]U.S. Bureau of the Census, "School Enrollment: October 1981."

[10]U.S. Bureau of the Census, "Population Profile of the United States: 1981," *Current Population Reports*, series P-20, no. 374 (Washington, DC: U.S. Government Printing Office, 1982), table 6–2; and U.S. Bureau of the Census, "School Enrollment—Social and Economic Characteristics of Students: October 1979," *Current Population Reports*, series P-20, no. 360 (Washington, DC: U.S. Government Printing Office, 1981), table A-2.

TABLE 4.3

Changes in Percentage of Degrees in Selected Fields of Study Conferred on Women

Field of Study	Bachelor's				Master's				Doctorate's			
	1965	1970	1975	1980	1965	1970	1975	1980	1965	1970	1975	1980
Architecture	8.2%	5.2%	17.4%	27.8%	7.8%	6.5%	20.2%	28.5%	10.0%	9.1%	15.9%	16.4%
Biological Sciences	29.2	27.8	33.1	42.1	27.0	31.5	30.0	37.0	11.9	14.2	22.0	26.0
Business	8.4	8.7	16.2	33.6	3.2	3.5	8.4	22.3	1.9	1.6	4.0	14.4
Education	76.5	75.0	73.3	73.8	47.5	55.3	62.2	70.2	19.5	20.3	30.8	44.3
Engineering	0.4	0.7	2.2	9.3	0.4	1.1	2.4	7.0	0.5	0.6	2.1	3.8
English and Literature	65.8	66.9	57.1	59.3	55.3	61.0	58.8	60.4	21.6	31.0	34.0	41.0
Fine and Applied Arts	58.9	57.2	61.9	63.2	41.7	47.0	46.8	53.3	15.9	19.3	31.3	36.9
Foreign Languages	70.5	73.4	76.6	75.5	53.6	62.7	67.0	70.2	27.8	33.4	46.9	57.4
Health Professions	93.1	78.0	77.7	82.2	43.9	52.0	61.7	72.2	9.2	16.2	28.6	44.6
Home Economics	97.9	97.2	95.9	95.3	97.8	94.2	89.3	91.3	79.3	71.6	67.3	76.0
Library Sciences	92.1	91.8	92.5	95.0	74.7	83.0	78.8	81.3	8.3	40.0	41.1	52.0
Mathematics	32.9	37.4	41.8	42.3	19.4	29.6	32.9	36.1	8.6	7.8	11.3	13.8
Physical Sciences	14.1	13.6	18.2	23.7	10.4	14.2	14.4	18.6	4.5	5.4	8.3	12.4
Psychology	41.0	43.3	52.6	63.2	32.7	38.0	42.8	56.8	18.8	22.3	30.9	42.1
Religion (Theology)	33.3	30.6	27.4	25.5	16.6	24.5	30.9	31.0	5.7	3.4	3.8	5.8
Social Sciences	33.9	37.1	37.3	43.6	22.7	35.3	30.0	36.1	9.3	13.0	20.8	27.1

SOURCE: National Center for Education Statistics, *Digest of Education Statistics* (Washington, DC: U.S. Government Printing Office, selected years).

women in the mid-1960s, but by the end of the 1970s, 9 percent of engineering bachelor's degrees were earned by women. In the physical sciences, the proportion of bachelor's degrees awarded to women rose from 14 to 24 percent between 1965 and 1980.

At one time mathematics was a typically "male" field, yet it now exceeds many other fields in the proportion of degrees granted to women. In the mid-1960s, 33 percent of bachelor's degrees in math went to women, and that proportion had increased to 42 percent by the late 1970s. Research conducted during the 1960s and 1970s tried to determine why girls do not do as well at math as boys. One finding is that girls withdraw from math training at an earlier age than boys, partly in response to the perception that math is intellectually a male domain. Some genetic advantage in spatial ability may exist for boys, but girls' lack of self-confidence and self-selection out of the field go farther toward explaining achievement differences than any inherited factors.[11] The fact that women are increasing their representation among math majors suggests that traditional sex-role stereotyping may be losing some of its power.

Despite the inroads that women have made into traditionally "male" fields, underrepresentation of women in some fields of undergraduate study persists. Business, for example, is still two-thirds male, while architecture, engineering, physical sciences, and religion are all more than two-thirds male. Five undergraduate majors are disproportionately (more than two-thirds) female: education, foreign languages, health professions, home economics, and library science. The male-dominated fields tend to lead to occupations which command higher earnings. For example, architects earned an average of $23,000 in 1979, while registered nurses earned $11,900. Mechanical engineers averaged $24,700, while elementary school teachers earned $12,600.[12]

By 1980 not only were women nearly as well represented as men among recipients of bachelor's degrees, but they also earned almost half of master's degrees. (See Figure 4.2.) Here also the content of those degrees was not sex-neutral. Over half of the master's degrees awarded to women were in the two fields of education and health

[11]M. E. Badger, "Why Aren't Girls Better at Math? A Review of Research," *Educational Research* 24 (November 1981):11–23.

[12]U.S. Bureau of the Census, "Earnings by Occupation and Education," *1980 Census of Population Subject Report*, PC80-2-8B (Washington, DC: U.S. Government Printing Office, 1984), table 1.

FIGURE 4.2

Trend in Percentage of Degrees Conferred on Women

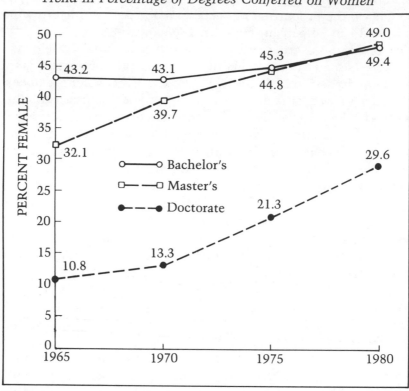

SOURCE: National Center for Education Statistics, *Digest of Education Statistics*, selected years.

professions. Among master's degrees granted to men in 1980, more than two-fifths were awarded in the fields of business, engineering, and biological and physical sciences.[13] Although the possession of an advanced degree is an achievement in and of itself, teaching and nursing degrees do not translate into as much future income as do business, engineering, or science degrees. Thus, an equal proportion of master's degrees went to men and women, but their content remained sex-typed.

Women have made great gains in earning professional degrees as well. Fewer than 1 percent of dentistry degrees were awarded to women in 1960 compared with 13 percent in 1980. (See Table 4.4.)

[13]National Center for Education Statistics, *Digest of Education Statistics 1982* (Washington, DC: U.S. Government Printing Office, 1982), table 108.

TABLE 4.4

Changes in Number and Percentage of Degrees in Dentistry, Medicine, and Law Granted to Women

Year	Dentistry		Medicine		Law	
	Number	Percent	Number	Percent	Number	Percent
1960	26	0.8%	387	5.5%	230	2.5%
1965	22	0.7	472	6.5	367	3.2
1970	34	0.9	699	8.4	801	5.4
1975	146	3.0	1,629	13.1	4,415	15.1
1980	700	13.3	3,486	23.4	10,754	30.2

SOURCE: National Center for Education Statistics, *Digest of Education Statistics* (Washington, DC: U.S. Government Printing Office, 1982), table 112.

The proportion of medical degrees granted to women rose from 6 percent in 1960 to 23 percent in 1980. The legal profession saw the greatest increase of all: from only 2 percent of all law degrees going to women in 1960 to 30 percent in 1980, that is, from 230 to over 10,000 degrees conferred on women between 1960 and 1980. Much of this change was concentrated in the latter half of the 1970s: The proportion of dental degrees awarded to women more than quadrupled, while the proportion of law degrees conferred on women doubled between 1975 and 1980.

Educational Attainment and Age at First Marriage

An entire field of sociological literature has been devoted to explaining differences in educational attainment.[14] Early studies had little to say about sex differences in educational attainment, because the majority of work was based on men only.[15] More recent research,

[14]Known collectively as "the Wisconsin Model" for the state in which the longitudinal data were gathered and the university at which they were analyzed, this research builds on the original Occupational Changes in a Generation model created by Blau and Duncan. See Peter M. Blau and Otis Dudley Duncan, *The American Occupational Structure* (New York: Wiley, 1967). An overview of the research is presented in William H. Sewell, Robert M. Hauser, and David L. Featherman, *Schooling and Achievement in American Society* (New York: Harcourt Brace Jovanovich, 1976).

[15]Karl L. Alexander, Bruce K. Eckland, and Larry J. Griffin, "The Wisconsin Model of Socioeconomic Achievement: A Replication," *American Journal of Sociology* 81 (September 1975):324–42; Larry J. Griffin and Karl L. Alexander, "Schooling and Socioeconomic Attainments: High School and College Influences," *American Journal of Sociology* 84 (September 1978):319–47; and Alan C. Kerckhoff and Robert A. Jackson, "Types of Education and the Occupational Attainments of Young Men," *Social Forces* 61 (September 1982):24–25.

however, has begun to include observations for women.[16] Of particular interest is the relationship between educational attainment and age at first marriage.

Early marriage and higher education tend to be incompatible in our society, particularly for women—the earlier the age at marriage, the lower the educational attainment. Partners in teenage marriages seldom complete college, although men are more likely to do so than women. The negative correlation between age at marriage and educational attainment has been documented at least since 1958.[17] However, there is disagreement about causality. Some argue that early marriage and lower educational attainment are both consequences of lower social origins,[18] while others propose that early marriage acts independently to lower educational attainment.[19] It has also been suggested that early marriage is more detrimental to women's educational attainment than to men's.[20]

Table 4.5 demonstrates the correlation between age at first marriage and completion of a college degree. In 1980 fewer than 4 percent of women who had married in their teens had finished four or more years of college; only 7 percent of teenaged grooms had a college degree. In contrast, persons who married after age 21 had much higher college completion rates. Those who married at age 24 or 25 had the highest completion rates among women, and men who married in their late 20s were the most likely to be college graduates.

An early marriage does not seem to adversely affect men who are already in college. For men, but not for women, greater educa-

[16]Karl L. Alexander and Bruce K. Eckland, "Sex Differences in the Educational Attainment Process," *American Sociological Review* 39 (October 1974):668–82.

[17]Paul C. Glick and Hugh Carter, "Marriage Patterns and Educational Level," *American Sociological Review* 23 (June 1958):294–300.

[18]Vaughn R. A. Call and Luther B. Otto, "Age at Marriage as a Mobility Contingency: Estimates for the Nye-Berardo Model," *Journal of Marriage and the Family* 39 (February 1977):67–79; and F. Ivan Nye and Felix M. Berardo, *The Family* (New York: Macmillan, 1973).

[19]Alan E. Bayer, "The College Drop-Out: Factors Affecting Senior College Completion," *Sociology of Education* 41 (Summer 1968): 305–15; Alan E. Bayer, "Marriage Plans and Educational Aspirations," *American Journal of Sociology* 75 (September 1969):239–44; John K. Folger, Helen S. Astin, and Alan E. Bayer, *Human Resources and Higher Education* (New York: Russell Sage Foundation, 1970); and Alan C. Kerckhoff and Alan A. Parrow, "The Effect of Early Marriage on the Educational Attainment of Young Men," *Journal of Marriage and the Family* 41 (February 1979):97–107.

[20]Karl L. Alexander and Thomas W. Reilly, "Estimating the Effects of Marriage Timing on Educational Attainment: Some Procedural Issues and Substantive Clarifications," *American Journal of Sociology* 87 (July 1981):143–56; and Margaret M. Marini, "The Transition to Adulthood: Sex Differences in Educational Attainment and Age at Marriage," *American Sociological Review* 43 (August 1978):483–507.

TABLE 4.5

Percentage of Women and Men Aged 25 and Over Who Completed Four or More Years of College by Age at First Marriage, 1980

	Percentage Completing College	
Age at First Marriage	Women	Men
Never Married	26.6%	27.7%
Under 18 Years	2.5	7.3
18 or 19 Years	4.0	7.4
20 or 21 Years	11.7	14.6
22 or 23 Years	21.4	23.2
24 or 25 Years	21.7	25.2
26 to 30 Years	19.5	26.0
Over 30 Years	12.5	18.1

SOURCE: 1960, 1970, and 1980 Census 1/1,000 Public Use Microdata Sample.

tional attainment prior to marriage increases the likelihood of continued education after marriage. In one national sample, 27 percent of men and 16 percent of women reported two or more years of additional schooling after marriage.[21] Level of attainment at the time of marriage was found to be almost as important as age at marriage in another sample of men.[22]

Not all women end their schooling when they marry. One national sample found that one married woman in five had attended high school or college since marriage, and two-fifths of women said they intended to continue schooling after marriage. Postnuptial education was higher than average for women who had married early, partly because they would be more likely to have had their education interrupted. Women who had attended college before marriage also had a high likelihood of continuing in school after marriage.[23]

Women's earlier average age at marriage seems to be a major factor contributing to sex differences in the effect of age at marriage on school interruptions, however.[24] In 1960 and 1970, for example, women's median age at first marriage was 20 and 21 years, respectively, while that for men was 23. This discrepancy means that

[21]Alexander and Reilly, "Effects of Marriage Timing."

[22]Kerckhoff and Parron, "Effects of Early Marriage."

[23]Nancy J. Davis and Larry L. Bumpass, "The Continuation of Education after Marriage Among Women in the United States: 1970," *Demography* 13 (May 1976):161–74.

[24]Alexander and Reilly, "Effect of Marriage Timing"; and Marini, "Transition to Adulthood."

women married about the time they would be finishing college, while men married some time after the average age of graduation. One study found that one American woman in three who dropped out of college in the 1960s did so to marry compared with only one man in ten.[25]

Alexander and Reilly report that women realize a significant increment to schooling for every year they defer marriage. The authors conclude that if women married at the same age as men (that is, about 2.5 years later), they would obtain almost a third of a year more schooling on average than they currently do. Delayed marriage for women could reduce the postmarriage educational gap between men and women by as much as three-quarters.[26]

There are reasons other than early marriage for which men and women interrupt their schooling. Taking time off between high school and college or dropping out of college for work, military service, or combining school with part-time work are all examples of the ways in which people make the transition from full-time schooling to full-time work.[27] Increasing numbers of men and women are choosing this nonlinear path, and marriage before the completion of schooling may be one of its components.

Educational Attainment and Fertility

The higher a woman's educational attainment, the more likely she is to remain childless or to have few children. The negative correlation between education and fertility has several explanations. The economic value of a college-educated woman's time is greater than that of a high school graduate's time, and thus years out of the labor force spent in childbearing have greater economic costs to highly educated women. Foregone income is greater the more highly educated a woman is.[28]

Schooling can also alter preferences for children and attitudes toward desired family size. The more educated the couple, the more

[25]John K. Folger and Charles B. Nam, *Education of the American Population: A 1960 Census Monograph* (Washington, DC: U.S. Government Printing Office, 1967).

[26]Alexander and Reilly, "Effects of Marriage Timing."

[27]James S. Coleman, "The Transition from School to Work," in Donald J. Treiman and Robert V. Robinson, eds., *Research in Social Stratification and Mobility*, vol. 3 (Greenwich, CT: JAI Press, 1984), pp. 27–60.

[28]Robert T. Michael, "Education and Fertility," in F. Thomas Juster, ed., *Education, Income and Human Behavior* (New York: McGraw-Hill, 1975), pp. 339–64.

TABLE 4.6

Birth Expectations of Women by Educational Attainment, 1982

Age and Years of School Completed	Births to Date	Lifetime Births Expected	Percentage Expecting No Births
Total, 18–34 Years	1.1	2.0	11.6%
Not High School Graduate	1.7	2.3	8.7
High School, 4 Years	1.2	2.0	10.3
College, 1 to 3 Years	0.8	2.0	13.1
4 Years	0.6	1.9	15.7
5 Years or More	0.6	1.7	18.7

SOURCE: U.S. Bureau of the Census, "Fertility of American Women: June 1982," *Current Population Reports*, series P-20, no. 387 (Washington, DC: U.S. Government Printing Office, 1984), table 4.

likely they are to use effective contraception, and highly educated couples use contraception earlier in their marriages.[29] During the 1960s the rate of oral contraceptive use was over twice as high among college-educated women as among those with an elementary education or less.[30]

Highly educated women may delay motherhood to accommodate their educational and career goals. Among women 30 to 44 with four or more years of college in 1982, about 22 percent of all births were first births. By comparison, 15 percent of births to all women aged 30 to 44 were first births.[31]

Table 4.6 demonstrates the relationship between educational attainment and fertility. The more education a woman has, the fewer births she has had to date, the fewer lifetime births she expects, and the greater the likelihood that she expects to have no children. In 1982 women who had not completed high school had already had 1.7 children on average and expected a total of 2.3 children; only 9 percent expected no children. Conversely, women with some graduate training had only 0.6 births to date and expected 1.7 births on average; 19 percent expected to remain childless.

Most researchers agree that educational attainment influences

[29]Pascal K. Whelpton, Arthur A. Campbell, and John E. Patterson, *Fertility and Family Planning in the United States* (Princeton, NJ: Princeton University Press, 1966).

[30]Norman B. Ryder and Charles F. Westoff, *Reproduction in the United States 1965* (Princeton, NJ: Princeton University Press, 1971).

[31]U.S. Bureau of the Census, "Fertility of American Women: June 1982," *Current Population Reports*, series P-20, no. 387 (Washington, DC: U.S. Government Printing Office, 1983), table D.

fertility,[32] but there is also evidence that a mother's young age at first birth deters future academic attainment.[33] The role of mother is even more time consuming than that of wife and can limit a woman's ability to continue in school. Waite and Moore found that 18-year-old girls who had borne a child at age 15 or younger completed approximately 1.5 fewer years of school compared with childless 18-year-olds. Slightly smaller losses accrued to women who had a first birth at age 16 or 17.[34] Longitudinal evidence reveals a negative relationship between educational aspirations and age at first birth.[35]

Rindfuss, Bumpass, and St. John argue that relatively few women get pregnant before age 17, and 40 percent of those in their sample who got pregnant had dropped out of school a year before becoming mothers. The researchers conclude that the reciprocal relationship between education and age at first birth is dominated by the effect from education to age at birth rather than the other way around. They suggest that education most directly affects fertility by postponing the first birth and thus reducing the total number of children ever born.[36] An older age at first birth is correlated with longer between-birth intervals,[37] more effective contraceptive use,[38] and preferences for fewer children.[39] It is the effect of education on these factors which ultimately influences completed family size.

[32]Ronald R. Rindfuss and James A. Sweet, *Postwar Fertility Trends and Differentials in the United States* (New York: Academic Press, 1977); Ronald R. Rindfuss, Larry L. Bumpass, and Craig St. John, "Education and Fertility: Implications for the Roles Women Occupy," *American Sociological Review* 45 (June 1980):431–47; and Charles F. Westoff and Norman B. Ryder, *The Contraceptive Revolution* (Princeton, NJ: Princeton University Press, 1977).

[33]Lloyd Bacon, "Early Motherhood, Accelerated Role Transition, and Social Pathologies," *Social Forces* 52 (March 1974):333–41; Linda J. Waite and Kristin A. Moore, "The Impact of an Early First Birth on Young Women's Educational Attainment," *Social Forces* 56 (March 1978):845–66.

[34]Waite and Moore, "Early First Birth."

[35]Josefina J. Card and Lauress L. Wise, "Teenage Mothers and Teenage Fathers: The Impact of Early Childbearing on the Parent's Personal and Professional Lives," *Family Planning Perspectives* 10 (July-August 1978):199–205; and Kimball P. Marshall and Arthur G. Cosby, "Antecedents of Early Marital and Fertility Behavior," *Youth and Society* 9 (December 1977):191–21.

[36]Rindfuss, Bumpass, and St. John, "Education and Fertility."

[37]Larry L. Bumpass, Ronald R. Rindfuss, and Richard B. Janosik, "Age and Marital Status at First Birth and the Pace of Subsequent Fertility," *Demography* 15 (February 1978):75–86.

[38]Barbara Vaughn, James Trussell, Jane Menken, and Louise Jones, "Contraceptive Failure Among Married Women in the U.S., 1970–1973," *Family Planning Perspectives* 9 (November-December 1977):251–57.

[39]Rindfuss, Bumpass, and St. John, "Education and Fertility."

The Role of the Same-Sex Parent

A third factor that has been shown to affect the educational attainment of women, in addition to age at marriage and age at first birth, is the educational attainment of their mother. Several studies support the role-model theory of educational attainment. That is, the mother's education has the most influence on a daughter's attainment while the father's education has the most influence on the son's.[40] Since traditionally a lower proportion of women have gone on to college, it may take several generations of more highly educated women to transmit higher educational goals to their daughters. As younger generations take advantage of greater opportunities, the proportion of women who complete college and graduate school should continue to grow, which in turn should increase the likelihood that their daughters will expect to attain college and postgraduate degrees.

Consequences of Higher Education

The clearest consequence of higher education for women is that it increases the likelihood of participation in the labor force. The more highly educated the woman, the more likely she is to work

[40]A panel study of Wisconsin high school students found that in addition to a variety of background variables, mother's education affects women's schooling. The direct effect of father's education on son's education is three times larger than its effect on daughter's education. See William H. Sewell, Robert M. Hauser, and Wendy C. Wolf, "Sex, Schooling, and Occupational Status," *American Journal of Sociology* 86 (November 1980):551–83. Another study of New York state high school students found that the education of the same-sex parent had a greater effect on adolescent educational expectations than the education of the opposite-sex parent. See Bernard C. Rosen and Carol S. Aneshensel, "Sex Differences in the Educational-Occupational Expectation Process," *Social Forces* 57 (September 1978):164–86. Findings from panel data on Illinois seniors suggested that the effects of father's education and family income were about equal for boys and girls, but that the effect of mother's education was consistently greater for girls than boys. See Marini, "Transition to Adulthood." The National Longitudinal Surveys of Labor Market Experience data also support the hypothesis that the educational level of the same-sex parent is most important in determining men's and women's eventual achievement. See Donald J. Treiman and Kermit Terrell, "Sex and the Process of Status Attainment," *American Sociological Review* 40 (April 1975):174–200. Only one study found no evidence that the same-sex parent has a strong influence on the child's attainment. See McKee J. McClendon, "The Occupational Status Attainment Processes of Males and Females," *American Sociological Review* 41 (February 1976):52–64.

outside the home, although the level of participation may vary with stage of the life cycle.[41]

An economic interpretation of the association between education and labor force activity is that the "cost" of staying home is greater for a college-educated woman than for a woman with a high school diploma, because more highly educated women are usually paid higher wages. It could also be argued that a woman with higher education usually has more occupational choices and thus may be more likely to seek work. The process of receiving a college degree can also widen a woman's aspirations to include more than work in the home, just as higher education may influence her preference for family size.

There is a positive relationship between level of education and labor force participation. The higher the level of educational attainment, the more likely a woman is to be in the labor force and work during some part of the previous year. Two-thirds of adult women with a college degree were in the labor force in 1980 compared with fewer than one-third of women who had not completed high school (Table 4.7). Participation has increased for all educational groups with at least a high school diploma, but more so for women with some college or a college degree than for those with a graduate school education. Hence, differences among women with varying amounts of college training have narrowed over time.

Women with five or more years of college have the highest labor force participation rates (73 percent in 1980), but are slightly less likely than college dropouts to work full time and year round (26 versus 30 percent in 1980). This discrepancy may be a result of the large proportion of women with graduate educations who enter teaching and would be reporting a part-year occupation. Women without a college degree would not be eligible to become teachers, and thus would more likely be in year-round occupations.

Labor force participation rates and labor force attachment are greater for younger women aged 25 to 34 than for all women. More than three-quarters of young women with a college degree were in the labor force in 1980, and just over one-third of college-educated

[41]William G. Bowen and T. Aldrich Finegan, *The Economics of Labor Force Participation* (Princeton, NJ: Princeton University Press, 1969); Glenn Cain and Arlene Leibowitz, "Education and the Allocation of Women's Time," in F. Thomas Juster, ed., *Education, Income, and Human Behavior* (New York: McGraw-Hill, 1975), pp. 171–98; and Linda J. Waite, "Working Wives and the Family Life Cycle," *American Journal of Sociology* 86 (September 1980):272–94.

TABLE 4.7

Changes in Labor Force Participation of Women by Educational Attainment

Age and Years of School Completed	In Labor Force			Worked Preceding Year			Worked Full-Time, Year-Round		
	1960	1970	1980	1960	1970	1980	1960	1970	1980
25 Years and Over	35.3%	40.8%	48.4%	41.0%	46.9%	52.5%	14.9%	17.3%	22.3%
Not High School Graduate	30.8	33.3	30.8	36.1	38.5	33.5	12.0	13.1	12.4
High School, 4 Years	39.1	46.7	53.6	45.1	52.9	57.9	19.5	21.9	26.6
College, 1 to 3 Years	40.9	44.8	58.8	47.5	51.9	64.0	18.0	20.4	29.6
4 Years	47.7	50.0	62.3	53.9	58.4	68.0	15.8	15.4	27.0
5 Years or More	66.6	66.0	72.7	71.8	73.0	77.9	19.7	21.7	26.5
25–34 Years	34.8	44.9	64.5	43.7	54.5	70.8	13.6	16.6	29.2
Not High School Graduate	33.2	39.3	48.6	41.6	47.3	53.2	10.7	12.5	16.8
High School, 4 Years	34.3	44.4	61.7	42.9	54.0	68.0	15.7	18.2	28.9
College, 1 to 3 Years	35.5	46.4	69.5	46.2	57.5	76.3	14.6	20.4	34.6
4 Years	41.6	53.4	74.8	52.5	66.2	81.3	14.6	14.9	35.0
5 Years or More	58.6	70.6	79.6	67.4	79.0	86.7	17.6	21.9	30.3

SOURCE: 1960, 1970, and 1980 Census 1/1,000 Public Use Microdata Sample.

women worked full time and year round. Labor force participation rates almost doubled between 1960 and 1980 for high school graduates and women with one to three years of college. Participation rates for women with higher educations also rose, although not as dramatically, because their rates were already higher than average in 1960.

Young children at home are correlated with lower labor force participation for women of all educational categories, but women with school-age children who are high school and college educated are more likely to stay out of the labor force than grade-school educated women.[42] Mothers with higher educational attainment spend more time in child care activities than women with less schooling. Time spent on other household tasks such as meal preparation and cleaning tends to fall as educational level increases, supposedly because these tasks are more readily taken over by a husband or housekeeper. Cain and Leibowitz found that "women with college degrees devote more than twice as many hours to childcare as women with fewer than twelve years of schooling, 83 percent more time than high school graduates, and 59 percent more time than women with one to three years of college."[43] Hill and Stafford found that more highly educated mothers of preschoolers spend more time playing with their children, reading to them, and taking them on educational outings than do less-well-educated mothers.[44] After more than a century of higher education for women, it appears that it is achieving its original goal of making women more effective mothers.

A higher education may mean that women's labor force participation rates are slightly closer to men's rates, but the returns to education are different for women and men who work. Research in the field of status attainment has shown repeatedly that equal numbers of years of school have different consequences for men and women.[45]

For example, women with 12 to 15 years of school may have higher-status first jobs than men with comparable education, be-

---

[42]Cain and Leibowitz, "Education."

[43]Cain and Leibowitz, "Education," p. 191.

[44]C. Russell Hill and Frank P. Stafford, "Parental Care of Children: Time Diary Estimates of Quality, Predictability, and Variety," *Journal of Human Resources* 15 (Summer 1980):219–39.

[45]Larry Suter and Herman Miller, "Income Differences Between Men and Career Women," *American Journal of Sociology* 78 (January 1973):962–74; David L. Featherman and Robert M. Hauser, "Sexual Inequalities and Socioeconomic Achievement in the U.S., 1962–1973," *American Sociological Review* 41 (June 1976):462–83; Sewell, Hauser, and Wolf, "Sex, Schooling"; and Treiman and Terrell, "Sex and Status Attainment."

cause jobs for women with 12 to 15 years of school tend to be white collar (clerical or sales), while those for men with comparable schooling tend to be blue collar. Although women hold jobs of higher status (though not of higher pay) at the time of the first job, men hold the advantage at mid-career. Later in life, women receive higher returns on their educational qualifications while men receive higher returns on previous work experience. A possible explanation is that women rely on early educational attainment because so many leave and reenter the labor force, whereas most men are able to build on occupational experience because of their continuous work history.[46]

Table 4.8 shows that regardless of educational level women are far more likely than men to be in administrative support occupations such as secretary, typist, or bookkeeper. Among high school graduates in 1980, 47 percent of women worked in this category compared with 8 percent of men. Forty-four percent of women with some college and 24 percent of women with a college degree worked in administrative support occupations compared with 9 and 8 percent of men with comparable educations.

Among persons with four or more years of college, women are less likely than men to be in managerial occupations and more likely to be in professional occupations. These professional occupations include the traditionally female jobs of teaching and nursing.

While differences within white-collar occupational categories partly explain persistent earnings differences between women and men with equal educational attainment, field of study in college also accounts for some of the wage differential. Men are disproportionately represented in those college curricula ranked highest on income, power, and prestige in the occupational structure.[47] Since the sex composition of the major field in college is the primary determinant of the sex composition in the field of later employment,[48] and field of employment largely determines income, sex inequalities in college can have prolonged effects on lifetime earnings. Daymont and Andrisani find that gender differences in preferences and preparation for various types of work account for a substantial portion of

---

[46]Sewell, Hauser, and Wolf, "Sex, Schooling."

[47]Kenneth L. Wilson and Eui Hang Shen, "Reassessing the Discrimination Against Women in Higher Education," *American Educational Research Journal* 20 (Winter 1983):529–51.

[48]Denise D. Bielby, "Career Sex-Atypicality and Career Involvement of College Educated Women: Baseline Evidence from the 1960s," *Sociology of Education* 51 (January 1978):7–28.

TABLE 4.8

Occupations of Full-Time, Year-Round Workers Aged 25 and Over, 1980 (percentage distribution)

Major Occupational Group	High School 4 Years		College 1 to 3 Years		College 4 Years		College 5 Years or More	
	Women	Men	Women	Men	Women	Men	Women	Men
Total	100.0%	100.0%	100.0%	100.0%	100.0%	100.0%	100.0%	100.0%
Executive, Managerial	10.4	10.8	15.1	20.5	20.7	34.3	16.2	26.7
Professional Speciality	3.3	3.1	14.7	8.3	38.0	21.4	59.5	51.3
Technicians	3.3	2.8	5.6	6.5	4.5	4.5	4.7	3.3
Sales	8.4	8.9	7.6	13.3	7.0	16.2	3.9	7.0
Administrative Support, Including Clerical	46.8	8.3	43.9	9.0	24.2	8.0	10.7	4.0
Private Household	0.3	0.0	0.2	0.0	0.3	0.0	0.0	0.0
Protective Service	0.4	3.0	0.5	4.4	0.4	2.1	0.4	1.1
Other Service	10.1	4.6	5.7	2.9	1.9	1.0	2.0	0.7
Farming, Forestry, Fishing	0.9	4.0	0.6	2.3	0.8	2.2	0.5	0.8
Precision Production, Including Craft	6.7	32.1	3.0	21.8	1.0	7.2	1.3	3.7
Machine Operators	7.3	15.0	2.2	7.6	0.8	2.0	0.6	0.9
Transportation Workers	0.2	3.1	0.1	1.1	0.1	0.5	0.0	0.2
Handlers, Laborers	1.9	4.3	0.8	2.3	0.3	0.6	0.2	0.3

SOURCE: 1980 Census 1/1,000 Public Use Microdata Sample.

the earnings gap between women and men who have recently graduated from college.[49] On the other hand, Angle and Wissman's analysis suggests that field of study is not as important a determinant of the earnings gap between women and men as gender per se.[50] Controlling for major field of study decreases slightly the negative impact on earnings of being female, but it does not significantly alter the fact that being female in and of itself results in substantially lower earnings.

Table 4.9 shows that among year-round, full-time workers with the same educational attainment, women consistently earn less than men. Nearly half of all female high school graduates who worked in 1979 earned less than $10,000 compared with only 13 percent of male high school graduates. Even among persons with some college, over one-third of the women earned less than $10,000 versus one-tenth of the men. The proportion of persons with low earnings declines steadily as education rises, but at all levels a higher proportion of women earn less than $10,000.

Conversely, men are much more likely than women to be at the higher end of the earnings scale. Nearly 9 percent of male high school graduates earned $30,000 or more in 1979 compared with less than 1 percent of female graduates. Among persons with some college, 14 percent of male and 1.5 percent of female full-time, year-round workers earned $30,000 or more. The discrepancy becomes especially pronounced among persons with four or more years of college. Twenty-nine percent of men and 3 percent of women with a college degree earned high incomes; nearly 38 percent of men and only 6 percent of women with graduate or professional training were in the top income brackets in 1979.

In 1979 a woman with graduate training who worked full time, year round earned less (8 percent less, on average) than a man with a high school education (see median earnings in Table 4.9). Full-time working women with a college degree earned only about three-quarters as much as men with a high school diploma. These differences partly reflect the different occupations chosen by women with a college education and men with a high school education. Highly educated women, for example, might be teachers or librarians with low

[49]Thomas Daymont and Paul J. Andrisani, "Job Preferences, College Major, and the Gender Gap in Earnings," *Journal of Human Resources* 19 (Summer 1984):408–28.

[50]John Angle and David A. Wissman, "Gender, College Major, and Earnings," *Sociology of Education* 54 (January 1981):25–33.

TABLE 4.9

Earnings of Full-Time, Year-Round Workers Aged 25 and Over, 1979 (percentage distribution)

Earnings	High School 4 Years		College 1 to 3 Years		College 4 Years		College 5 Years or More	
	Women	Men	Women	Men	Women	Men	Women	Men
Total	100.0%	100.0%	100.0%	100.0%	100.0%	100.0%	100.0%	100.0%
Less Than $10,000	47.6	13.3	35.4	10.5	22.6	6.1	13.6	6.3
$10,000 to $14,999	35.5	22.2	39.2	20.6	38.1	13.8	28.3	10.1
15,000 to 19,999	11.8	25.9	16.9	24.2	23.7	19.5	29.5	16.2
20,000 to 24,999	3.2	20.2	5.6	19.6	9.8	18.4	15.5	17.1
25,000 to 29,999	1.0	9.7	1.4	11.4	3.0	13.1	6.7	12.3
30,000 to 34,999	0.3	4.3	0.9	5.7	1.5	10.2	2.7	10.2
35,000 to 49,999	0.3	2.8	0.5	5.0	0.8	11.3	2.7	14.8
50,000 and Over	0.3	1.6	0.1	3.0	0.5	7.6	1.0	13.0
Median (1979 $)	$10,338	$17,799	$11,862	$18,050	$13,596	$22,880	$16,373	$25,122

NOTE: Medians interpolated from distributions shown.

SOURCE: 1980 Census 1/1,000 Public Use Microdata Sample.

salaries, while less well-educated men might be union workers with higher wages. Occupational differences alone, however, cannot account for such large discrepancies in annual earnings.

Summary

The American population is becoming increasingly well educated, although women are still less likely than men to finish college or attain graduate and professional degrees. By 1980, 21 percent of women aged 25 to 34 had completed four or more years of college compared with 26 percent of young men.

Although women are not yet as likely to finish college, they have caught up with men in terms of college attendance. Enrollment rates for women aged 18 to 24 rose from 12 percent in 1960 to 25 percent in 1981; comparable rates for young men were 20 percent in 1960 and 25 percent in 1981 (a decline from the high of 29 percent about 1970). Now that the gap in college enrollment has closed, there may eventually be a smaller gap between completion rates as well.

Despite gains in enrollment and number of degrees granted, there are still large differences between men and women in the major field of college study. Majors in which more than two-thirds of the students are male include architecture, engineering, physical sciences, and religion, while those in which over two-thirds are female include education, foreign languages, health professions, home economics, and library science. Each of the traditionally "male" fields of study has increased in the proportion female since 1960, and women have made particularly large gains in the professions. The proportion of medical and law degrees conferred on women more than doubled during the 1970s.

Educational attainment for women is related to several factors. One is age at first marriage: On average, the younger a woman is when she marries, the less formal education she achieves. Among women who have married, those with the least education have the highest fertility. Women with a college degree have an average of one child less than women with less than a high school diploma, and highly educated women are almost three times as likely to be childless as women without a high school education. The years of school completed by a woman's mother is also an important influence on her own educational attainment.

The higher a woman's education, the more likely she is to be in the labor force. Women with a college degree are more than twice as likely to be working outside the home as women who did not finish high school. Within the labor force, women are concentrated in specific occupations regardless of educational achievement. Among female college graduates, for example, 24 percent were in administrative support jobs in 1980 compared with 8 percent of male college graduates. Just over one-third of male college graduates were in executive or managerial positions in 1980 compared with one-fifth of female college graduates.

In addition to differences in occupational distribution by sex (and partly because of such differences), there are large differences in earnings between men and women with the same educational attainment. Among year-round, full-time workers, women consistently earn less than men with comparable years of schooling. Among persons with a college degree, 84 percent of women earned less than $20,000 in 1979 compared with 39 percent of men. Nearly 8 percent of male college graduates earned $50,000 or more compared with fewer than 1 percent of female college graduates. A woman with graduate training, working full time and year round, did not earn as much as a man with a high school education in 1979.

5

LABOR FORCE PARTICIPATION AND OCCUPATIONAL COMPOSITION

WOMEN have entered the labor force in dramatic numbers since World War II and the very fabric of American society has been revolutionized. But is the increase in women's participation really a new story? Yes and no. The upswing in female labor force participation was evident by the time Gertrude Bancroft wrote the 1950 Census monograph on the labor force. However, in the mid-1950s no one was predicting how the age pattern and quality of that participation would be altered in subsequent decades. The projections in the Bancroft monograph did not anticipate the rise in age at first marriage, decline in fertility, and increase in educational attainment of women—all of which contributed to a dramatic alteration in the labor force participation rates of young women over the ensuing decades. Nor was anyone predicting that mothers of small children would remain in the labor force during their childrearing years. To quote from the Bancroft monograph:

> Typically, in the 1950's American girls seek jobs on leaving school, marry shortly thereafter, and continue working until they start having children, when they retire for a period of years. While they are in the labor force at the beginning of their work-

TABLE 5.1

Projected and Actual Civilian Labor Force Participation Rates for 1975

Sex and Age	Projected in 1958	Actual	Difference (Actual–Projected)
WOMEN	38.2%	46.3%	8.2%
14–19 Years	28.1	49.1	—
20–24 Years	47.8	64.1	16.3
25–34 Years	38.9	54.6	15.7
35–44 Years	48.9	55.8	6.9
45–54 Years	53.2	54.6	1.4
55–64 Years	41.0	41.0	0.0
65 Years and Over	11.6	8.3	−3.3
MEN	78.9	77.9	−1.0
14–19 Years	43.4	59.1	—
20–24 Years	86.8	84.6	−2.2
25–34 Years	96.8	95.3	−1.5
35–44 Years	97.3	95.7	−1.6
45–54 Years	95.6	92.1	−3.8
55–64 Years	87.1	75.8	−11.3
65 Years and Over	30.6	21.7	−8.9

NOTE: Figures shown in the first column represent the average of four projections based on 1920 and 1950–55 data made by Gertrude Bancroft in 1958; the difference between the actual and projected labor force participation rate of the youngest age group is not calculated because the 1958 projection is for the 14-to-19-year age group whereas the actual participation rate available for 1975 is for the 16-to-19-year age group.

SOURCE: U.S. Department of Labor, Bureau of Labor Statistics, *Handbook of Labor Statistics* (Washington, DC: U.S. Government Printing Office, 1983), table 4; Gertrude Bancroft, *The American Labor Force: Its Growth and Changing Composition* (New York: Wiley, 1958), table 91.

ing lives, they are probably doing clerical or secretarial work in an office or selling in a retail store. It is probable that after they send their last child off to school they will return to the labor force, voluntarily and with enthusiasm, not to pursue a career for which they have been prepared by school and college but to supplement the family income at whatever kind of work is both available and agreeable.[1]

As illustrated in Table 5.1, the end result was that these mid-1950 projections of labor force participation rates proved much too low by 1975 for women under 35. Actual participation of women in their 20s and early 30s in 1975 was 16 percentage points higher than projected!

[1]Gertrude Bancroft, *The American Labor Force: Its Growth and Changing Composition* (New York: Wiley, 1958), pp. 38–40.

The "new" story of the past two decades has been the rise in participation by younger women and the increased continuity of participation over their life course. Many women now postpone family formation to complete education and establish themselves in the labor force. Despite family obligations, a majority of women work outside the home during their childrearing years. Women's labor market involvement is still dissimilar to men's involvement, but the convergence in many of the indicators is truly the remarkable story of the 1960s, and even more so of the 1970s. It is to this story that we now turn.

Trends in Labor Force Participation

During this century, the number of women in the labor force has increased dramatically—from about 5 million women in 1900 to 48.5 million in 1983. (See Table 5.2.) At the turn of the century,

TABLE 5.2

Women in the Labor Force, Selected Years Since 1900

Year	Number (in thousands)	Percentage of Total Labor Force	Percentage of All Women
1900	4,999	18.1%	20.0%
1910	8,076	21.2	23.4
1920	8,229	20.4	22.7
1930	10,396	21.9	23.6
1940	13,007	24.6	25.8
1950	18,389	29.6	33.9
1955	20,548	31.6	35.7
1960	23,240	33.4	37.7
1965	26,200	35.2	39.3
1970	31,543	38.1	43.3
1975	37,475	40.0	46.3
1980	45,487	42.5	51.5
1983	48,503	43.5	52.9

NOTE: Labor force data for 1900–30 refer to gainfully employed workers aged 10 and over; data for 1940 include the labor force aged 14 and over; data for 1950–83 refer to the civilian labor force aged 16 and over and are based on annual averages derived from the Current Population Survey; data for 1900–40 are based on the decinnial census.

SOURCE: U.S. Department of Labor, Bureau of Labor Statistics, "Women in the Labor Force: Some New Data Series," report 575 (October 1979), table 1; *Handbook of Labor Statistics* (Washington, DC: U.S. Government Printing Office, 1983), tables 1 and 2; *Employment and Earnings* vol. 31 (January 1984), table 1; U.S. Bureau of the Census, *Historical Statistics of the United States* (Washington, DC: U.S. Government Printing Office, 1976), series D11-25 and D29-41.

about one worker in five was a woman. By the mid-1970s, two workers in five were female, and the representation of women in the work force has continued to increase since that time. The proportion of women in the labor force, which was about 20 percent in the early part of the century, increased only slightly until the 1940s. Since World War II, participation of women in the paid work force has accelerated greatly.

Women are less likely to be in the labor force than men, but as women's rates have increased, men's participation rates have decreased. In 1948, 87 percent of men were in the labor force compared with 33 percent of women—a difference of over 50 percentage points. By 1983, 76 percent of men and 53 percent of women were in the labor force—a difference of a little over 20 percentage points. (See Table 5.3.)

The decline in men's participation rates is accounted for almost entirely by rates of older men. Rates for men aged 25 to 54 remained about 95 percent, but rates have declined from 71 to 43 percent for those 55 and over. This reflects, among other things, the increased number of workers covered by Social Security, private pension plans, and disability benefits, allowing for earlier withdrawal from the labor force than was possible in the past.

Women's labor force participation has increased at all ages under 65, but there have been significant changes in the age groups accounting for the increase. Figure 5.1 shows 1950–80 changes in the age pattern of labor force participation of women and men. Typically, men's patterns look like an arch or an inverted U. That is, rates increase as men finish school and enter the labor force. By their late 20s most men are in the labor force and most will remain there more or less continuously until they retire in their late 50s and 60s. Women's patterns, on the other hand, have often been described as U-shaped, at least up to age 50. That is, they are highest in the early 20s before women start having children. They drop off as women leave the labor force to have children, but begin to increase again as some of these women return to work after their children have entered school. This is the sort of pattern Bancroft refers to as typifying women's participation in the 1950s.

Women's labor force participation increased in each decade shown in Figure 5.1, and this U pattern is apparent in 1950, 1960, and 1970. During the 1950s and early 1960s the increase in women's labor force participation was largely the result of the increase in the

TABLE 5.3

Male-Female Differences in Civilian Labor Force Participation Rates,
Selected Years

Age and Year	Men	Women	Difference (M–W)	Ratio (W/M)
Total, 16 Years and Over				
1948	86.6%	32.7%	53.9%	0.378
1950	86.4	33.9	52.5	0.392
1955	85.3	35.7	49.6	0.419
1960	83.3	37.7	45.6	0.453
1965	80.7	39.3	41.4	0.487
1970	79.7	43.3	36.4	0.543
1975	77.9	46.3	31.6	0.594
1980	77.4	51.5	25.9	0.665
1983	76.4	52.9	23.5	0.692
16–24 Years				
1948	75.7	43.9	31.8	0.580
1950	77.3	43.9	33.4	0.568
1955	72.3	43.1	29.2	0.596
1960	71.7	42.8	28.9	0.597
1965	69.0	44.0	25.0	0.638
1970	69.4	51.3	18.1	0.739
1975	72.4	57.2	15.2	0.790
1980	74.4	61.9	12.5	0.832
1983	72.5	61.9	10.6	0.854
25–54 Years				
1948	96.6	35.0	61.6	0.362
1950	96.5	36.8	59.7	0.381
1955	97.4	39.8	57.6	0.409
1960	97.0	42.9	54.1	0.442
1965	96.7	45.2	51.5	0.467
1970	95.8	50.1	45.7	0.523
1975	94.4	55.1	39.3	0.584
1980	94.2	64.0	30.2	0.679
1983	93.8	67.1	26.7	0.715
55 Years and Over				
1948	70.6	17.2	53.4	0.244
1950	68.6	18.9	49.7	0.276
1955	64.8	21.6	43.2	0.333
1960	60.9	23.6	37.3	0.388
1965	56.9	24.6	32.3	0.432
1970	55.7	25.3	30.4	0.454
1975	49.3	23.1	26.2	0.469
1980	45.6	22.8	22.8	0.500
1983	43.0	22.4	20.6	0.521

SOURCE: U.S. Department of Labor, Bureau of Labor Statistics, *Handbook of Labor Statistics* (Washington, DC: U.S. Government Printing Office, 1983), tables 2 and 3; *Employment and Earnings*, vol. 31 (January 1984), table 3.

FIGURE 5.1

Trend in Labor Force Participation Rates by Age and Sex

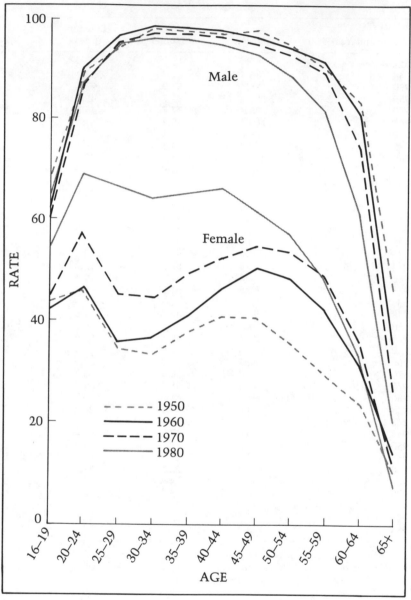

SOURCE: Gertrude Bancroft, *The American Labor Force: Its Growth and Changing Composition* (New York: Wiley, 1958), tables A-1, D-1, and D-1A; U.S. Department of Labor, Bureau of Labor Statistics, "Labor Force and Employment in 1960," *Special Labor Force Report*, no. 14 (Washington, DC: U.S. Government Printing Office, 1961), table A-2; "Employment and Unemployment in 1970," *Special Labor Force Report*, no. 129 (Washington, DC: U.S. Government Printing Office, 1971), table A-2; and *Employment and Earnings*, vol. 28 (January 1981), table 3.

rates of older women—women over age 45, beyond the years of most intensive childrearing responsibilities. But in the mid-1960s this pattern began to change. Since then the largest increase has been among women in their 20s and 30s—women most likely to be raising small children. The increase in the 1970s was particularly dramatic—so much so that the age pattern of labor force rates has lost the U-shaped pattern and is beginning to resemble men's pattern, albeit at a much lower level.

The disappearance of the drop in women's participation during the childbearing years is significant in relation to women's earnings. One reason given for women's lower wages is that women leave the labor force to have children and lose seniority and valuable experience in the labor market. A generation of young women is currently emerging for which this explanation will be less adequate because they will have worked continuously over their lifetime in contrast to previous cohorts of women. If continuity of work experience serves to explain wage differentials by sex, women's wages vis-à-vis those of men would be expected to rise.

Black-White Differences in Participation

Figure 5.2 depicts the trends in labor force participation of Black and White men and women. Historically, Black women have been more likely than White women to participate in the labor force, but the difference has narrowed. In recent decades participation has risen faster for White women than for Black women. Hence, rates have converged over time.

The age profile of labor force participation for Black women has not exhibited the U-shaped pattern that has characterized White women's participation. There is no trough in the childbearing years for Black women as evidenced in both period and cohort data.[2] Studies of women's labor force participation rates, such as Sweet's, have noted that children do not seem to be the deterrent to Black women's participation that they have been to White women's participation.[3] The 1970–80 change in the age profile of participation of White

[2]U.S. Department of Labor, Bureau of Labor Statistics, *Handbook of Labor Statistics* (Washington, DC: U.S. Government Printing Office, 1983), table 4; and J. Gregory Robinson, "Labor Force Participation Rates of Cohorts of Women in the United States: 1880 to 1979," paper presented at the annual meeting of the Population Association of America, Denver, 1980.

[3]James A. Sweet, *Women in the Labor Force* (New York: Seminar Press, 1973).

FIGURE 5.2

Trend in Labor Force Participation Rates by Race and Sex

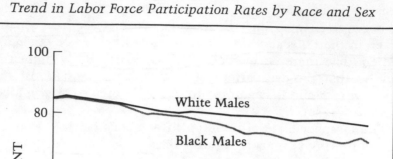

NOTE: Black and other races; persons aged 16 and over.

SOURCE: U.S. Department of Labor, Bureau of Labor Statistics, *Employment and Training Report of the President* (Washington, DC: U.S. Government Printing Office, 1982), table A-5; *Employment and Earnings*, vol. 29 (January 1982), table 3.

women, with the loss of the trough in the childbearing years, is another way in which White women's participation has become more similar to that of Black women.

Cohort Patterns

Thus far we have focused on measures of the increase in female labor force participation over time, but the data can be rearranged to show how birth cohorts compare in terms of their labor force participation at each age. This is done in Figure 5.3, which shows the age profiles of participation of five-year birth cohorts of women born between 1901 and 1960. Age profiles for later cohorts are incomplete since these women have not yet reached older ages.

The cohort patterns suggest that the upturn in female labor force participation has resulted in large part from the fact that, at least for

FIGURE 5.3

Labor Force Participation Rates of Birth Cohorts

SOURCE: U.S. Department of Labor, Bureau of Labor Statistics, *Perspectives on Working Women:A Databook*, bulletin 2080 (Washington, DC: U.S. Government Printing Office, 1980), table 5; *Employment and Earnings*, vol. 27 (January 1980), table 1; J. Gregory Robinson, "Labor Force Participation Rates of Cohorts of Women in the United States: 1890 to 1979," paper presented at the annual meeting of the Population Association of America, Denver, April 1980, table 2.

cohorts born since 1930, each succeeding group of women started out with higher rates of participation and maintained higher rates at older ages than their predecessors. Analyses of cohort patterns for women born since 1870 show that even the gradual increase in labor force participation prior to World War II occurred because each cohort was a little more likely to participate at young ages than the previous one. Age patterns were quite similar for these cohorts but were shifting slowly upward.[4]

[4]James P. Smith and Michael P. Ward, "Women's Wages and Work in the Twentieth Century," report prepared for the National Institute of Child Health and Human Development, R-3119–NICHD (Santa Monica, CA: Rand Corporation, 1984); and Robinson, "Labor Force Participation Rates."

Smith and Ward show that for cohorts born in 1870 and 1880, women's participation rates peaked about age 20 and then declined and remained relatively flat throughout the rest of their lives.[5] But for cohorts born in 1890 and 1900, there was a surge in participation which coincided with World War II (that is, a surge just after age 50 for women born in 1890 and just after age 40 for women born in 1900). These cohorts of women remained in the labor force as they aged, and hence their age profiles of labor force participation exhibit a double peak or U-shape. Thus, the first appearance of the U-shaped pattern actually came with the war and continued to characterize women's employment until only recently.

There is disagreement as to how much World War II per se affected the work patterns of women. Bancroft argued that the experience women gained in the labor market during World War II changed both individual workers' and employers' attitudes about women's place in the labor force.[6] Hence, World War II was crucial in creating a more hospitable environment for women workers and thus contributed to the higher labor force participation rates of cohorts reaching labor force age after the war. But others point to factors operating throughout the twentieth century, such as the increasing educational attainment of women and the increase in wages, as the more important inducements to women to work outside the home.[7]

Labor force patterns for the most recent cohorts of women reinforce the picture derived from the period data. There have been dramatic upward shifts in the participation rates at young ages of successive cohorts of women, and these high initial rates have a lasting effect, raising rates throughout life. The dip in labor force participation during childrearing years is disappearing in the cohort as well as the period patterns. Clogg has argued that cohort effects have been even stronger in recent years than the increases indicate because period effects have served to dampen the actual increases.[8]

Cohort patterns, disaggregated by marital status, illustrate that the largest changes have been among married women, in particular White married women.[9] Even during the high fertility baby boom

[5]Smith and Ward, "Women's Wages."

[6]Bancroft, *American Labor Force.*

[7]Smith and Ward, "Women's Wages"; and Claudia Goldin, "The Changing Economic Role of Women: A Quantitative Approach," *Journal of Interdisciplinary History* 13 (Spring 1983):707–33.

[8]Clifford C. Clogg, "Cohort Analysis of Recent Trends in Labor Force Participation," *Demography* 19 (November 1982):459–79.

[9]Robinson, "Labor Force Participation Rates"; and Smith and Ward, "Women's Wages."

years, participation rates of young married women rose but because more young women were marrying, and married women have lower participation rates than single women, overall labor force participation of young women did not increase.

The suggestion from both period and cohort data is that the continuity of employment over the life cycle has been increasing for women. With each succeeding cohort, women's participation has increased and their profiles are becoming similar to the inverted U-shape which characterizes men's patterns.

Trends in Women's Attachment to the Labor Force

Labor force participation rates provide a preliminary look at how women's work roles have changed, but questions about the nature of that participation remain. A particularly important issue is whether or not work experience or continuity of labor force attachment over the life course has increased for women. Have women's propensities to stay in the labor force once they have entered risen over time or were women just as likely to drop out of the labor force to rear children in 1980 as in 1950?

Trends in aggregate participation rates provide indirect evidence on worker attachment. For example, the disappearance of the drop in participation during the childbearing years among recent cohorts of young women strongly suggests more continuity in labor force participation over the life course than was true in the past. However, women's rates of labor force participation can increase either because women workers become less likely over time to exit the work force or because more nonworkers are induced to enter. If the labor force is growing because women are more firmly attached than they were in the past—that is, they are more likely to enter at young ages and less likely to exit as they age—then the female labor force becomes more experienced over time. If, on the other hand, the female labor force is growing because more women who have never worked before—and who in previous eras would not have worked—are now entering the labor force in great numbers, the average experience of female workers declines.

Expectations about the trend in earnings of women depend on which process is seen as dominant. If the increase in labor force participation coincides with an increase in average work experience of women workers, then earnings of women workers should rise. If the average experience of women workers is being diluted over time by the entry of more and more inexperienced workers, women's wages would not be expected to rise, or at least would not rise as precipitously as in the former situation.

Change over time in worker attachment to the labor force is extremely difficult to assess because the requisite data do not exist. Neither Current Population Survey nor decennial census data contain detailed work histories of the population. This type of information is necessary to answer definitively whether the continuity in women's participation has changed over time.

Some information on labor force turnover is available from the Current Population Survey and decennial censuses. For example, it is possible to assess whether those employed, unemployed, or out of the labor force in the spring of one year were employed for all or part of the previous year. Since the late 1960s persons who are not currently in the labor force have been asked about the length of time they have been out of the labor force. From these data, probabilities of exiting the labor force can be estimated.

Lloyd and Niemi have shown that exit and entrance rates have been declining for women, which suggests that the female labor force has become more stable and firmly attached, at least since the late 1960s.[10] We recalculate and extend their series in Table 5.4, which shows estimates of labor force entrants and exits for the years between mid-1968 and mid-1982. The columns which show entrants and exits as a percentage of the labor force in each year are particularly illuminating. The percentage of women workers who enter and exit the labor force in any given year is much higher than the percentage of men. But whereas women's rates of exit and entry were three times those of men in the late 1960s, they are now only about twice those of men. Men's rates did not change more than a percentage point or two over this period, while women's rates declined significantly. In the late 1960s, depending on whether exits or entrants are measured, one-fifth to one-quarter of the female labor force "turned over" each year. By 1981–82 only 12 percent of women workers exited and 14 percent entered the labor force for the first time or after a period of nonparticipation. Blau has pointed out that labor force turnover does not dilute the average experience level of

[10]Cynthia B. Lloyd and Beth T. Niemi, *The Economics of Sex Differentials* (New York: Columbia University Press, 1979), table 2–7.

TABLE 5.4

Changes in Labor Force Entrants and Exits (numbers in thousands)

Year	Women			Men		
	Labor Force	Entrants as Percentage of Labor Force	Exits as Percentage of Labor Force	Labor Force	Entrants as Percentage of Labor Force	Exits as Percentage of Labor Force
1968–69	29,859	26.2%	21.8%	49,877	8.7%	7.4%
1969–70	31,028	24.2	20.9	50,725	9.2	7.2
1970–71	31,873	22.1	20.1	51,704	9.0	7.2
1971–72	32,841	22.3	18.5	52,868	9.3	6.7
1972–73	34,142	22.4	18.5	54,090	8.8	6.9
1973–74	35,508	22.3	18.3	55,182	8.9	6.8
1974–75	36,843	20.3	16.9	56,019	8.0	7.0
1975–76	38,229	19.5	15.6	56,737	8.1	6.6
1976–77	39,798	19.5	15.4	57,785	8.7	6.5
1977–78	41,622	19.9	15.0	59,008	8.4	6.3
1978–79	43,433	18.2	14.5	60,173	8.1	6.2
1979–80	44,861	17.0	14.2	61,090	7.4	6.2
1980–81	46,092	15.6	13.0	61,714	7.0	6.1
1981–82	47,226	14.2	12.0	62,212	6.8	6.1

NOTE: Exits estimated from persons out of the labor force who left a job within the previous 12 months (for example, to estimate the number who left between mid-1968 and mid-1969, an average of the four quarterly figures for 1969 is taken; because these four quarterly figures include persons who left jobs from the beginning of 1968 to the end of 1969, an average gives a more accurate estimate of the flow between two mid-years); entrants calculated as the sum of the number of exits and the net change in the civilian labor force between the two years; labor force figures represent the average size in the two-year period spanned by the exits.

SOURCE: *Employment and Earnings*, January, April, July, and October issues, 1968–83, quarterly data on recent work experience of persons not in the labor force; U.S. Department of Labor, Bureau of Labor Statistics, *Handbook of Labor Statistics* (Washington, DC: U.S. Government Printing Office, 1983), table 3.

151

the work force as much as it might at first appear: Entrants tend to be women with previous work experience, and exits tend to be selective of female participants with lower levels of previous work experience.[11]

Smith and Ward have recently used CPS data to estimate worker experience. Based on these estimates, they argue that the increase in female labor force participation has primarily resulted from the movement of inexperienced housewives into the labor force.[12] As women's labor force participation increased, the average work experience of all women increased but the average experience of women workers did not rise. Their calculations for recent cohorts born in 1940 and 1950 are at odds with this interpretation, however, and suggest that the experience of women workers has increased, though at a slower rate than for all women of these birth cohorts.[13]

Smith and Horvath have used rates of labor force turnover, that is, probabilities of being in the labor force in one year and being out of the labor force one year later, and vice versa, calculated from matched CPS samples from two consecutive years, to estimate the work-life expectancies of men and women.[14] Women are much more likely to allocate time to nonlabor market activities than men, but women spent 38 percent of their lifetimes in the labor force in 1980 compared with only 13 percent at the turn of the century. Smith and Horvath note that the expansion of the female labor force has dampened increases in the average work-life expectancy of women workers. But their estimates show that the lifetime work expectancy of women workers has been increasing, although not as rapidly as has the average for all women.

The Smith and Ward estimates of experience and the Smith and Horvath estimates of work-life expectancy are derived from Current Population Survey data and hence are not based on actual measurement of work histories. More direct measures of labor force experi-

[11]Francine D. Blau, "Occupational Segregation and Labor Market Discrimination," in Barbara F. Reskin, ed., *Sex Segregation in the Workplace: Trends, Explanations, Remedies* (Washington, DC: National Academy Press, 1984), pp. 117–43.

[12]Smith and Ward, "Women's Wages," p. xi.

[13]Smith and Ward, "Women's Wages," figure 10.

[14]Shirley J. Smith, "New Worklife Estimates Reflect Changing Profile of Labor Force," *Monthly Labor Review* 105 (March 1982):15–20; Shirley J. Smith and Francis W. Horvath, "New Developments in Multistate Working Life Tables," paper presented at the annual meeting of the Population Association of America, Minneapolis, 1984; and Shirley J. Smith, "Revised Worklife Tables Reflect 1979–80 Experience," *Monthly Labor Review* 108 (August 1985):23–30.

ence come from the longitudinal data bases such as the National Longitudinal Surveys (NLS) and the Social Security Administration's Continuous Work History Sample (CWHS). O'Neill, using NLS data, has shown that between 1967 and 1978 the proportion of years women had worked after leaving school increased for employed women as well as for all women, though again increases were greater for all women. There was also a decrease in the absolute number of years women spent out of the labor force.[15] Mallan's analysis of the CWHS data also shows that the proportion of women who work every year of a ten-year period has increased, particularly among younger women.[16]

To summarize, the increase in women's labor force participation has resulted from the replacement of successive cohorts of women, each with higher rates of participation and average work experience than preceding generations. At least since the late 1960s, the period for which we have actual measures of labor force experience from the NLS and exit rates from the CPS, the increase in female labor force participation has coincided with an increased likelihood that once women enter the labor force, they remain there. Recent cohorts of women workers are exhibiting more continuous attachment to the work force than did women of earlier generations.

Sex Differences in Labor Force Participation

Women's participation in the labor force over the life course still remains more discontinuous than men's, as women continue to exit and reenter the labor force more times than men. Estimates from 1980 suggest that the average man will enter the labor force 3.9 times and exit voluntarily 3.6 times. The average woman will enter 5.5 times and exit voluntarily 5.4 times. In the teenage years, women's and men's entry and exit rates are similar with the pace of entries slowing by age 20 for both sexes. However, female exit rates start to rise so that by age 25 the share of men in the labor force substantially exceeds that of women.[17]

[15]June O'Neill, "The Trend in the Sex Differential in Wages," paper presented at the Conference on Trend in Women's Work, Education, and Family Building in Cherwood Gate, Sussex, England 1983, tables 10 and 11.

[16]Lucy B. Mallan, "Labor Force Participation, Work Experience, and the Pay Gap Between Men and Women," *Journal of Human Resources* 17 (Summer 1982):437–48.

[17]Smith, "Worklife Estimates"; and Smith, "Revised Worklife Tables."

Women's higher quit rates are often regarded as one reason why women earn less then men. Employers pay women less because women are less experienced, less stable workers, and employers believe they will lose investments that they make in the skills of these workers. But the causality is probably not unidirectional: Women earn less than men because they have less experience, but their lower wages also increase their probability of quitting a job. Recent studies of voluntary exit rates of men and women show that women with job characteristics equivalent to those of men are no more likely to quit their jobs than are men.[18] Osterman finds that women's voluntary exit rates are greatly reduced in industries in which there is greater pressure from the federal government for affirmative action programs. This suggests that if women perceive opportunities for advancement, they are less likely to change jobs or exit the labor force altogether.[19]

The average number of years that women work over their lifetime is lower than the number for men. Recent estimates, based on 1980 CPS data, suggest that a female born in 1980 is likely to spend 29.4 years in the labor force compared with 39.8 years for a male—a difference of almost 10 years. However, as with labor force participation rates, there has been convergence in the work-life expectancies of women and men. Women's work-life expectancy increased from only 32 percent of men's in 1940 to 59 percent in 1970. Trends accelerated during the 1970s, primarily because of the strengthening of female labor force attachment, so that by 1980 women's work-life expectancy was up to 76 percent of that of men's.[20]

Table 5.5 shows sex differences in the distribution of weeks worked last year and hours worked in the preceding week as reported in the 1960, 1970, and 1980 Censuses of Population. Variations in the business cycle affect hours and weeks worked. In interpreting

[18]Francine D. Blau and Larry Kahn, "Race and Sex Differences in Quits by Young Workers," *Industrial and Labor Relations Review* 34 (July 1981):563–77; and W. Kip Viscusi, "Sex Differences in Worker Quitting," *Review of Economics and Statistics* 62 (August 1980):388–98.

Also, Haber, Lamas, and Green look at overall separation rates (quits + layoffs) using CPS data and find only small sex differences. Women are more likely to leave the labor force entirely, however, whereas men are more likely to leave one job to take another. Sheldon E. Haber, Enrique J. Lamas, and Gordon Green, "A New Method for Estimating Job Separation by Sex and Race," *Monthly Labor Review* 106 (June 1983):20–27.

[19]Paul Osterman, "Affirmative Action and Opportunity: A Study of Female Quit Rates," *Review of Economics and Statistics* 64 (November 1982):604–12.

[20]Smith "Revised Worklife Tables."

TABLE 5.5
Changes in Hours and Weeks Worked for Women and Men

Hours and Weeks	1960 Women	1960 Men	1970 Women	1970 Men	1980 Women	1980 Men
Hours Worked Last Week	100.0%	100.0%	100.0%	100.0%	100.0%	100.0%
1–14	9.2	3.7	3.1	3.7	6.9	3.1
15–29	11.4	4.3	13.6	5.2	15.9	6.6
30–34	6.7	3.0	8.9	5.2	7.4	3.3
35–39	11.8	4.6	11.4	4.9	11.3	3.9
40	42.9	41.8	45.5	43.8	45.5	47.8
41–48	11.9	20.2	7.9	17.8	7.2	13.6
49–59	2.9	10.7	2.3	9.9	3.5	12.1
60+	3.2	11.7	2.1	9.5	2.4	9.6
Percentage Who Worked No Hours	67.2	23.5	61.6	26.8	54.3	30.3
Index of Dissimilarity	24.6		20.3		24.6	
Weeks Worked Last Year	100.0%	100.0%	100.0%	100.0%	100.0%	100.0%
1–13	17.6	5.7	15.5	6.6	11.3	6.2
14–26	12.5	5.8	11.9	5.3	11.7	7.0
27–39	12.3	7.6	11.9	6.0	10.7	6.6
40–47	9.9	8.8	10.4	7.8	10.6	8.4
48–49	4.9	5.9	5.8	6.1	4.4	4.5
50–52	42.8	66.2	44.5	68.1	51.4	67.3
Percentage Who Worked No Weeks	57.0	14.2	50.2	16.4	44.2	20.1
Index of Dissimilarity	24.4		24.0		16.1	

SOURCE: 1960, 1970, and 1980 Census 1/1,000 Public Use Microdata Sample.

155

changes in Table 5.5, it should be kept in mind that economic conditions were much better and unemployment much lower in the late 1960s than in either the late 1950s or the 1970s. Workers were more likely to be employed throughout the entire year in 1969 when the unemployment rate stood at 3.5 percent than in 1959 or 1979 when unemployment was at 5.5 and 5.8 percent, respectively.[21]

At each point in time women were less likely to work overtime and more likely than men to work part time. The index of dissimilarity, which shows the proportion of women workers who would have to move into the higher hours-worked categories in order for the distribution of women workers to be the same as that of men, shows that dissimilarity in the distribution of hours worked between the sexes was as great in 1980 as in 1960. However, the percentage of women not working at all decreased over the period while the proportion of men not working at all increased.

Over the two decades women have become increasingly likely to work the entire year. In 1960, 43 percent of those who worked were employed for 50 to 52 weeks during the year. By 1980, 51 percent of working women were employed all year. Women are still less likely than men to work the entire year and more likely not to work at all, but there has been convergence between men and women in the extent of their employment throughout the year. As shown in Table 5.5, dissimilarity in the distribution of weeks worked during the year by men and women declined substantially, with all of the decline occurring in the 1970s.

In the Current Population Survey, workers are defined as working full time, year round if they usually work 35 or more hours per week during at least 50 weeks of the year. An increasing proportion of women workers are full-time, year-round employees. (See Table 5.6.) Whereas in 1950, 37 percent of women workers worked full time, year round, 45 percent did so in 1980. By 1983 almost half of employed women were full-time, year-round workers.[22] Almost two-thirds of working men are in the labor force full time, year round; this has not changed during the past three decades.

---

[21]U.S. Department of Labor, *Handbook*, table 24.

[22]In 1983 19 percent of women workers worked full time for only part of the year (a decline from 37 percent in 1950); 13 percent worked part time, year round, and 20 percent worked part time for part of the year. U.S. Department of Labor, Bureau of Labor Statistics, press release, June 26, 1984.

TABLE 5.6

*Percentage of Workers Who Worked Full Time, Year Round,
Selected Years*

Year	Women	Men	Diff (M-W)
1950	36.8%	65.4%	28.6%
1955	37.9	67.5	29.6
1960	36.9	63.9	27.0
1965	38.8	67.3	28.5
1970	40.7	66.1	25.4
1975	41.4	63.8	22.4
1980	44.7	65.2	20.5
1983	47.7	64.2	16.5

SOURCE: U.S. Department of Labor, Bureau of Labor Statistics, *Handbook of Labor Statistics* (Washington, DC: U.S. Government Printing Office, 1983), table 45; and press release, June 26, 1984 (1983 data).

Sex Differences in Experience, Tenure, and On-the-Job Training

The work force in general was composed of less experienced individuals in the 1970s and early 1980s as the young, large baby boom cohorts entered the labor force for the first time. However, there is no reason to expect that this entry effect was any greater for women than for men and hence no reason to suggest that women were less experienced workers relative to men by the end of the 1970s. In fact, the CPS data on exit rates and full-time, year-round employment suggest just the opposite: Women workers gained in average work experience relative to men during the decade.

Longitudinal data on work experience from the Panel Study of Income Dynamics (PSID) suggest that sex differentials in experience increase with age and that there is much more variation in the experience distribution of women than of men. Hence, averages are less representative for women. Sex differences are lower if one restricts comparisons to those currently working than if one looks at all adults. Duncan and Hoffman report that among their sample of working household heads and wives, White men had 20 years of work experience since age 18 compared with 18 years for Black men, 14 years for White women, and 16 years for Black women.[23]

[23]Work experience was defined as the number of years in which a person had worked 500 hours or more since turning 18. See Greg J. Duncan and Saul D. Hoffman, "On-the-Job Training and Earnings Differences by Race and Sex," *Review of Economics and Statistics* 61 (November 1979):594–603.

Women have less tenure with their current employer than men do. Lloyd and Niemi show that the sex differences in tenure widened in the 1950s, narrowed in the late 1960s, and remained fairly stable into the latter 1970s.[24] As with the PSID experience data, the employer tenure data from the Current Population Survey show that sex differentials widen with age. Recently, questions about tenure in one's current occupation—not just with one's current employer—have been asked in the Current Population Survey. Rytina has shown that whereas 30 percent of men had been in their current occupation less than 3 years, the comparable figure for women was 38 percent. On the other hand, 38 percent of men had 10 years or more experience in their particular line of work compared with 27 percent of women.[25]

A crucial component of experience levels is the extent of learning or on-the-job training that takes place during those years in the labor force. That is, it is not just the differential quantity of time men and women spend in the labor force but also the differential quality of that time which may be a key to wage differentials between the sexes. Although imperfect, a measure of on-the-job training was ascertained in the 1976 PSID: Respondents were asked to indicate how long it would take the average new employee to learn the respondent's job. Duncan and Hoffman analyze this indicator and find that White males are in jobs which are reported to require an average of two and one-quarter years of training; all other race-sex groups are in jobs requiring less than one year of training. When years of training are subtracted from tenure on the job to arrive at a measure of who is receiving training, Duncan and Hoffman find that 25 percent of White men are receiving on-the-job training compared with 14 percent of White women and 9 percent of Black men and women. Their multivariate results suggest that all race-sex groups receive similar payoffs for on-the-job training. However, commitment to the labor force, as measured by past years of work experience, does not increase the probability that a worker will receive on-the-job training for minorities and women as much as it does for White males. Women (and Black men) receive less on-the-job train-

[24]Lloyd and Niemi, *Economics of Sex Differentials*, table 3.7.
[25]Nancy F. Rytina, "Tenure as a Factor in the Male-Female Earnings Gap," *Monthly Labor Review* 105 (April 1982):32–34.

ing than White men and part of the reason is that their work experience is treated differently.[26]

Occupations

One of the most striking features of the U.S. labor market is the dissimilarity in the occupations of men and women. Many jobs are filled almost entirely by women; others have few women in them. This occupational concentration of women may explain a significant proportion of the male-female wage gap.[27] Many of the typically female occupations are relatively low paying. Why this is the case is an important question. Answers focus on either women's choices or labor market discrimination.

Studies of occupational sex concentration covering the 1900–70 period suggest that small declines occurred in the occupational concentration of women in all decades except the 1920s and 1950s.[28] Treiman and Terrell's investigation of occupational change shows that women were concentrated in fewer occupations than men throughout the 1940–70 period. Occupations with large concentrations of women tended to pay workers—men as well as women— poorly relative to occupations with fewer women. During this period the occupational distribution of Black women became more similar to White women as Black women moved out of private household and farm laboring occupations and into clerical and service sector jobs. Thus, the occupational distribution of Whites and Blacks became much more similar while occupational differences between women and men changed rather minimally.[29]

What has happened to the occupational distribution of women since 1970? Have women moved into male-dominated occupations in greater numbers than they had in previous decades? The analysis

[26]Duncan and Hoffman, "On-the-Job Training."

[27]Donald J. Treiman and Heidi I. Hartmann, *Women, Work, and Wages: Equal Pay for Jobs of Equal Value* (Washington, DC: National Academy Press, 1981), pp. 33–40.

[28]For a review as well as a discussion of the methodological differences among various studies, see Paula England, "Assessing Trends in Occupational Sex Segregation, 1900–1976," in Ivar Berg, ed., *Sociological Perspectives on Labor Markets* (New York: Academic Press, 1981), pp. 273–94. See also Gregory Williams, "The Changing U.S. Labor Force and Occupational Differentiation by Sex," *Demography* 16 (February 1979):73–88.

[29]Donald J. Treiman and Kermit Terrell, "Women, Work, and Wages—Trends in the Female Occupational Structure," in Kenneth C. Land and Seymour Spilerman, eds., *Social Indicator Models* (New York: Russell Sage Foundation, 1975), pp. 157–200.

TABLE 5.7

Growth in the Percentage of Women in Major Occupational Groups,
1970–1980

Major Occupational Group	1970	1980	1970–80 Net Growth
Executives, Managers	18.5%	30.5%	46.9%
Professional Specialty	44.3	49.1	61.2
Technicians	34.4	43.8	57.5
Sales	41.3	48.7	75.4
Administrative Support, Including Clerical	73.2	77.1	89.2
Private Household	96.3	95.3	
Protective Service	6.6	11.8	23.2
Other Service	61.2	63.3	67.5
Farming, Forestry, Fishing	9.1	14.9	
Precision Production, Including Craft	7.3	7.8	10.2
Machine Operators	39.7	40.7	48.5
Transportation Workers	4.1	7.8	23.9
Handlers, Laborers	17.4	19.8	38.8
Total	38.0	42.5	57.5

NOTE: Percentage shown in column 3 is calculated in the following way: the number of women in the occupational group in 1970 is subtracted from the number in 1980 to form the numerator of the fraction; the denominator is the total civilian labor force in the occupational group in 1980 minus the total in 1970; this fraction is multiplied by 100; percentage female is not calculated for occupational groups which declined in size between 1970 and 1980.

SOURCE: U.S. Bureau of the Census, "Detailed Occupation of the Experienced Civilian Labor Force by Sex for the United States and Regions: 1980 and 1970," *Census of Population: 1980*, Supplementary Report, PC80-S1-15 (Washington, DC, U.S. Government Printing Office, 1984).

of occupational trends is complicated by the fact that the classification system for occupations was changed considerably in 1980. Fortunately, a sample of 1970 data was coded into both the old and the new occupational systems, making it possible to reallocate 1970 data into the new 1980 classification and hence to analyze occupational change during the 1970s.[30] The data shown in Table 5.7 come from the 1970 and 1980 decennial censuses, with the 1970 data converted to the 1980 occupational scheme. Data shown refer to occupations of the experienced civilian labor force, that is, the current occupation of those employed at the time of the census as well as the last oc-

[30]For more detail on the reclassification and its effects, see Nancy F. Rytina and Suzanne M. Bianchi, "Occupational Reclassification and Changes in Distribution by Gender," *Monthly Labor Review* 107 (March 1984):11–17; and Suzanne M. Bianchi and Nancy F. Rytina, "Occupational Change, 1970–80," paper presented at the annual meeting of the Population Association of America, Minneapolis, 1984.

cupation of the unemployed if they had been employed within the last five years.

The percentage female in the experienced civilian labor force increased from 38 to 43 percent between 1970 and 1980, which follows from the fact that 58 percent of the workers added during the decade were women. During the 1970s women increased their representation among most major occupational groups. A very significant increase occurred in the proportion of managers who were women—an increase from 19 to 31 percent. Another large increase took place among technicians: In 1970, 34 percent of technicians were women; by 1980 this was up to 44 percent.

Relative to the overall increase in the female proportion in the labor force, there was very little change in the percentage female within two of the major occupational groups with very high proportions of male workers—handlers (laborers) and precision production (craft) workers. Likewise, among major groups that are largely composed of women—administrative support (clerical) and private household workers—there was little change in the female proportion during the decade.

Overall, as shown in the third column of Table 5.7, women accounted for more than half of the growth in professional specialties, technical and related support, sales, administrative support, and other service occupations. Among protective service and transportation major groups, the percentage of women among workers added during the decade was low, but much higher than the overall percentage of women in these groups in 1970. The percentage female was lowest among net additions to the precision production (craft) major group. In 1970 only 7 percent of precision production workers were women, and of the workers added to this group during the decade 10 percent were women.

Because major groups encompass large aggregations of occupations and workers, trends at the major group level can mask as much as they reveal. Therefore, we turn our attention to changes at the three-digit detailed occupational level. If we divide detailed occupations within major groups into those in which the percentage female decreased (that is, by more than 5 percentage points between 1970 and 1980), remained about the same (that is, the 1980 figure is within 5 percentage points of the 1970 figure), or increased significantly (that is, by more than 5 percentage points), we find that in about half of the detailed occupations no change occurred in the proportion female. However, this varied widely by major group. In 22 out of 25 managerial categories, the percentage of women increased. Among the more male-dominated, "blue collar" groups—that is, precision production, machine operator, transportation occupations—only 20 to 30 percent of the occupations experienced increases in the percentage female.[31]

The index of dissimilarity, which indicates what proportion of the female (or male) labor force would have to change occupations in order for the occupational distribution to be the same for each sex, declined from 67.7 to 59.3, a decline of 8.4 percentage points, between 1970 and 1980 (see Table 5.8). Blau and Hendricks estimate a decline in the index of dissimilarity during the 1960s of about 3 percentage points. Our estimate for the 1970s is much greater than this, suggesting much greater change in the 1970s than the 1960s.[32]

This is not to say that occupational differentiation by sex was disappearing by 1980. Almost three-fifths of women workers would have had to be in different occupations than they were in 1980 for women to have the same occupational distribution as men. And if net additions to occupational categories during the 1970s had been filled indiscriminately by sex—that is, if the proportion of workers added to each occupation who were women was equal to the propor-

---

[31]Bianchi and Rytina, "Occupational Change," table 5.

[32]In our focus on 1970–80 change, we follow many of the methodological procedures used by Blau and Hendricks, who have investigated occupational change between 1950 and 1970. Francine D. Blau and Wallace E. Hendricks, "Occupational Segregation by Sex: Trends and Prospects," *Journal of Human Resources* 14 (Spring 1979):197–210. These include weighting occupations by their size, calculating how much of a decline in the index there would have been if net additions to each occupation had been "sex blind" additions, and decomposing change over time into "mix" and "sex composition" factors. Unlike Blau and Hendricks, we are not forced to restrict our analysis to a subset of comparable occupational categories at each point in time. We use virtually all occupations representing the entire 1970 and 1980 labor force.

Our figures are not strictly comparable to those calculated by Blau and Hendricks for 1950, 1960, and 1970 because we use the full occupational distribution and 1980 coding scheme. For example, their estimates of dissimilarity for 1970 using all occupations and the 1970 code categories is about 2 percentage points lower than ours: 65.8 percent. When they restrict analysis to the 183 categories that are comparable across the 1950–70 censuses, the index for 1970 is 3 percentage points higher than our calculation: 70.7 percent. Although point estimates differ, changes over decades using comparable categories at the beginning and end of the decade would seem reasonable to compare.

A significant decline in the index of dissimilarity of occupational distributions of men and women has also been noted in studies using CPS data for the 1970s. See Andrea Beller, "Trends in Occupational Segregation by Sex: 1960–1981," in Barbara F. Reskin, ed., *Sex Segregation in the Workplace: Trends, Explanations, Remedies* (Washington, DC: National Academy Press, 1984), pp. 11–26; and Jerry Jacobs, "Changes in Sex-Segregation in the 1970s," unpublished manuscript, Department of Sociology, Harvard University, 1983.

TABLE 5.8

Index of Occupational Dissimilarity Between Women and Men
and Components of Change, 1970–1980

	Index		Total Change (1980–1970)	Due to Changing Occupational Mix	Due to Decline in Sex Segregation	Interaction
	1970	1980				
Actual	67.7%	59.3%	−8.4%	−1.4%	−6.4%	−0.6%
Predicted If Hiring "Sex Blind"	—	47.8	−19.9			

NOTE: Index of dissimilarity is weighted by the size of the occupation; if all occupations are weighted equally, the index is 62.1 in 1970 and 55.3 in 1980, a decline of 6.8 percentage points.

SOURCE: See Table 5.7.

tion female in the entire "hiring pool"[33]—then we estimate that the index would have declined an additional 11.5 percentage points to 47.8 by 1980 (see Table 5.8). Of course, this is a hypothetical calculation and provides only a rough indication of occupational change possible if all new hiring were "sex blind." Men and women in the hiring pool are not equally qualified for each occupation. Very likely a much higher proportion of women have the skills necessary for clerical jobs whereas a higher proportion of men have the requisite training (usually involving apprenticeships) for precision production jobs. The question arises: Why haven't men and women acquired the same skills on average so that "sex blind" hiring would be feasible? It appears that a mix of preferences, socialization, institutional factors, and discrimination have resulted in different training and occupational outcomes for women and men.[34]

Was the decline in occupational dissimilarity between men and women in the 1970s the result of women moving into formerly male-dominated spheres or just a change in the occupational structure such that integrated occupations grew faster than segregated ones? Further evidence is given by decomposing change in the index of dissimilarity into mix and sex composition components. Whereas the mix component, a changing occupational distribution, did con-

---

[33]The "hiring pool" is composed of net additions to growing occupations and net losses from declining occupations.

[34]Barbara F. Reskin, ed., *Sex Segregation in the Workplace: Trends, Explanations, Remedies* (Washington, DC: National Academy Press, 1984); and Barbara F. Reskin and Heidi Hartmann, eds., *Women's Work, Men's Work: Sex Segregation on the Job* (Washington, DC: National Academy Press, 1985).

tribute to the decline, the much larger component was an actual change in the sex composition within detailed occupations. About three-quarters of the 8.4 percentage point decline in the index was attributable to the more equal distribution of men and women within occupational categories in 1980 than in 1970.

In sum, the change that occurred in the sex composition of detailed occupations that resulted in a decline in the index of dissimilarity arose from the fact that some women moved into male-dominated occupational spheres. The reverse did not occur. Men did not rush into jobs typically filled by women. Indeed, some occupations, such as office clerks, that had a higher than average proportion female in 1970 became even more female by 1980.[35]

In 1980, 46 percent of the female experienced civilian labor force was still concentrated in occupations which were 80 to 100 percent female. Nearly 50 percent of male workers in 1980 remained in occupations which had been 0 to 10 percent female in 1970. But these male-dominated occupations did become more female by 1980, so that only 37 percent of male workers were in occupations which remained 0 to 10 percent female in 1980.

Beyond Occupation: Sex Differentiation in Specific Job Titles

Although census data provide information on 503 occupations, this still represents the aggregation of many jobs in many different types of work settings. Hence, although women increased their representation among most of the managerial occupations, the data do not necessarily indicate that men and women within managerial specialties were filling the same job titles within the same type of organization,

An interesting study by Bielby and Baron looked at specific jobs held by men and women. Using a sample of business and manufacturing establishments in California studied by the U.S. Employment Service between 1959 and 1979, they show that the vast majority of women workers are in completely different job titles than men.

---

[35]U.S. Bureau of the Census, "Detailed Occupation of the Experienced Civilian Labor Force by Sex for the United States and Regions: 1980 and 1970," *1980 Census of Population Supplementary Report*, PC80–S1–15 (Washington, DC: U.S. Government Printing Office, 1984).

Rather than the indexes of dissimilarity in the range of 60 to 70 percent as are found with the three-digit census occupational categories, the mean index for the establishments studied was 93. That is, 93 percent of women would have had to change jobs in the late 1960s and early 1970s to have had the same job titles as men. Though these data are limited in geographic coverage and somewhat limited in the types of firms studied, the pervasiveness of sex-typed jobs and occupational ladders in nonmanufacturing as well as manufacturing firms is noteworthy. Fewer than one-fifth of the establishments had indexes of dissimilarity lower than 90. Only 10 percent of the workers they studied were even in job titles which had both men and women assigned to them. Often, establishments had only one or two job titles which included both sexes.[36]

The relationship between organizational size and the index of dissimilarity was found to be curvilinear: Women and men were highly concentrated in different job titles within huge bureaucracies as well as in very small entrepreneurial firms at the economic margins. Bielby and Baron also report "that they repeatedly encountered instances of sex segregation of jobs leading to gender specific promotion lines: an orderly progression through jobs of successively greater authority and responsibility for men and 'dead end' careers for women."[37]

The authors provide statistical evidence for what casual observation of work settings suggests: The workplace is substantially more segregated by sex than has been shown by studies of occupational concentration. The census three-digit occupational categories, upon which most studies are based, are aggregates of job titles. Often an occupation appears rather sex neutral when, in fact, a great degree of sex differentiation exists among the specific job titles included in the occupation. It would be useful to see if, as with occupational titles, specific jobs actually have experienced noticeable declines in sex concentration since the early 1970s. Unfortunately, data like those used in the Bielby and Baron study are very scarce. Establishments are reluctant to supply information on the sex composition of specific job titles.

---

[36]William T. Bielby and James N. Baron, "A Woman's Place Is with Other Women: Sex Segregation within Organizations," in Barbara F. Reskin, ed., *Sex Segregation in the Workplace: Trends, Explanations, Remedies* (Washington, DC: National Academy Press, 1984), pp. 27–55.
[37]Bielby and Baron, "Woman's Place."

Summary

Women's labor force participation has increased dramatically over the century and, in recent years, the continuity of attachment over the life course also appears to be increasing. What has brought about these changes?

Perhaps the most important factor explaining the increase in labor force participation throughout this century has been the increase in the wages paid to women working outside the home.[38] Smith and Ward argue that few married women were in the labor force at the turn of the century because wages of married women were so much lower than those of single women. As this differential narrowed, married women increased their participation dramatically.[39] Rising educational attainment of women has also increased women's "tastes" for market work and increased the costs to them of not working outside the home, since better educated persons tend to command higher salaries in the workplace. The development and lowered cost of labor and time-saving devices in the home may also be related to the increase in women's market work. However, it is difficult to determine whether new technology was a cause or response to women's increased work outside the home.[40]

The importance of World War II—and the greater need for women workers during that time—has been noted as a catalyst for participation at older ages in the 1950s. Economic growth during the 1950s also created many jobs. Oppenheimer has argued that the 1940–60 period was one of immense growth in clerical and service sector jobs, jobs typically filled by women.[41] This increased demand for female workers coincided with a period of relative shortage of the type of female worker preferred in the past—young single women or married women without children. That is, just as the demand for female labor was growing to new heights, young women of the 1950s were marrying and starting families earlier. Hence, older women, who had their appetites for paid work awakened during the war and whose families were already grown, filled the gap.

[38]Victor Fuchs, *How We Live* (Cambridge, MA: Harvard University Press, 1983), pp. 127–40.

[39]Smith and Ward, "Women's Wages."

[40]Fuchs, *How We Live*, pp. 130–31; and Glen G. Cain, "Women and Work: Trends in Time Spent in Housework," Discussion Paper no. 747–84 (Madison: Institute for Research on Poverty, University of Wisconsin, 1984).

[41]Valerie K. Oppenheimer, *The Female Labor Force in the United States* (Westport, CT: Greenwood Press, 1970).

How does one explain the large influx of young women workers during the past two decades and the more continuous labor force participation of these women? Some of the suggested explanations have been touched on in the preceding chapters on changing marriage, childbearing, and educational patterns. These include the rising educational attainment of women, the increasing divorce rate and women's ensuing realization that they must be able to support themselves financially, the women's movement and changing attitudes about the desirability of working outside the home, the slow wage growth of males during the past decade, rising consumption aspirations requiring both husbands and wives to be in the labor force, lower fertility, and later marriage.

We have noted that in recent years young women have been waiting longer to marry and start families than did women of their mother's generation. However, these would seem reasonable responses to, as much as causes of, an increased desire to participate in the labor force. Demographers, who point to the importance of the marriage squeeze or to the postponement of marriage because of the poor labor force prospects facing young men of the baby boom generation as they entered the job market, contend that young women funneled the time they would have otherwise spent in marrying and rearing children into getting a college education and starting a job. However, such an explanation paints a very passive picture of women, suggesting that they spend their lives waiting to marry and have children and everything else is secondary. More reasonable, in our estimation, is that as more women became aware of alternatives to marriage and early childbearing, and as they were increasingly able to exert effective control over the timing of these events, particularly childbearing, more women invested in education and acted on desires to enter the world of paid work. Indeed, as we have shown, delayed marriage and childbearing are not the real key to labor force increases among women, for the sharpest growth in rates has been among married women with children. Michael has shown that standardizing for changing marital and parity statuses of women does not diminish the increase in women's labor force participation rates.[42] Increased educational attainment of women does, however,

---

[42]Robert T. Michael, "Consequences of the Rise in Female Labor Force Participation Rates: Questions and Probes," *Journal of Labor Economics* 3 (January 1985 supplement):S117–46.

contribute to the explanation of labor force increases and accounts for about one-quarter of the growth.

Changing attitudes about women's place and about equality between the sexes have no doubt influenced women's propensity to earn higher degrees and subsequently embark on a career track. Additionally, legislative initiatives may have opened doors previously closed to women.

Women may also be assessing the possible costs attached to discontinuous labor force participation and making a realistic appraisal of their need to be able to support themselves. Divorce rates remain high by historical standards. Behavior of women, such as staying in school longer, working for pay, and working more continuously throughout life, certainly seems economically rational in a world in which half of women who marry eventually divorce and the other half tend to outlive their husbands. Greater attachment to work provides women more independence and marital choice—they can delay marriage or leave an unhappy marriage more easily. Working also provides women with more financial security in those situations in which they are propelled by circumstances beyond their control into providing for a family on their own.

Finally, some would point to the slow or nonexistent growth in wage rates for men during the past decade as an additional impetus for wives to enter the labor force. (See chapter 6.) Also, rising standards of living and desires for consumer goods have contributed to the perceived need among married couples for two wage earners rather than one. In general, women's labor force participation is more responsive to their own wage opportunities than to those of their spouse—and this has become more the case over time.[43] Still, families do save and spend as a unit and labor supply decisions are influenced by such things as mortgage payments and college tuition. More women are working today because they want to, but also because they feel they have to. The perceived pressure to work outside the home is another way in which women's work motivations have become similar to those of men.

---

[43]June O'Neill and Rachel Braun, "Women and the Labor Market: A Survey of Issues and Policies in the United States," United States Country Report to the Conference on "Regulation of the Labor Market: International Comparison of Labor Market Policy Related to Women," IIMV/LMP, Berlin, 1983.

6

EARNINGS

ISCUSSION of the changing labor force participation of women in the preceding chapter alluded to the earnings differential by sex. Working women do not earn as much as working men. In 1983 women who worked full time, year round averaged about $14,000 compared with $22,000 for men. (See Table 6.1.) Common explanations for women's lower earnings are that they enter and leave the labor force more frequently than men, resulting in less work experience; women's skills and educational background are not equal to those of men; and women are discriminated against in hiring, promotion, and pay. Research conducted in the last two decades has tried to explain why earnings differences persist as more and more women earn college degrees, women's attachment to the labor force increases, and discrimination lessens. Although it is possible to quantify variables such as work experience, on-the-job training, and educational attainment, it is difficult to measure differences in hiring and promotion practices, motivational factors, and qualitative differences in the jobs of men and women.

In this chapter we take an individualistic look at women as wage earners, that is, we focus primarily on their wage-related characteristics compared with those of men. We begin this chapter by

TABLE 6.1

Changes in Ratio of Women's Earnings to Men's Among Full-Time, Year-Round Workers (current dollars)

Year	Median Annual Earnings			Median Weekly Earnings		
	Women	Men	Ratio (W/M)	Women	Men	Ratio (W/M)
1955	$2,719	$4,252	0.64			
1956	2,827	4,466	0.63			
1957	3,008	4,713	0.64			
1958	3,102	4,927	0.63			
1959	3,193	5,209	0.61			
1960	3,257	5,368	0.61		[Not available]	
1961	3,315	5,595	0.59			
1962	3,412	5,754	0.59			
1963	3,525	5,980	0.59			
1964	3,669	6,203	0.59			
1965	3,828	6,388	0.60			
1966	3,946	6,856	0.58			
1967	4,150	7,182	0.58	$78	$125	0.62
1968	4,457	7,664	0.58			
1969	4,977	8,227	0.60	86	142	0.61
1970	5,323	8,966	0.59	94	151	0.62
1971	5,593	9,399	0.60	100	162	0.62
1972	5,903	10,202	0.58	106	168	0.63
1973	6,335	11,186	0.57	116	188	0.62
1974	6,772	11,835	0.57	124	204	0.61
1975	7,504	12,758	0.59	137	221	0.62
1976	8,099	13,455	0.60	145	233	0.62
1977	8,618	14,626	0.59	156	252	0.62
1978	9,350	15,730	0.59	166	271	0.61
1979	10,169	17,045	0.60	180	297	0.61
1980	11,197	18,612	0.60	201	309	0.65
1981	12,001	20,260	0.59	217	345	0.63
1982	13,014	21,077	0.62	240	363	0.66
1983	13,915	21,881	0.64	252	379	0.66

NOTE: Annual earnings collected in March CPS; weekly earnings collected of wage/salary workers in May CPS for years 1967 and 1969–78; beginning in second half of 1979, figures represent average of quarterly averages (weekly earnings collected monthly).

SOURCE: U.S. Bureau of the Census, "Money Income of Households, Families, and Persons in the United States," *Current Population Reports*, series P-60, nos. 37, 39, 41, 43, 47, 51, 53, 60, 66, 75, 80, 85, 90, 97, 101, 105, 114, 118, 129, 132, 137, 142, and 146 (Washington, DC: U.S. Government Printing Office, 1960–85), data on work experience by total money earnings; U.S. Department of Labor, Bureau of Labor Statistics, "Labor Statistics Derived from the Current Population Survey: A Databook," bulletin 2096 (September 1982); table C-19, U.S. Department of Labor, Bureau of Labor Statistics, "Perspectives on Working Women: A Databook," bulletin 2080 (October 1980), table 52; U.S. Department of Labor Bureau of Labor Statistics, "Handbook of Labor Statistics," Bulletin 2217 (June 1985), table 41.

reviewing trends in the earnings of women and men. Next, we look at earnings differences between men and women in the same occupation. Finally, we discuss some of the theories and research findings that have been posited to explain how sex differentials arise and why they persist.

Many labor force decisions by men and women are made within a family context. A wife's wage is an important component of the economic well-being of husband-wife families. And the labor force participation and earnings of women who manage families on their own are increasingly important to another large group of families. We reserve discussion of women's economic contribution to families until the following chapter, however.

Trends in the Sex Differential in Earnings

Women are paid about 60 cents for every dollar paid to men. Table 6.1 shows year-to-year variation and the trend over time in median earnings measures for men and women. Comparisons are restricted to full-time workers who worked year round. The annual earnings series, which extends back to 1955, shows considerable stability in the earnings ratio of women to men. Since 1955 the annual earnings of women have averaged between 57 and 64 percent of those of men, with the ratio close to 60 percent in most years. Women lost some ground vis-à-vis men in the 1960s and 1970s, but may have recouped that loss in the early 1980s. By 1983 women's median earnings were 64 percent of men's, the same as in 1955.

Table 6.1 also shows median weekly earnings of wage and salary workers, a series which extends back to the late 1960s. The ratio of weekly earnings of women to men is slightly higher than the one based on the annual measure.[1] Women who worked full time earned two-thirds of what men did in 1983. Since women on full-time work

---

[1] Reasons for differences in the annual and weekly earnings series are discussed in Nancy F. Rytina, "Comparing Annual and Weekly Earnings from the Current Population Survey," *Monthly Labor Review* 106 (April 1983):32–36. The standard errors for the weekly data are smaller than for the annual data. The reference period for the weekly data is the previous week, whereas it is the previous 2 to 14 months for the annual data. The annual estimates are based on the actual earnings of all individuals who were usually employed full time, year round the previous year, whereas the weekly estimates are based on the usual earnings of those who were employed full time in the week prior to the monthly CPS survey. The weekly data refer to earnings from primary job, whereas the annual data refer to earnings from the longest job held during the previous year. Income from self-employment is included in the annual data but excluded from the weekly data.

schedules average about four hours less per week than men who work full time, some of the weekly earnings gap between the sexes can be attributed to differences in hours worked. However, the fact that men take home a weekly paycheck that is one and one-half times that of women on average cannot be explained solely by the additional hours they work each week. O'Neill has adjusted the median weekly earnings series for sex differences in hours worked and calculated that, in 1983, the adjusted ratio was 72 percent.[2]

In sum, what is most striking about Table 6.1 is not only how large the earnings differential is, no matter which measure is used, but also how little movement there has been in the ratio of women's earnings to men's over nearly three decades.

Smith and Ward have recently addressed the question of why the relative wages of women versus men remained constant at the same time that female labor force participation expanded rapidly.[3] They argue that the influx of inexperienced workers dominated the increase in female labor force participation between 1950 and 1980, which held down the relative wages of working women. They show that the increase in working women's educational attainment did not keep pace with that of men, and they estimate that the average experience of women workers increased by only one-half year relative to men between 1950 and 1980. According to their estimates, the hourly wage of female workers was 63 percent of that of male workers in 1950 and 60 percent in 1980. The stability in the ratio of female to male earnings, they argue, is consistent with the stability in the relative skills of women workers over this period.

The trend is somewhat different when they consider all women, not just those who are working. They estimate that the relative experience of all women increased by 2 or 3 years and educational attainment declined by only one-half year relative to men between 1950 and 1980. Hourly wages increased from 48 percent of men's wages in 1950 to 53 percent by 1980. That is, the wage rate of all women relative to men is lower than the 60 percent figure for workers, but has increased slightly over time.

---

[2]June O'Neill, "The Trend in the Male-Female Wage Gap in the United States," *Journal of Labor Economics* 3 (January 1985 supplement):S91–116.

[3]James P. Smith and Michael P. Ward, "Women's Wages and Work in the Twentieth Century," report prepared for the National Institute of Child Health and Human Development, R-3119–NICHD (Santa Monica, CA: Rand Corporation, 1984). Part of this report is published in James P. Smith and Michael P. Ward, "Time Series Growth in the Female Labor Force," *Journal of Labor Economics* 3 (January 1980 supplement):S59–90.

The Smith and Ward explanation may be accurate for the post-war period prior to about 1970, but is less satisfactory as an interpretation of stability in the overall ratio of working women's earnings to men's since that time. Women's college enrollment has been increasing as men's enrollment has dropped off. Available cross-sectional data on exit rates and estimates of work-life expectancy suggest that women's attachment to the labor force has increased substantially since the late 1960s while men's attachment has remained unchanged. As women's participation in the world of paid work has become much more similar to that of men, there has not been corresponding movement in the overall ratio of working women's earnings to men's.

Age, Education, and Earnings Differences by Sex

Given the narrowing of sex differences in educational attainment during the 1970s and early 1980s, the great increase in labor force participation of young women, and the disappearance of the dip in participation rates during childbearing years, we might expect to see more equalization over time in the wages of younger men and women than for all workers. Table 6.2 focuses on available earnings and income series for young, college-educated workers.

The median annual income series for persons aged 25 to 34 (extending back to 1955) indicates, as does the series for the total, that women's income as a percentage of men's income deteriorated between 1955 and the mid-1960s. However, among this young age group, there was somewhat more improvement by the early 1980s than there was in the overall trend reported in Table 6.1.

The median income series for college-educated persons which extends back to 1967 also suggests improvement. Among college-educated workers aged 25 to 34, for example, median income of women increased from 67 to 75 percent of that of men between 1967 and 1982. The ratio of female to male income was higher among young, college-educated persons than it was for the overall labor force in 1982. However, women still received only about three-quarters of the income of men.

Table 6.3 provides a closer look at age-earnings profiles within levels of educational attainment in 1982. The striking features are these: the relative flatness of the profiles for women as compared

TABLE 6.2

Changes in Ratio of Women's Income and Earnings to Men's Among Full-Time, Year-Round Workers Aged 25–34

| Year | All Workers | | College-Educated Workers | |
	Median Annual Income	Mean Annual Earnings	Median Annual Income	Mean Annual earnings
1955	0.66			
1956	0.68			
1957	0.67			
1958	0.63			
1959	0.64			
1960	0.65			
1961	0.64			
1962	0.63			
1963	0.62			
1964	0.62			
1965	0.62			
1966	0.60			
1967	0.62		0.67	
1968	0.63		0.67	
1969	0.62		0.65	
1970	0.65		0.68	
1971	0.65		0.68	
1972	0.65		0.67	
1973	0.63		0.68	
1974	0.63		0.69	
1975	0.66	0.65	0.71	0.69
1976	0.68	0.65	0.71	0.68
1977	0.68	0.65	0.71	0.66
1978	0.66	0.64	0.70	0.66
1979	0.66	0.65	0.71	0.68
1980	0.69	0.69	0.74	0.71
1981	0.70	0.69	0.73	0.71
1982	0.72	0.71	0.75	0.72

SOURCE: U.S. Bureau of the Census "Money Income of Households, Families, and Persons in the United States" *Current Population Reports*, series P-60, nos. 23, 27, 30, 33, 35, 37, 39, 41, 43, 51, 53, 60, 66, 75, 80, 85, 90, 97, 101, 105, 114, 118, 129, 132, 137, 142, and 146 (Washington, DC: U.S. Government Printing Office, 1955–84), data on educational attainment by total money income and earnings.

with those for men, the great amount of deterioration in the female to male earnings ratios with age, especially among women with a college degree or some graduate training, and the large gap in earnings separating men and women in every age-educational category.

If one takes this cross-sectional snapshot as a rough picture of cohort patterns—realizing that ratios for older age groups may be poor approximations of the future ratios for those now in the young

TABLE 6.3
Age-Earnings Profiles of Women and Men, 1982 (mean earnings)

Age	All Educational Levels			High School Graduate			College Graduate			Graduate/Professional Training		
	Women	Men	Ratio	Women	Men	Ratio	Women	Men	Ratio	Women	Men	Ratio
Total, 18 Years and Over	$14,331	$23,653	0.61	$12,993	$20,480	0.63	$17,331	$29,547	0.59	$21,871	$36,079	0.61
18–24 Years	10,903	13,225	0.82	10,235	13,088	0.78	14,436	17,984	0.80	—	—	—
25–29 Years	14,276	19,501	0.73	12,634	17,556	0.72	16,232	21,975	0.74	19,702	23,953	0.82
30–34 Years	15,536	22,993	0.68	13,507	20,171	0.67	18,063	25,988	0.70	21,458	30,337	0.71
35–39 Years	15,803	26,326	0.60	14,287	22,857	0.63	19,608	29,232	0.67	22,452	36,059	0.62
40–44 Years	14,751	27,409	0.54	13,069	24,188	0.54	19,244	32,775	0.59	21,612	40,036	0.54
45–49 Years	14,843	27,401	0.54	13,791	23,451	0.59	17,561	37,246	0.47	24,050	41,315	0.58
50–54 Years	14,824	27,194	0.55	13,816	22,744	0.61	18,521	37,265	0.50	23,867	42,489	0.56
55–59 Years	14,771	26,805	0.55	14,312	23,800	0.60	17,217	39,849	0.43	23,578	43,645	0.54
60–64 Years	14,319	25,265	0.57	14,084	23,379	0.60	17,040	34,546	0.49	—	40,770	—
65 Years and Over	12,553	20,712	0.61	12,812	19,123	0.67	—	28,281	—	—	34,095	—

NOTE: Mean earnings of full-time, year-round workers; "All Educational Levels" includes those with less than a high school education.

SOURCE: U.S. Bureau of the Census, "Money Income of Households, Families, and Persons in the United States: 1982," *Current Population Reports*, series P-60, no. 142 (Washington DC: U.S. Government Printing Office, 1984), table 48.

age groups—it suggests that women begin their work lives at a disadvantage, that is, making only about 80 percent of what men of comparable age and educational attainment earn, and that this initial disadvantage worsens with advancing age. This happens because men's earnings increase as they age but women's earnings do not. Hence, the ratio of female to male earnings declines. By the time women are in their 50s, those with a high school diploma are earning only about 60 percent of what men with a high school diploma are earning. The deterioration is even more substantial for college-educated women who earn only 45 to 50 percent of what men do at older ages. In the past, college-educated men have continued to make sizable average earnings gains until age 60, whereas college-educated women's earnings reach a small peak much earlier. The story is similar for those with graduate training, though not quite as accentuated.[4]

The diagonals of Table 6.4 allow limited cohort comparisons of women's earnings relative to men's earnings. Estimates are derived from census data and are somewhat lower for 1980 than those based on the 1982 Current Population Survey reported in the previous table. In the past, women have experienced a sizable decline in their earnings position relative to men between age 30 and age 40. For those with college degrees or graduate training, declines have been 10 percentage points or more. The declines observed within cohorts are similar—though in some cases slightly smaller—to those suggested by the cross-sectional picture.

Whether the greater labor force attachment of women aged 25 to 34 in 1980 will result in less earnings deterioration relative to men in the future remains to be seen. In the past, the failure of earnings to increase as women aged may have been due, in part, to the fact that they interrupted their labor force participation to raise children. When they reentered at older ages, they received wages similar to those they had earned at the time they left the labor force. To the extent that recent cohorts of women will work more continuously over their lifetime than women of previous generations did and to the extent that intermittency is a cause of the flat age-earnings profiles of women, women currently in their 20s and early 30s will be

---

[4]If one believes that a college education today has less of a payoff for men than it did in the past, the steep age-earnings profile for college-educated men which is evident in the cross-sectional data may overstate the wage appreciation that young men today will realize over their lifetime.

TABLE 6.4

Changes in Women's Earnings as a Percentage of Men's Within Age and Educational Groups (mean earnings)

Age and Education	1960	1970	1980
Total			
25–34 Years	59%	59%	63%
35–44 Years	50	47	52
45–54 Years	52	50	50
55–64 Years	55	55	54
Not High School Graduate			
25–34 Years	55	56	66
35–44 Years	53	53	56
45–54 Years	55	53	52
55–64 Years	55	58	57
High School Graduate			
25–34 Years	63	59	63
35–44 Years	54	51	55
45–54 Years	54	54	56
55–64 Years	54	55	58
Some College			
25–34 Years	59	63	66
35–44 Years	49	49	56
45–54 Years	47	52	52
55–64 Years	52	52	56
College Graduate			
25–34 Years	57	62	68
35–44 Years	45	45	52
45–54 years	46	47	45
55–64 Years	45	52	51
Graduate Training			
25–34 Years	64	68	69
35–44 Years	48	52	57
45–54 Years	45	56	53
55–64 Years	57	57	53

NOTE: Percentage based on earnings ratios of full-time, year-round workers.

SOURCE: 1960, 1970, 1980 Census 1/1,000 Public Use Microdata Sample.

expected to realize more wage growth as they age than suggested by past trends.

Black-White Differences in Earnings

The trend in the relative earnings of Black women has been quite different from that of White women. Figure 6.1 illustrates the trend in the income of Black and White males and females, and Table 6.5 shows changes over time in the ratio of the earnings of Black

FIGURE 6.1

Trend in Median Income of Year-Round, Full-Time Workers
by Race and Sex (1982 dollars)

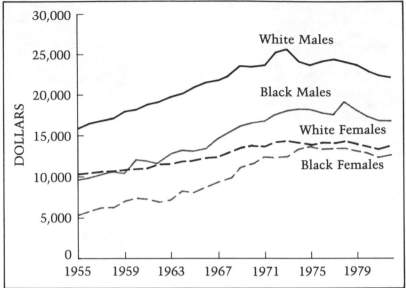

NOTE: "Black" includes other races.

SOURCE: U.S. Bureau of the Census, "Money Income of Households, Families, and Persons in the United States: 1982," *Current Population Reports*, series P-60, no. 142 (Washington, DC: U.S. Government Printing Office, 1984), table 40.

women to all the other race-sex groups.[5] Black women in 1955 were at the bottom of the income hierarchy. In 1982 they remained the least-well-remunerated of the four race-sex groups, but the relative improvement they witnessed during the period was substantial. Between 1955 and 1982 Black women's average income increased from 51 to 91 percent of that of White women. Black women also improved their income position relative to men. Whereas in 1955 they received only 55 percent of the income of Black men, by 1982 their

[5]Data for Blacks actually include Blacks and other races. Figures have been converted to constant dollars by adjusting dollar amounts using the Consumer Price Index. The trend in median annual income is shown because this is the only series which extends back to 1955 for the various race-sex groups. Median earnings would be preferable to median income but the data are unavailable. Among year-round, full-time workers almost all annual income is derived from earnings, and hence we assume that the two series would be quite similar. Series of median income and median earnings are available for total workers and are virtually identical.

TABLE 6.5

Changes in Ratios of Median Annual Income of White and Black Women and Men

Year	BF/WM	BF/BM	BF/WF	WF/WM	WF/BM	BM/WM
			Ratio			
1955	0.34	0.55	0.51	0.65	1.07	0.61
1956	0.35	0.59	0.56	0.63	1.06	0.60
1957	0.37	0.61	0.58	0.64	1.04	0.61
1958	0.37	0.58	0.59	0.63	1.00	0.63
1959	0.39	0.67	0.64	0.61	1.05	0.58
1960	0.41	0.62	0.68	0.61	0.92	0.66
1961	0.39	0.61	0.66	0.59	0.93	0.63
1962	0.36	0.61	0.61	0.60	1.00	0.60
1963	0.37	0.57	0.62	0.59	0.92	0.64
1964	0.41	0.63	0.69	0.59	0.91	0.66
1965	0.39	0.63	0.68	0.58	0.92	0.63
1966	0.41	0.65	0.71	0.58	0.92	0.63
1967	0.43	0.65	0.75	0.57	0.86	0.67
1968	0.43	0.63	0.74	0.58	0.85	0.69
1969	0.47	0.70	0.82	0.58	0.85	0.68
1970	0.49	0.70	0.84	0.59	0.83	0.70
1971	0.52	0.74	0.90	0.58	0.82	0.71
1972	0.49	0.70	0.87	0.57	0.81	0.69
1973	0.49	0.69	0.87	0.56	0.80	0.70
1974	0.55	0.73	0.94	0.58	0.78	0.75
1975	0.57	0.75	0.98	0.58	0.76	0.77
1976	0.55	0.75	0.94	0.59	0.80	0.73
1977	0.55	0.77	0.95	0.58	0.80	0.72
1978	0.56	0.70	0.94	0.59	0.75	0.79
1979	0.55	0.73	0.93	0.59	0.78	0.75
1980	0.56	0.74	0.94	0.59	0.79	0.75
1981	0.55	0.74	0.92	0.60	0.80	0.74
1982	0.57	0.75	0.91	0.62	0.83	0.75

NOTE: Data are for full-time, year-round workers; BF = Black and other race females; WF = White females; BM = Black and other race males; WM = White males.

SOURCE: U.S. Bureau of the Census, "Money Income of Households, Families, and Persons in the United States: 1982," *Current Population Reports*, series P-60, no. 142 (Washington, DC: U.S. Government Printing Office, 1984), table 40.

income reached 75 percent of that of Black men on average. It rose from 34 to 57 percent of the income of White men during this same period.

White women, on the other hand, lost ground vis-à-vis men. In 1955 White women's income was about 65 percent of that of White men. This declined to a low of 56 percent in the early 1970s and had risen somewhat to 62 percent by 1982. The relative income position of White women compared with White men was thus worse in 1982 than in 1955. And the absolute dollar gap separating women's income from men's increased from $5,000 to $8,000 among Whites.

It is easier to explain the relative improvement for Black women over the past three decades than it is to explain the lack of significant change for White women. Blacks as a group have made substantial gains in educational attainment and occupational mobility. Employment of Black women in private household occupations began to decline during the 1940s, but 40 percent of employed Black women were still in low-paying, domestic service jobs in 1960.[6] In the subsequent two decades, Black women increasingly moved into better paid clerical jobs—the kinds of jobs held by White women. The civil rights legislation of the 1960s probably helped to open educational and occupational opportunities to Black women that were closed to them in 1955, when they earned only half as much as White women. As Black women have achieved parity with White women in jobs and earnings, sex differences, much more than race differences, have come to account for remaining earnings gaps between Black women and White men. And the earnings of Black women may have improved relative to those of Black men, but they still earn only 75 percent as much as Black men—again, suggesting the importance of gender rather than racial differences for Black women.

Earnings Differences Within Occupations

A frequently voiced concern with overall earnings comparisons, such as those just reviewed, is that they are really not comparisons of men and women doing similar jobs. We know that women and men are concentrated in different types of occupations and the suspicion is that if we compare women and men in similar lines of work, we will find lower, perhaps nonexistent, pay differentials.

[6]Jane R. Wilkie, "The Decline in Occupational Segregation Between Black and White Women," in Cora B. Marrett and Cheryl Leggon, eds., *Research in Race and Ethnic Relations*, vol. 4 (Greenwich, CT: JAI Press, 1985), pp. 67–90; Allyson S. Grossman, "Women in Domestic Work: Yesterday and Today," *Monthly Labor Review* 103 (August 1980):17–21; and Donald J. Treiman and Kermit Terrell, "Women, Work, and Wages—Trends in the Female Occupational Structure Since 1940," in Kenneth C. Land, ed., *Social Indicator Models* (New York: Russell Sage Foundation, 1975), pp. 157–200.

The occupational data from the 1980 census afford an opportunity to look at male-female pay differentials in more detail. In the 1980 Census of Population 503 occupational categories within 13 major groups were used to classify workers. Table 6.6 considers the hourly earnings differences of men and women in the 13 major occupational groups. The average within-occupation earnings gap between men and women was $2.50 among full-time, year-round workers aged 18 and over. This translates into approximately a $5,000 earnings gap over the course of a year. However, the gap in the earnings of younger workers aged 25 to 34 was much smaller ($1.62).

Table 6.6 allows us to assess whether occupational earnings differences between the sexes are smaller on average within the detailed occupations of certain major groups. That is, using occupations as the unit of analysis, the average occupational earnings differences across the detailed categories within each of the 13 major occupational groups are shown. For example, for the 26 managerial detailed occupations, the average within-occupation earnings of women 18 and over who worked full time, year round in 1979 was $6.67, whereas for men it was $10.47, a difference of $3.80 per hour. Among the 26 managerial specialties, earnings of women were about 64 percent of those of men on average and tended to lag behind the average for all occupations.

Another group of occupations which offer particularly poor earnings prospects for women vis-à-vis men are sales occupations in which women's average earnings were only 61 percent of those of men. The ratio is higher among young workers, but women still lag farther behind men in this group of occupations than among all other categories except private household occupations.

Table 6.6 clearly demonstrates that the income position of young women relative to young men is much better than for the labor force as a whole. Within the detailed categories of all major groups, ratios of female to male earnings among those aged 25 to 34 tend to be higher than ratios for the population aged 18 and over. Among professional, technical, and protective services specialties, the relative earnings of young women are over 80 percent of those of young men on average. Young women in managerial and farming occupations were also paid much better relative to men than older women in these occupations.

The seemingly much more equal treatment of younger women, particularly in occupations requiring advanced schooling, such as

TABLE 6.6

*Mean Hourly Earnings and Sex Differences in Earnings
Among Detailed Occupations, 1980*

Occupation and Age	Mean Hourly Earnings		Gap (M-W)	Ratio (W/M*100)
	Women	Men		
All Occupations (503)				
18 Years and Over	$5.63	$8.13	$2.50	70
25–34 Years	5.65	7.27	1.62	78
Managerial (26)				
18 Years and Over	6.67	10.47	3.80	64
25–34 Years	6.53	8.48	1.94	77
Professional (106)				
18 Years and Over	7.25	10.57	3.32	70
25–34 Years	6.91	8.30	1.39	85
Technical (22)				
18 Years and Over	6.12	8.75	2.63	71
25–34 Years	6.19	7.70	1.51	81
Sales (23)				
18 Years and Over	5.09	8.56	3.47	61
25–34 Years	5.28	7.70	2.42	69
Administrative Support (57)				
18 Years and Over	5.26	7.60	2.34	70
25–34 Years	5.32	6.92	1.60	77
Private Household (5)				
18 Years and Over	2.44	3.93	1.49	63
25–34 Years	2.64	4.30	1.66	65
Protective Service (11)				
18 Years and Over	5.62	7.33	1.70	77
25–34 Years	5.80	6.75	0.97	86
Other Service (28)				
18 Years and Over	4.05	5.54	1.49	74
25–34 Years	4.22	5.41	1.19	78
Farming (19)				
18 Years and Over	4.06	5.94	1.89	68
25–34 Years	4.51	5.63	1.13	78
Precision Production (103)				
18 Years and Over	5.48	7.66	2.18	72
25–34 Years	5.60	7.39	1.79	76
Machine Operative (62)				
18 Years and Over	4.68	6.84	2.16	69
25–34 Years	4.75	6.70	1.95	71
Transportation (25)				
18 Years and Over	5.68	7.66	1.98	75
25–34 Years	5.81	7.35	1.54	79
Handlers (16)				
18 Years and Over	4.84	6.38	1.54	76
25–34 Years	5.16	6.41	1.25	80

NOTE: Unit of analysis is detailed occupations noted in ( ); earnings of full-time, year-round workers.

SOURCE: 1980 Census of Population, special tabulations.

professional, managerial, and technical jobs, may be signaling real improvement in the earnings status of women vis-à-vis men, at least for those who receive training beyond high school. Entry-level, white collar jobs, with the exception of sales, appear to be opening up to women with the requisite credentials. However, many of the full-time, year-round working women aged 25 to 34 in 1980 have delayed marriage and childbearing and hence have not had a work interruption. And most of them have not yet tried to move up job ladders into mid-level and top positions. The age-earnings profiles reviewed previously showed that in the past women started their work lives earning 80 percent of what men earned, but this ratio deteriorated substantially by the time these women were in their 40s and 50s. The important question which will begin to be answered with the 1990 census is whether women in the cohort aged 25 to 34 in 1980 will be more successful in holding onto their earnings position relative to men as they age. The past suggests that they will run into difficulties, but, as previously noted, the past may not be a good indicator because continuity of labor force attachment is increasing for women.

Table 6.7 reinforces the finding in Table 6.6 that young women have earnings considerably closer to those of men—but by no means equal to men—than do women in general. Whereas fewer than 1 percent of all women workers were in occupations in which women's earnings were at least 90 percent those of men, 10 percent of young women workers were in such occupations. This is not a large percentage, even among young women, but it does suggest more equality for younger women than older women.

An earnings gap of $1.00 or less an hour among full-time, year-round workers translates into an annual earnings difference of $2,000 or less. The average hourly earnings of male and female workers differed by less than $1.00 in about 7 percent of occupations and for about 3 percent of all women in the full-time labor force. In 18 percent of the detailed occupations with enough young men and women aged 25 to 34 to compare, the earnings gap was less than $1.00. Seventeen percent of young women were in these occupations.

On the other hand, an hourly wage gap of $2.50 or more suggests an annual earnings difference of $5,000 or more. In 25 percent of all occupations average earnings gaps between the sexes were this great. In only 5 percent of occupations were earnings differences so large for young workers. Thirty-seven percent of all women, but only 2

TABLE 6.7

Cumulative Percentage Distribution of Occupations Across Categories of Mean Hourly Earnings Gaps and Ratios, 1980

Earnings	Occupations		Female Workers		Male Workers	
	18 Years Old and Over	25–34 Years Old	18 Years Old and Over	25–34 Years Old	18 Years Old and Over	25–34 Years Old
Mean Hourly Earnings Gap (M–F)						
Less Than $1.00	6.8%	17.5%	2.8%	16.5%	4.8%	12.7%
$1.00–$1.49	19.1	45.1	20.5	35.5	15.0	31.6
1.50–1.99	36.8	71.9	36.3	73.4	29.5	60.9
2.00–2.49	60.5	89.2	52.5	87.7	54.6	83.9
2.50–2.99	74.8	94.6	63.3	97.6	63.4	96.6
3.00–3.99	89.9	99.0	89.1	99.8	82.2	99.5
4.00–4.99	94.5	99.0	92.2	99.8	85.4	99.5
5.00 and Over	100.0	100.0	100.0	100.0	100.0	100.0
Mean Hourly Earnings Ratio (F/M*100)						
100% and Over	0.0	1.0	0.0	0.1	0.0	0.1
90–99	1.1	9.8	0.8	10.2	0.9	6.6
80–89	12.2	39.7	12.9	25.9	12.0	28.8
75–79	22.3	59.8	19.6	47.0	22.2	51.9
70–74	49.2	79.6	40.2	86.4	49.2	83.7
65–69	65.4	93.8	63.8	97.0	65.3	96.5
60–64	79.2	97.2	74.5	98.8	79.2	99.3
50–59	99.5	99.5	99.4	99.9	99.5	99.9
Less Than 50%	100.0	100.0	100.0	100.0	100.0	100.0

NOTE: Based on earnings of full-time, year-round workers and on a subsample of occupations in which there were at least 250 persons of each sex; 456 occupations for earnings of persons aged 18 and over, representing 99.9% of the female work force and 99.2% of the male work force; 388 occupations for earnings of persons aged 25–34 representing 99.5% of the female work force and 96.0% of the male work force.

SOURCE: 1980 Census of Population, special tabulations.

percent of young women, were in occupations with male-female earnings gaps as large as $2.50 an hour.

Tables 6.8 and 6.9 list the 25 occupations with the highest male/female earnings ratios and the 25 occupations with the lowest ratios for all workers aged 18 and over and for workers aged 25 to 34.[7] The highest ratio for those aged 18 and over was for the occupation of waiter or waitress in which women earned 99 percent on average of what men earned. Among those aged 25 to 34, there were actually two occupations in which women earned 100 percent or more of what men earned: announcers and waiter's assistants.

Among the population aged 18 and over, very few professional occupations and no managerial occupations made the list of the top 25 occupations in terms of earnings ratios. The professional occupations with fairly high relative earnings of women to men included occupational therapists (92 percent), social workers (83 percent), and secondary school teachers (83 percent).

The list of professional occupations which were included in the 25 occupations with the highest earnings ratios was much more extensive among those aged 25 to 34, though here again no managerial occupations made the list. The professional occupations included announcers, clergy, musicians, urban planners, a residual category of social scientists, biological scientists, librarians, pharmacists, archivists, social workers, counselors, registered nurses, secondary school teachers, and actors. In fact, 14 of the 25 occupations with the highest rankings of female to male earnings were professional occupations.

What about the other side of the ledger—occupations in which women have the lowest earnings relative to men? At the top of the list for persons aged over 18 and second on the list for younger workers is the occupation of dentist. Lawyers and veterinarians also appear on the list for persons aged 18 and over, though not on the list for those aged 25 to 34. Several management and sales occupations appear on both lists, suggesting that women still have quite a way to go before they achieve equality with men in the financial and business world. This is all the more interesting because of the changes

---

[7]Occupations with fewer than 1,000 workers of either sex have been eliminated from consideration. About one person in five responding to the 1980 Census was selected to answer the occupation question. Such a restriction ensures that at last 200 individuals form the base for each mean hourly earnings amount in the ratio of female to male earnings.

TABLE 6.8

*25 Detailed Occupations with the Highest and Lowest Ratios of
Women's Mean Hourly Earnings to Men's Among Full-Time,
Year-Round Workers Aged 18 and Over, 1980*

Occupations with Highest Rankings	Ratio (W/M*100)	Occupations with Lowest Rankings	Ratio (W/M*100)
Waiters/Waitresses	98.9	Dentists	42.3
Miscellaneous Food		Health Practitioners (n.e.c.)	45.7
Preparation Workers	94.8	Sales Workers, Securities	46.2
Occupational Therapists	92.3	Communications	
Postal Clerks	91.5	Equipment Operators	47.8
Public Transportation		Medical Scientists	47.9
Attendants	87.4	Dental Assistants	49.0
Welfare Eligibility Clerks	86.6	Horticultural Farmers	50.2
Library Clerks	86.1	Veterinarians	50.7
Helpers, Construction	85.9	Managers (n.e.c.)	51.4
Automobile Mechanics	85.8	Rolling Machine Operators	52.0
Mail Carriers	85.5	Stenographers	52.8
Sheriffs, Bailiffs, etc.	85.1	Managers, Property/Real	
Meter Readers	85.1	Estate	52.9
Industrial Truck Operators	84.5	Farmers	53.1
Construction Trades		Sales Workers, Insurance	53.4
Workers (n.e.c.)	84.0	Material Recording Clerks	53.8
Supervisors, Farm Workers	83.9	Other Financial Officers	53.8
Barbers	83.7	Athletes	54.2
Licensed Practical Nurses	83.4	Photoengravers	54.9
Social Workers	83.3	Managers, Marketing	55.1
Surveying/Mapping		Sales Workers, Apparel	55.3
Technicians	83.2	Lawyers	55.3
Metal Layout Workers	83.2	Air Traffic Controllers	55.5
Teachers, Secondary	83.1	Sales Counter Clerks	55.8
Knitting Machine		Underwriters	55.9
Operators	82.8	Sales Workers, Other	
Lab Technicians	82.7	Commodities	56.1
Correctional Officers	82.6		
Messengers	82.5		

NOTE: Restricted to occupations with at least 1,000 male and 1,000 female full-time, year-round workers; n.e.c. = not elsewhere classified.

SOURCE: 1980 Census of Population, special tabulations.

we noted in earlier chapters: That is, by 1980 many more women were in management fields and professional fields such as dentistry. Based on the data presented for young workers, however, it appears that not all of this movement has resulted in equal earnings for women and men entering these fields.

What explains the earnings differences within detailed occupations? First, as is clear from the titles listed in Tables 6.8 and 6.9, the 503 detailed occupations used to categorize jobs in the 1980 census are quite general, covering a variety of specific jobs and work

TABLE 6.9

25 Detailed Occupations with the Highest and Lowest Ratios of
Women's Mean Hourly Earnings to Men's Among Full-Time,
Year-Round Workers Aged 25–34, 1980

Occupations With Highest Rankings	Ratio (W/M*100)	Occupations With Lowest Rankings	Ratio (W/M*100)
Announcers	104.4	Private Household	
Waiters'/Waitresses'		Cleaners	47.2
Assistants	100.8	Dentists	53.9
Clergy	96.6	Child Care Workers	57.0
Public Transportation		Athletes	57.5
Attendants	96.5	Sales Workers, Securities	58.4
Short-Order Cooks	96.1	Farmers	59.5
Postal Clerks	94.3	Sales Workers, Apparel	60.4
Supervisors, Farm Workers	93.6	Managers, Property/Real	
Musicians and Composers	93.4	Estate	60.4
Urban Planners	93.1	Sales Workers, Other	
Library Clerks	92.4	Commodities	60.4
Meter Readers	92.4	Managers, Farm	62.1
Social Scientists (n.e.c.)	92.4	Precious Stones/Metal	
Biological/Life Scientists	92.2	Workers	63.6
Licensed Practical Nurses	92.2	Sales Workers, Hardware	63.7
Lab Technicians	92.1	Folding Machine Operators	63.9
Librarians	91.9	Sales Counter Clerks	64.1
Pharmacists	91.8	Fabricating Machine	
Archivists, Curators	91.5	Operators	64.7
Social Workers	91.0	Supervisors, Cleaning	
Miscellaneous Food		Workers	64.9
Preparation Workers	90.0	Butchers/Meat Cutters	65.1
Counselors, Vocational		Artists, Performers	65.3
Education	90.9	Material Recording Clerks	65.4
Registered Nurses	90.8	Stenographers	65.4
Teachers, Secondary	90.4	Slicing Machine Operators	65.5
Automobile Mechanics	90.1	Printing Machine	
Actors and Directors	89.5	Operators	65.7
		Miscellaneous Printing	
		Machine Operators	65.9
		Sales Workers, Real Estate	65.9
		Production Inspectors	66.2

NOTE: Restricted to occupations with at least 1,000 male and 1,000 female full-time, year-round workers; n.e.c. – not elsewhere classified; child care workers excludes those working in private homes.

SOURCE: 1980 Census of Population, special tabulations.

settings and making no distinctions as to whether a person in those occupations is in an entry level or higher level position. For example, over half of all managers are classified into the residual category, "Managers, not elsewhere classified." Such a group is so amorphous as to be almost meaningless. Women may earn 51 percent of what men in this category earn in part because they are in very different work settings.

Blau has shown that women in the same occupation as men tend to be concentrated in lower-paying firms.[8] This suboccupational level—the firm—is a very important unit of analysis in studying wage differentials. Unfortunately, there is very little empirical data at the firm level of analysis. Often the detailed occupational categories offered by the census are the most disaggregated data available.

Why Do Women Earn Less Than Men?

Knowing that women earn less than men because they are concentrated in lower-paying occupations or that women's earnings within the same occupation are lower than men's because they are concentrated in lower-paying firms merely refocuses the issues. The more general question remains: Why do women earn less than men? Why are women in different occupations and lower-paying firms within occupations? There are at least two competing explanations: Women are discriminated against in the labor market versus women make choices about family roles that limit their labor market productivity and constrain their occupational choices.

A large body of research in economics and sociology has been devoted to analysis of sex differences in earnings. A very influential economic framework for viewing earnings differences is the human capital tradition. The argument, as formulated in a 1974 article by Mincer and Polachek, is that because women do not expect to work as much as men throughout their lives, they invest less in acquiring labor market skills.[9] Women anticipate having children and leaving the labor force to raise them and therefore take jobs which have relatively high initial wage rates but offer little on-the-job training or potential wage growth. When women leave the labor force to rear children, the skills they have deteriorate and they suffer a wage penalty when they reenter. Employers may also choose to invest less in women workers because they believe women will work less continuously than men and hence, they, the employers, will not realize the return on investment in women workers that they will in male workers.

Mincer and Ofek revised the original argument by postulating

[8]Francine D. Blau, *Equal Pay in the Office* (Lexington, MA: Heath, 1977).

[9]Jacob Mincer and Solomon Polachek, "Family Investment in Human Capital: Earnings of Women," in Theodore W. Schultz, ed., *Marriage, Family Human Capital, and Fertility* (Chicago: University of Chicago Press, 1974), pp. S76–108.

that human capital that depreciates during periods of nonparticipation in the labor force can be, and often is, restored and restored rather quickly and fairly extensively once women reenter the labor force after a period of absence.[10] They still claim that there is a cost associated with spending time outside the labor force but short-run costs are much greater than the long-run costs due to this restoration of depreciated human capital.

To the lay person, the discussion of workers, specifically women workers, as machines that depreciate but then with some reinvestment have their productive capacity restored may seem a bit strange. Nonetheless, the human capital explanation of earnings differences has been useful in pointing out the importance of work histories. Although the size of the costs associated with discontinuous labor force participation has been disputed,[11] and the interpretation of costs as "depreciation" has been questioned,[12] most would agree that work experience is significantly related to earnings. Thus, the fact that women spend less time in the labor market is related to why they earn less than men. The question arises in the interpretation of this relationship. Does work experience merely serve as a proxy for seniority—are people just paid more the longer they remain with an organization? Or is there significant enhancement of skills with years on the job so that a worker's productivity actually increases with experience, making it economically rational to pay an individual more the longer he or she has been on the job? The human capital tradition places major emphasis on the latter interpretation of

---

[10]Jacob Mincer and Haim Ofek, "Interrupted Work Careers: Depreciation and Restoration of Human Capital," *Journal of Human Resources* 17 (Winter 1982):3–24.

[11]Sandell and Shapiro suggest that several methodological flaws in the original Mincer and Polachek study resulted in an overestimation of the effects of depreciation for time spent out of the labor force. Sandell and Shapiro's estimates are about half the size of those of Mincer and Polachek. See Steven H. Sandell and David Shapiro, "The Theory of Human Capital and the Earnings of Women: A Reexamination of the Evidence," *Journal of Human Resources* 13 (Winter 1978):103–17.

[12]Corcoran and Duncan offer an alternative explanation to the depreciation-restoration explanation for what happens to wages upon exit from and reentry to the labor force. They suggest that when a person first reenters it takes time to become aware of all available job opportunities. A woman who reenters at a lower rate than she can command begins searching for better alternatives, and her wages go up when she settles into a more suitable job. See Mary Corcoran and Greg J. Duncan, "Work History, Labor Force Attachment, and Earnings Differences Between the Races and Sexes," *Journal of Human Resources* 14 (Winter 1979):3–20. Treiman argues that women's discontinuous labor force participation places them at a serious bargaining disadvantage in negotiating for position and salary when seeking a job. It is as if every job is a first job. See Donald J. Treiman, "The Work Histories of Women and Men: What We Know and What We Need to Find Out," in Alice Rossi, ed., *Gender and the Life Course* (New York: Aldine, 1985), pp. 213–32.

work experience. Hence, skill accumulation, or on-the-job training, is a major variable in this research. Given the importance of on-the-job training, it is rather disappointing to find that in most of the literature training has been equated with years of work experience—work experience itself being measured more or less well depending on the data at hand.

Human capital theorists note that women have flatter age-earnings (or experience-earnings) profiles than men and that married women have flatter age-earnings profiles than non-married women. This is taken as evidence, albeit indirect, that investment, skill accumulation, and then depreciation are occurring. The problem is that flat experience-earnings profiles are as compatible with an explanation that women are discriminated against in obtaining training and securing promotions in the work setting as with an explanation that women choose not to invest in acquiring job skills because they anticipate future withdrawal from the labor force.

Finally, even if one accepts the human capital explanation for how earnings differences arise and work experience as a perfect proxy for skill investment and accumulation, it is disconcerting to find that much—probably half—of the wage gap between men and women remains unexplained. We turn to a review of a study that represents one of the most thorough of those aimed at explaining earnings differences by productivity-related variables.

Work Experience As a Factor in Male-Female Wage Gaps

In 1979 Corcoran and Duncan published an ambitious analysis of the relationship of work experience to earnings and to the male-female earnings gap.[13] Their measures are the most detailed available and their analysis one of the most complete that exists. They measured the number of years workers had spent outside the labor force, the number of years in their current position (job tenure), the number of years with their current employer prior to their current job, and the number of years of work experience prior to those with a current employer. They also measured whether those years of work experience were full time or part time.[14] The data used were from

---

[13]Corcoran and Duncan, "Work History."

[14]Part time was defined as fewer than 1,500 hours per year, that is, an average of fewer than 30 hours per week.

the 1976 Panel Study of Income Dynamics (PSID), a longitudinal survey of the economic well-being of 5,000 American families which has been conducted annually since the late 1960s.

In addition to actual years of work experience, they included several variables measuring other aspects of labor force attachment. Many speculate that women earn less than men because they place special constraints on the hours they work, or how far they will travel to work, in order to combine family and work responsibilities. In the PSID survey, respondents were asked whether limitations had been placed on hours or job location and these factors were entered into the analysis. Respondents were also asked if they planned to quit their jobs in the near future. Additionally, absenteeism due to one's own illness or that of a family member was considered in the analysis as a predictor of earnings.

As discussed above, on-the-job training or skill accumulation is a crucial aspect of the human capital formulation of how wages are set. All other studies equate on-the-job training with years of work experience, Corcoran and Duncan used a separate measure of on-the-job training, the respondent's report of how long it would take the average person to learn his or her job. In addition to on-the-job training, educational attainment—the mechanism by which job-related skills are accumulated prior to entry into the labor market—was also entered into the analysis.

Corcoran and Duncan predictably find that work experience and on-the-job training are directly related to earnings. However, certain segments of experience are more valuable than others—time in current position and with current employer, for example, appears more valuable than time with previous employers. Full-time work is significantly more valuable than part-time work. Years of nonparticipation is found to be only weakly related to earnings.[15]

---

[15]Corcoran and Duncan dispute the importance of the skills depreciation interpretation of wage loss for years out of the labor force because their variable on years of nonparticipation is only weakly related to earnings. Corcoran, Duncan, and Ponza find that while there is an initial 4 or 5 percent wage loss for each year out of the labor force, the PSID data show a rebound effect of similar magnitude for each year back in. See Mary Corcoran, Greg J. Duncan, and Michael Ponza, "Work Experience and Wage Growth of Women Workers," in Greg J. Duncan and James N. Morgan, eds., *Five Thousand American Families: Patterns of Economic Progress, vol. 10* (Ann Arbor: Institute for Social Research, 1983), pp. 249–311.

Mincer and Ofek, using longitudinal data, continue to find that there is a 1.5 percent long-run wage loss per year out of the labor force. See Mincer and Ofek, "Interrupted Work Careers."

As for the work attachment variables, most of them do not explain much about the earnings gap because most are either not related or are only weakly related to earnings.[16] Differences in educational attainment between White men and women are so slight that they explain little of the wage gap. Educational differences are more significant in explaining wage gaps between Black women and White men and very significant in explaining wage gaps between White and Black men.

Contrary to some other findings, results from this study suggest that men and women of either race receive almost identical payoffs to training and work experience. But work experience and training differences do explain some of the sex (and race, but more of the sex) differential in earnings because women receive less training and have less work experience. The problem with interpreting these differences, however, is that it is not clear, particularly in the case of on-the-job training, whether differences arise because workers choose to invest less in skill accumulation or because discriminatory practices keep women from receiving the same training as men.

What is the end result of entering all these work experience, training and education, and work attachment variables into the analysis of sex differences in earnings? A large part of the wage differential between White men and the other race-sex groups remains unexplained by this long list of productivity-related variables. Over 50 percent of the wage differential between White men and women remains and closer to 70 percent of the wage differential between Black women and White men remains after taking into account all the productivity-related variables. In the regression equations, even though coefficients representing wage payoffs to various characteristics are similar for all groups, the constants differ significantly. That is, at any given skill level, White men earn more than women and Blacks.

Corcoran and Duncan are not alone in being able to explain only about half of the earnings differential with experience and training variables. Mincer and Polachek and Mincer and Ofek themselves ex-

---

[16]Absenteeism because of the illness of a family member is not related to earnings and absenteeism because of one's own illness is only very weakly related and then only for Whites. Planning to quit a job lowers earnings, but so few persons of either sex plan to quit that this at most explains only 2 percent of the wage gap. Whether a person limits job hours or restricts job location is only weakly related to earnings and hence explains only 1 or 2 percent of the gap in wages between the sexes.

plain only about half of the earnings differential between the sexes with their "human capital" differences. What can we conclude? Given their lower levels of work experience, women might be expected to earn 80 percent of what men earn on average. Instead, they earn only 60 percent.

Some would take the unmeasured differences between the sexes, particularly in studies such as Corcoran and Duncan's that have gone a long way toward actually measuring the supposed productivity differences between men and women, as a measure of the wage differential that is attributable to discrimination. However, even Corcoran and Duncan's careful measurement of many variables leaves others unmeasured. For example, the education measure is just years of schooling completed and hence leaves out any consideration of content and quality differences which vary across race-sex groups.

Corcoran and Duncan also do not measure individual worker differences in ability, diligence, and motivation. It seems unlikely that women and men differ greatly in ability. And one might hypothesize that women are more diligent on the job—they work harder because they have to prove themselves, especially in work settings dominated by men. But there may be systematic differences in commitment to jobs or work between men and women resulting from the fact that women often have a legitimate alternative use of time— that is, raising children. Men might also view childrearing as an alternative, but the traditional division of labor within families, firmly embedded in our values and culture, has viewed this as women's responsibility. In sum, one must at least entertain the likelihood that all factors affecting the productivity of men and women have not been entered into the analysis—and that some variables have been imperfectly measured. To the extent that characteristics accounting for justifiable wage differences are left out of existing analyses, taking the residual as a measure of discrimination could overestimate its importance in explaining male-female wage differentials.

The unexplained residual also could be an underestimate of discrimination. To allow that the explained portion of the wage gap represents only wage differences which are deserved because of productivity differences between male and female workers, one must assume that no discrimination exists in the differential acquisition of education and training and that no discrimination has entered into promotions and selection for certain jobs. To the extent that women have faced discrimination in educational programs, job training, and selection for certain occupations, existing wage differentials explained by differences in on-the-job training or tenure in current job are not solely due to productivity differences between workers. If women workers are not as productive on average, it may be because they have been denied promotions and access to education and training.

Several studies have tried to add to the explanation of the sex differentials in wages by focusing on aspects of jobs themselves as explanatory factors in earnings regressions.[17] The general impression from these studies is that they do not move very far beyond the strictly human capital models in explaining the mechanisms generating wage differentials. They shift the question from why women earn less than men to why women are concentrated in jobs which pay poorly by comparison to those held by men.

The human capital explanation of job segregation by sex is that it arises because of women's choices about family roles, which in turn influence their decisions about investments in training and job choice.[18] Women who plan to work intermittently choose jobs which do not penalize discontinuity in labor force participation. That is, they select jobs requiring either little investment in training and/or in which the atrophy of skills during time out of the labor force is minimal. The end result is a concentration of women in low-paying, dead-end occupations.

This argument assumes that women who expect discontinuous

[17]For example, Wolf and Fligstein report that women are much less likely to be in supervisory positions—to have jobs in which they have control over the pay of employees or in which they exercise the right to hire and fire personnel. See Wendy C. Wolf and Neil D. Fligstein, "Sex and Authority in the Workplace: The Causes of Sexual Inequality," *American Sociological Review* 44 (April 1979):235–52.

Ferber and Spaeth find that having control over money and having a male supervisor are related to earnings. When they add characteristics of jobs such as these to the usual productivity variables in human capital models, they explain 57 percent of the male-female wage gap. That is, job characteristic differences between men and women add significantly to the explanation of earnings differentials, but a very large unexplained gap still remains. See Marianne A. Ferber and Joe L. Spaeth, "Work Characteristics and the Male-Female Earnings Gap," *American Economic Review* 74 (May 1984):260–64.

Roos, too, has attempted to go beyond the myriad of sociological studies of sex earnings differences which include occupation, indexed by prestige. Her proxies for women's concentration in low-wage jobs, lack of control of the means of production, and lesser authority explain some of the wage gap—but the majority remains unexplained. See Patricia A. Roos, "Sex Stratification in the Workplace: Male-Female Differences in Economic Returns to Occupation," *Social Science Research* 10 (September 1981):195–224.

[18]Solomon W. Polachek, "Occupational Self-Selection: A Human Capital Approach to Sex Differences in Occupational Structure," *Review of Economics and Statistics* 63 (February 1981):60–69.

careers are concentrated in traditionally female jobs. England finds that women who have spent a lot of time out of the labor force are no more likely to be in female occupations than women who are employed more continuously.[19] Wolf and Rosenfeld find only a weak correlation between the sex composition of a woman's first and current occupation and the number of years she has spent outside the labor force.[20] Findings from the PSID data suggest that there is considerable mobility between male and female typed occupations.[21]

The human capital explanation also predicts that wage growth for female occupations is lower because women who plan intermittent work careers concentrate in occupations which supposedly have relatively high initial wage rates and little depreciation. England finds, however, that earnings of women in predominantly female occupations do not show lower rates of either depreciation or appreciation than do earnings of women in occupations containing more men.[22]

In sum, it may be argued that the wage and occupational differentials between the sexes are primarily the result of women's choices concerning family roles. There is no denying that some women make choices about home and childrearing responsibilities that negatively affect their market equality with men. And it is easy to believe that there is much less discriminatory treatment of women in the workplace today than there was even a decade ago. But it is just as easy to believe that discrimination continues to exist and that its existence is part of the reason that repeated attempts to explain male-female wage differentials have resulted in our ability to attribute only about half of the existing differential to factors that might legitimately be thought to be related to wage structures.

Pay Equity for Women

Cases of women being paid less than men in identical jobs are becoming rare and are explicitly illegal under the Equal Pay Act and Title VII of the 1964 Civil Rights Act. Until now, two basic strate-

---

[19]Paula England, "The Failure of Human Capital Theory to Explain Occupational Sex Segregation," *Journal of Human Resources* 17 (Summer 1982):356–70.

[20]Wendy C. Wolf and Rachel Rosenfeld, "Sex Structure of Occupations and Job Mobility," *Social Forces* 56 (March 1978):823–44.

[21]Greg J. Duncan, *Years of Poverty, Years of Plenty* (Ann Arbor: Institute for Social Research, 1984), chap. 6.

[22]England, "Failure of Human Capital Theory."

gies have been used to ameliorate the male-female pay differential. First, attempts have been made, supported by the courts, to alter the opportunity structure facing women entering the labor market—to guarantee equal, or in some cases even preferential, access to educational and employment opportunities. Second, emphasis has been placed on paying essentially similar jobs (for example, nursing aides and orderlies) the same and on desegregating occupations and specific jobs within occupations.[23]

It is clear from the data presented in this chapter and the previous one that, whereas these measures may eventually reduce earnings disparities between men and women, change occurs slowly. In addition, these types of strategies will not be very effective for older women workers, particularly those who have invested heavily in skills that are not now highly rewarded.

Not surprisingly, then, one increasingly hears talk of the need for further intervention in the labor market. Some are now arguing that women are not paid fairly for the work that they do and that the intent of the employment provisions in the Civil Rights Act was far broader than had heretofore been interpreted. The new call is for pay equity among jobs of comparable worth, with job evaluation plans as one mechanism for determining comparability. The comparable worth notion is that the wages paid to persons holding any given job should be based on the skill, effort, responsibility, and working conditions of the job. Jobs which are dissimilar in content but similar in productivity requirements should be paid comparably.

Opponents of the comparable worth concept object to the fact that external market forces, which affect the supply of labor and the price employers must pay to attract and retain workers, are ignored by a system of remuneration based solely on job content.[24] Proponents argue that there is ample evidence that institutional factors such as unionization and discrimination enter into the wage setting process. Current wages cannot be taken as a measure of a job's worth because these wages reflect a systematic undervaluing of certain jobs merely because they are deemed "women's work" and not because of productivity-related factors pertaining to the work performed.

[23]George T. Milkovich, "The Male-Female Pay Gap: Need for Reevaluation," *Monthly Labor Review* 104 (April 1981):42–44.

[24]Charles Waldauer, "The Non-Comparability of the "Comparable Worth" Doctrine: An Inappropriate Standard for Determining Sex Discrimination in Pay," *Population Research and Policy Review* 3 (June 1984):141–66.

The verdict is still out as to whether a workable means for comparing dissimilar jobs in terms of worth can or should be accomplished. It is not clear what the ultimate effect on employment and the economy would be or if, on balance, the effect would be positive or negative for women. There is no assurance that the wages of women will be raised vis-à-vis men because there is no direct empirical evidence as to whether "women's work" has been systematically undervalued.[25] One also does not know what hiring decisions would be made by employers if the wage rates of certain occupations were elevated.

Despite the disagreement surrounding the pay equity issue, considerable legislative activity has taken place at the state and local level of government. As of early 1985 all but five states had taken some action on the issue of comparable worth. In eight states the activity was rather minimal and involved monitoring what other states were doing or holding public hearings on the issue. Fifteen states had gone a step further and established a task force or commission to address the issue. Sixteen states had undertaken job evaluation studies which could be used to address pay equity concerns. And six states (Idaho, Iowa, Minnesota, New Mexico, South Dakota, and Washington) had actually appropriated or set aside funds for implementing some form of pay equity salary adustments. In 1982 Minnesota became the first state to amend its state civil service law, establish a policy of equitable compensation between female and male job classes, and appropriate funds to be used to that end. As of the writing of this monograph, two years of a four-year plan had been implemented and funds were pending for the second two years.[26]

Summary

The preceding discussion leaves one major question unanswered: Why has there been so little improvement in the earnings of women relative to men in the last decade? There is some indication that younger, well-educated women entering professional jobs did

25Milkovich, "Male-Female Pay Gap."
26National Committee on Pay Equity, *Who's Working for Working Women? A Survey of State and Local Government Initiatives* (Washington, DC: National Committee on Pay Equity, 1984); and National Committee on Pay Equity, "Pay Equity Newsnotes," May 1985, pp. A–D.

better relative to men than previous cohorts of women, but their gains were not overwhelmingly large.

Prior to 1970 the relative inexperience of the female worker entering the labor force may have accounted for the stability in the ratio of women's earnings to men's but this explanation is not satisfactory for the period since 1970. During the 1970s changing characteristics of women workers as a group should have made for earnings improvements relative to men in any but unfavorable times. Rather than a rush of former housewives with little or no market skills into the labor force, we have been witnessing the increasing commitment of women to the labor force for longer periods of their lives. Relative to men, the female labor force has become more skilled, not more marginal, since 1970.

The 1970s were plagued by periodic recessions and slow wage growth as many new workers, men as well as women, of the baby boom generation were absorbed into the labor force. Increasing pressures on husband-wife families served to move both partners to work outside the home, with the resultant skyrocketing of labor force participation rates of married women. It is possible that sluggish economic conditions combined with an overabundance of new workers did make this a particularly "unfortunate" decade for women. These conditions weighed heavily against large gains for any group. Industries which absorbed the largest influx of women workers—those in the rapidly expanding service sector—were those with traditionally low hourly earnings.[27]

There are indicators, albeit indirect, that institutional factors, including discrimination, at least partly explain continued male-female wage differentials. These consist of the extreme concentration of women in different occupations, the earnings gap by sex within occupations, and the inability of productivity-related factors such as work experience and on-the-job training to explain half of the wage gap.

Whether earnings parity between the sexes will come quickly or will be far-reaching is really the question for women in the 1980s and 1990s. Much will probably depend on how well the overall economy does during these years.

---

[27]Howard Davis, "Employment Gains of Women by Industry, 1968–78," *Monthly Labor Review* 103 (June 1980):3–9.

7

INCOME, POVERTY,
AND PER CAPITA WELL-BEING

O UT OF all the trends we have reviewed in previous chapters, two developments—the increase in divorce and the increase in labor force participation of wives—are perhaps most important in relation to the economic position of women. Why? Because these two trends have revolutionized the economic contribution women make to families: An increasing proportion of adult women assume a "breadwinner" role in addition to the "caregiver" role women have traditionally filled.

Although the husband's earnings are still the major source of income in the majority of husband-wife families, the importance of the earnings of wives has increased. Additionally, an increased proportion of families do not include a male breadwinner and must rely instead on a female wage earner. Both working wives and women who are maintaining families without a spouse must balance the need to provide income to their family with the need to devote time to the care and nurturance of that family.

Over their lifetime, many women will experience the pressures inherent in both breadwinner roles: Wives who divorce will maintain families, and many women who manage families by themselves will eventually marry. One can speculate that part of the motivation

for married women to work outside the home is the growing awareness that they may at some point be raising a family on their own.

In this chapter the changing economic activity of working wives
and women who maintain families are examined. There are signs of
a growing divergence in the economic well-being of the families of
these two groups of women: As married women increase the income
available to their families through their labor force participation, unmarried women and their families are becoming more economically
disadvantaged relative to dual-earner, husband-wife families.

Trends in Labor Force Participation and Earnings of Wives

The increased participation of married women has accounted for
much of the rise in labor force rates among women during the post–
World War II period. In 1947 about one-fifth of all wives were in the
labor force, but by 1982 over one-half of all wives were working for
pay. Labor force participation rates of married women are still much
lower than those of married men, but there has been a distinct convergence in these trends over time. (See Figure 7.1.)

The majority of married women do not hold full-time, year-
round jobs, but the percentage who do has increased. As shown in
Figure 7.1, 26 percent of all wives in 1981 worked year round, full
time, up from 15 percent in 1961.[1] Participation is still substantially
lower for wives than for husbands (two-thirds of whom worked year
round, full time in 1981), but, as with overall participation rates,
rates of full-time, year-round employment are also converging.

The increased labor force participation of wives has resulted in
a significant change in the way husband-wife couples amass income.
In most households, the majority of income comes from earnings.
Table 7.1 shows the proportion of family earnings contributed by the
wife in husband-wife households with earnings. The estimates are
derived from the 1960, 1970, and 1980 censuses and refer to earnings
in the preceding year. The proportion of families relying solely on
the husband's earnings has declined substantially. In 1960 over

---

[1]Estimates are calculated by multiplying the proportion of employed wives (husbands) who worked full time, year round in 1981 times the proportion employed during
the year times the total number of wives (husbands) in the civilian population in March
of the following year.

FIGURE 7.1

Trend in Labor Force Participation and Full-Time, Year-Round Employment of Husbands and Wives

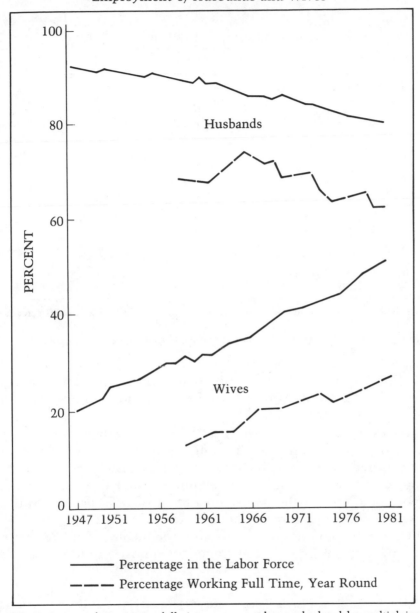

NOTE: Estimates of percentage full time, year round are calculated by multiplying the proportion of wives (husbands) who worked full time, year round in 1981 times the proportion employed during the year times the total number of wives (husbands) in the civilian population in March of the following year.

SOURCE: U.S. Department of Labor, Bureau of Labor Statistics, *Labor Force Statistics Derived from the Current Population Survey: A Databook, Volume I*, bulletin 2096 (Washington, DC: U.S. Government Printing Office, 1982), tables C-3 and C-6.

TABLE 7.1

Changes in Percentage of Family Earnings Contributed by Wives
(numbers in thousands, percentage distribution)

Wife's Contribution	1960	1970	1980
Total Husband-Wife Families with Earnings	37,221	40,536	43,572
Percentage of Earnings Wife Contributes	100.0%	100.0%	100.0%
0%	61.2	49.5	38.9
1–10	8.3	9.7	10.3
11–20	5.6	7.7	9.2
21–30	6.2	8.9	10.4
31–40	6.5	8.9	10.7
41–50	5.4	6.6	8.1
51–60	2.7	3.5	4.9
61–75	1.4	1.7	2.2
76–99	1.0	1.2	2.0
100	1.6	2.2	3.2
Percentage who Contribute More Than Half	6.7	8.6	12.3

NOTE: Husband-wife families with no earnings or earnings losses excluded 6 percent of all husband-wife families in 1960, 7 percent in 1970, and 11 percent in 1980.

SOURCE: 1960, 1970, and 1980 Census 1/1,000 Public Use Microdata Sample.

three-fifths of husband-wife households received no earned income from the wife. By 1980 only two-fifths had no earnings from the wife.

Wives on average earn only 42 percent as much as their husbands—63 percent as much when only full-time, year-round workers are compared.[2] It is still the atypical case in which the wife is the major contributor to family income. But between 1960 and 1980 the proportion of wives who contributed more than 50 percent to their household's earnings almost doubled: from 6.7 to 12.3 percent.

Current Population Survey data for the income year 1981 reveal that wives were primary breadwinners in almost 6 million couples.[3]

[2]U.S. Bureau of the Census, "Money Income of Households, Families, and Persons in the United States: 1982," *Current Population Reports,* series P-60, no. 142 (Washington, DC: U.S. Government Printing Office, 1984), table 31.

[3]For a discussion of the characteristics of couples in which the wife is the primary breadwinner see Suzanne M. Bianchi, "Wives Who Earn More Than Their Husbands," *Special Demographic Analyses,* CDS-80–9 (Washington, DC: U.S. Government Printing Office, 1983).

The husband contributed no earnings in 2 million households. Most of these couples consisted of a retired, ill, or disabled husband married to a younger wife who was still in the paid labor force. Another 2 million wives shouldered the major breadwinning role in families in which the husband had difficulty securing full-time, year-round employment. Finally, 2 million wives earned more than their husbands in 1981 even when he worked full time, year round. Such women may be in the vanguard at this time, but it can no longer be assumed that men are always primary breadwinners in their respective households or that wives' earnings are discretionary components of income. Wives no longer work just for "pin money"—if, in fact, they ever did.

For a growing number of couples, a wife's earnings are an essential component of a family's level of well-being for extended periods of time. Even when the wife earns substantially less than her husband, her contribution may be necessary to pay the mortgage and maintain a certain standard of living. A wife's employment can also serve as an important buffer against a husband's unemployment and poverty, though the margin of safety is eroded during economic recessions.[4] Because women on average earn much less than men, a family forced to rely on the wife's income may experience a serious reduction in their standard of living if a husband's labor force difficulty is prolonged.

To date, most analyses of wives' employment and earnings have emphasized the secondary nature of their labor market involvement. For example, Oppenheimer has pointed out the significance of a wife's earnings during life cycle squeezes such as the early stage of marriage when a couple incurs the expense of setting up a new household and, again, at a later stage when children reach high school and college age.[5] This focus suggests that wives' labor force participation is easily influenced (up or down) by family economic constraints. A "life cycle squeeze" interpretation of wives' economic contribution to families seems much more in line with the U-shaped

---

[4]Deborah P. Klein, "Trends in Employment and Unemployment in Families," *Monthly Labor Review* 106 (December, 1983):21–25.

[5]Valerie K. Oppenheimer, "The Life-Cycle Squeeze: The Interaction of Men's Occupational and Family Cycles," *Demography* 11 (May, 1974):237–45; Valerie K. Oppenheimer, "The Sociology of Women's Economic Role in the Family," *American Sociological Review* 42 (June 1977):387–405; and Valerie K. Oppenheimer, *Work and the Family* (New York: Academic Press, 1982).

age profiles of labor force participation which characterized women in the 50s and 60s than with the age pattern of participation that typified women by 1980.

Family needs still influence the market roles of wives: The overwhelming majority of women not in the labor force give home responsibilities as their major reason for not working.[6] The probability of a wife being employed is inversely related to her husband's earnings, but over time the responsiveness of a wife's employment to the employment and earnings of her husband has declined and the importance of her own market characteristics has increased.[7] Increasingly, career goals and the perceived need by women to be able to take care of themselves financially in the event of a marital disruption are also important determinants of their labor force participation. As more women complete college and graduate training, more view work in much the same way as men do—as something they will continue throughout their adult lives. And at a time when one-half of all marriages end in divorce, married women cannot rest assured that their financial needs will always be met by their husbands.

To be sure, not all the movement of wives into the labor force during the 1970s and early 1980s is accounted for by workers planning a life-long attachment to the work force. If all the increase in working wives had occurred because of the entrance of career-minded, well-educated, well-paid wives—wives who would typically be married to husbands with similar educational credentials and earnings potential—we might have seen increased inequality in the distribution of family income among husband-wife couples. Instead, several studies have shown that wives' earnings actually served to slightly reduce income inequality among husband-wife families during the 1960s and 1970s[8]—evidence that there was movement into

[6]U.S. Department of Labor, Bureau of Labor Statistics, *Perspectives on Working Women: A Databook*, bulletin 2080 (Washington, DC: U.S. Government Printing Office, 1980), table 14.

[7]June O'Neill and Rachel Braun, "Women and the Labor Market: A Survey of Issues and Policies in the United States," United States Country Report to the Conference on "Regulation of the Labor Market: International Comparison of Labor Market Policy Related to Women," IIMV/LMP, Berlin, 1981.

[8]Francis W. Horvath, "Working Wives Reduce Inequality in the Distribution of Family Earnings," *Monthly Labor Review* 103 (July 1980):48–50; Sheldon Danziger, "Do Working Wives Increase Family Income Inequality?" *Journal of Human Resources* 15 (Summer 1980):444–51; James P. Smith, "The Distribution of Family Earnings," *Journal of Political Economy* 87 (October 1979):S162–92; and Jacob Mincer, *Schooling, Experience, and Earnings* (New York: Columbia University Press, 1974).

the labor force of wives of lower-income husbands as well. The 1970s were a period of relatively slow wage growth for men, and hence some wives (who in better times might not have worked outside the home) entered the labor force out of economic necessity.

Nonetheless, the labor force patterns of married women, particularly those with children, do seem to be changing. Over time, younger generations of wives and mothers with greater lifetime commitment to the labor force are replacing older generations for whom market work was almost always secondary to nonmarket work. The career paths and labor force expectations of these younger women are not the same as their husbands'. Among couples in which the wife commands a salary considerably lower than her husband, for example, it may continue to be economically rational for her to adjust her labor force participation downward to accommodate children. But the breadwinner role wives play is becoming more important and more similar to that of their husbands.

Trends in Labor Force Participation and Earnings of Female Householders

As the economic role of married women has changed, so also has that of unmarried women. An increasing number of unmarried women are raising families by themselves. As noted in chapter 3, the increase in female family householders accelerated during the 1970s. Women who maintained families were younger on average in 1980 than in 1970. More of them were divorced or separated rather than widowed. And during the 1970s the largest percentage increase in the number of female family householders was among those with at least some college education. In 1981 female family householders were still somewhat less well educated than women in general, but 24 percent had completed at least one year of college compared with only 13 percent in 1970.[9]

Because female householders were better educated in 1980 than they had been previously, they were presumably in a better position

[9]U.S. Bureau of the Census, "Families Maintained by Female Householders, 1970–79," *Current Population Reports, Special Studies,* series P-23, no. 107 (Washington, DC: U.S. Government Printing Office, 1980), table 10; and U.S. Bureau of the Census, "Educational Attainment in the United States: March 1981 and 1980," *Current Population Reports,* series P-20, no. 390 (Washington, DC: U.S. Government Printing Office, 1984), table 4.

to find employment. Not surprisingly, then, women who maintained families increased their labor force participation (from 50 to 61 percent in the labor force) between 1960 and 1982. The increase was not as sizable as for wives, but women who maintain families without a spouse present are still more likely to be in the labor force than are married women.[10]

Within households maintained by women, some important labor force shifts have had an impact on the income situation in these households. Most female-maintained families rely on earned income rather than transfers, either public or private, for the major portion of their financial well-being. The proportion of female-maintained families in which the householder provides earnings has increased. Concomitantly, a decrease in the proportion which receive earnings from other adult household members has occurred. As shown in Table 7.2, in households with earned income 31 percent of female householders contributed no earnings to their household in 1960. This declined to 18 percent in 1980. Conversely, the proportion of these households which received all earnings from the female householder increased from 37 to 47 percent during this period.

TABLE 7.2

Changes in Percentage of Family Earnings Contributed by Female Family Householders (numbers in thousands, percentage distribution)

Householder's Contribution	1960	1970	1980
Total Female-Maintained Families with Earnings	3,251	4,376	6,480
Percentage of Earnings Householder Contributes	100.0%	100.0%	100.0%
0%	30.5	22.1	18.3
1–25	6.7	5.1	4.8
26–50	9.1	8.8	8.9
51–75	8.6	10.5	10.7
76–99	8.0	10.9	9.9
100	37.1	42.5	47.3

NOTE: Female-maintained families with no earnings or earnings losses excluded 21 percent of all female-maintained families in 1960, 23 percent in 1970, and 22 percent in 1980.

SOURCE: 1960, 1970, and 1980 Census 1/1,000 Public Use Microdata Sample.

[10]U.S. Department of Labor, Bureau of Labor Statistics, *Handbook of Labor Statistics*, bulletin 2175 (Washington, DC: U.S. Government Printing Office, 1983), tables 50 and 56.

As husband-wife households increasingly rely on the earnings of two persons, female-maintained families are becoming more and more dependent upon the wage earnings of only one earner, the householder. Although female-maintained families have become more middle class—at least as indexed by the educational attainment of the householder—their income situation relative to husband-wife households has deteriorated. Median income in husband-wife families, which was already twice as high as in female-maintained families in 1967, increased to 2.3 times that of female-maintained families by the early 1980s.[11] Since income growth in female-maintained families has not kept pace with that of other types of households, poverty has become more concentrated in families maintained by a woman.

Female-Maintained Families and Poverty

In studies from the Panel Study of Income Dynamics (PSID), a longitudinal survey of 5,000 American families, it has been observed repeatedly that the single most important factor affecting changes in individual economic well-being is family composition.[12] And the economic status of women is affected more by a divorce than is that of men—because women earn much less than men, women usually retain custody of dependent children after a divorce, and child-support payments are often inadequate.

Nowhere are the economic problems of unmarried women more evident than in the official poverty statistics. Figure 7.2 shows the trend in the poverty rate of persons living in female-maintained households compared with persons in other types of households (husband-wife and male-maintained households). These estimates make use of the official poverty levels which relate total money income to a measure of need based on family food budgets. They do not include any measurement of in-kind transfers such as food stamps.[13] Poverty rates declined in all types of households during the

[11]Estimates based on Current Population Survey data. Ratios of median family income. U.S. Department of Labor, Bureau of Labor Statistics, *Handbook*, table 58.

[12]Greg J. Duncan, *Years of Poverty, Years of Plenty* (Ann Arbor: Institute for Social Research, 1984), chap. 1.

[13]For a discussion of issues involved in incorporating in-kind benefits into the estimates of poverty, see U.S. Bureau of the Census, "Estimates of Poverty Including the Value of Noncash Benefits: 1979 to 1982," *Technical Paper 51* (Washington, DC: U.S. Government Printing Office, 1984).

FIGURE 7.2

*Trend in Percentage of Persons in Female-Maintained Households
Who Live in Poverty*

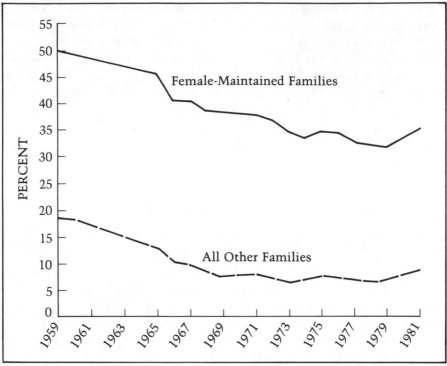

SOURCE: U.S. Bureau of the Census, "Characteristics of the Population Below the Poverty Level: 1982," *Current Population Reports*, series P-60, no. 144 (Washington, DC: U.S. Government Printing Office, 1984), table 1.

1960s, tended to level off some in the 1970s, and rose slightly in the early 1980s. In 1982 rates were much lower than they were in 1959 in both female-maintained and other households. However, the likelihood of being poor remains much higher for persons in female-maintained households. In 1982, 36 percent of the persons living in female-maintained households were in poverty compared with 10 percent of persons in other households.

Figure 7.3 illustrates the substantial differences that exist between the poverty rates of Black and White female-maintained households. In 1982, 57 percent of persons in Black households with a female householder were in poverty compared with 29 percent in White households. The probability of being poor has declined since the late 1950s, but the racial differential has not narrowed.

FIGURE 7.3

Trend in Percentage of Black and White Persons
in Female-Maintained Households Who Live in Poverty

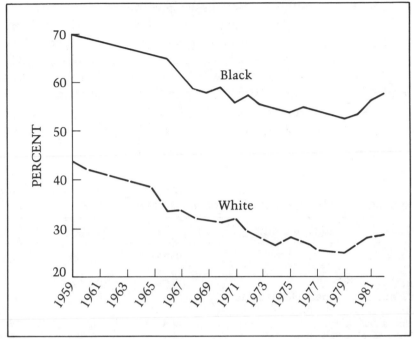

SOURCE: U.S. Bureau of the Census, "Characteristics of the Population Below the Poverty Level: 1982," *Current Population Reports*, series P-60, no. 144 (Washington, DC: U.S. Government Printing Office, 1984), table 1.

Since the late 1960s increases in Social Security income, disability benefits, and Medicare have greatly improved the economic situation of the elderly and the disabled, two other groups which have traditionally had high rates of poverty.[14] As a result, elderly and disabled householders and their families have become much less likely to reside in poverty. Little has been done to alleviate the economic strains in families maintained by a woman, and hence their likelihood of residing in poverty has remained high. An increasing proportion of the poverty population resides in families maintained by

[14]Lee Bowden and Frank Levy, "The Economic Well-Being of Families and Individuals," in John L. Palmer and Isabel V. Sawhill, eds., *The Reagan Experiment* (Washington, DC: Urban Institute Press, 1982), pp. 459–83, table 16–4; and Irvin Garfinkel and Sara McLanahan, *Single-Mother Families and Public Policy: A New American Dilemma?* (Washington, DC: Urban Institute, forthcoming).

women and, indeed, the term "feminization of poverty" has been used to describe changes among the poor.

Table 7.3 shows the changing composition of the poverty population. Between 1959 and 1982 the proportion of the poverty population which lived in female-maintained families increased from 18 to 36 percent, with most of this shift occurring in the 1960s. Among Blacks the increase was particularly dramatic: 60 percent in 1982, up from 24 percent in 1959. One would expect some increase in the share of the poverty population living in female-maintained families during this period simply because of the rapid growth in these families compared with other types of households. In 1959, for example,

TABLE 7.3

Changing Composition of the Black and White Poverty Population, Selected Years (numbers in thousands, percentage distribution)

Race and Household Status	1959	1972	1982
ALL RACES	39,490	24,460	34,398
Total Persons in Poverty	100.0%	100.0%	100.0%
In Families—Female Householder	17.8	33.2	35.5
Females Not in Families	8.5	14.2	12.0
In Families—Other	69.8	46.8	45.7
Males Not in Families	3.9	5.8	6.8
WHITE	28,484	16,203	23,517
Total Persons in Poverty	100.0%	100.0%	100.0%
In Families—Female Householder	14.9	23.3	25.9
Females Not in Families	10.1	18.0	14.0
In Families—Other	70.9	52.4	52.7
Males Not in Families	4.1	6.3	7.4
BLACK	9,927	7,710	9,697
Total Persons in Poverty	100.0%	100.0%	100.0%
In Families—Female Householder	24.3	53.7	59.9
Females Not in Families	4.9	6.9	7.5
In Families—Other	67.5	35.0	27.4
Males Not in Families	3.3	4.4	5.2

SOURCE: U.S. Bureau of the Census, "Characteristics of the Population Below the Poverty Level: 1982," *Current Population Reports*, series P-60, no. 144 (Washington, DC: U.S. Government Printing Office, 1984), table 1.

19 percent of all Blacks lived in families maintained by women compared with 36 percent in 1982—an increase of 17 percentage points.[15] However, the increase in the share of the poverty population living in female-maintained families is much larger than that accounted for by changing living arrangements.

Poverty rates calculated from the Current Population Survey only provide snapshots of the poor at one-year intervals. They do not allow one to assess the persistence of poverty for individuals in differing types of living arrangements. Fortunately, we now have fairly good information on the turnover of the poverty population from the PSID longitudinal study of 5,000 families. This study indicates that a fairly high proportion of the American population—one-quarter— experience poverty some time over a ten-year period. But for most, it is a temporary state, lasting for no more than one or two years. However, a subgroup of the poverty population remains in poverty for extended periods—the chronically poor. Whereas the temporarily poor do not differ much in composition from the general American public, the persistently poor are heavily concentrated in two overlapping groups: Black households and households maintained by women. Only about one-fifth of the population live in families maintained by a woman, but persons in these families account for over three-fifths of those who are persistently poor.[16]

Persistent poverty is concentrated more among Black than White women. One reason Black women are more likely to remain in poverty for extended periods is that they are much less likely to remarry following a divorce. In the longitudinal panel study, remarriage constituted the single most important event for raising the income of poor or near-poor female-maintained families. Estimates of how many such families would be raised from poverty if the householder worked full time showed that wage rates of these female householders were so low that the additional income often would not pull them out of poverty.[17]

[15]U.S. Bureau of the Census, "Characteristics of the Population Below the Poverty Level: 1982," *Current Population Reports*, series P-60, no. 144 (Washington, DC: U.S. Government Printing Office, 1984), table 1.

[16]Duncan, *Years of Poverty*, table 2.2.

[17]Duncan, *Years of Poverty*, chap. 2; Mary Corcoran and Martha S. Hill, "Unemployment and Poverty," *Social Service Review* 54 (September 1980):407–13; and Frank Levy, "The Intergenerational Transfer of Poverty," Working Paper no. 1241–02 (Washington, DC: Urban Institute, 1980).

Child Support

Because women generally earn much less than men, they frequently do not have sufficient earnings to adequately support a family. But women raising children by themselves face another serious economic problem: They often receive no child support from the absent father.

Data on the award and receipt of child support, collected in the April 1981 Current Population Survey, show that only about three-fifths of women raising a child under 21 were awarded child support for that child. Therefore two-fifths of women with dependent children have no legal claim, either via a court order or voluntary agreement, to receive support from an absent father. Of those who should have received payments in 1981, fewer than half of the women report receiving the full amount.[18] One-quarter received partial payment and a little over one-quarter received no payment at all.

In 1981 among those who were supposed to receive support payments the annual amount received was about $1,500 as compared with an annual amount actually due of $2,500. That is, on average payments made were almost $1,000 less than the amount due.[19]

Table 7.4 shows differences in award, recipiency, and amounts of child support received among women by race. Also shown are differences between all women and those in poverty. Black women are much less likely than White women to be awarded child support in the first place. Only 34 percent of Black women have been awarded support compared with 69 percent of White women.

The percentage of women who actually received support due differed far less between the racial groups than did the percentage awarded support. Whereas 73 percent of White women entitled to receive support in 1981 actually received some or all of that support, 67 percent of Black women in similar circumstances received support. The average annual amount received by Black women was considerably less than for White women, however: $1,600 compared with $2,200.

---

[18]Some women awarded child support are not entitled to receive it because children are past the age of eligibility or the absent father is deceased. U.S. Bureau of the Census, "Child Support and Alimony: 1981," *Current Population Reports, Special Studies*, series P-23, no. 124 (Washington, DC: U.S. Government Printing Office, 1983), tables A and 2.

[19]Those who received none of the support to which they were entitled are included in these calculations but excluded from the calculation of means in Table 7.4. U.S. Bureau of the Census, "Child Support," tables A and 2.

TABLE 7.4

Child Support Experience of White and Black Women, 1981

Women with Child Under 21, Father Absent	Total	White	Black
TOTAL WOMEN			
Percentage Awarded Child Support	59.2%	69.2%	33.8%
Percentage of Awarded Who Were Entitled to Receive Support	81.4	83.2	70.7
Percentage of Entitled Who Actually Received Support	71.8	72.5	67.0
Mean Amount Received by Recipients in 1981	$2,106	$2,180	$1,640
WOMEN BELOW POVERTY			
Percentage Awarded Child Support	39.7%	51.3%	26.6%
Percentage of Awarded Who Were Entitled to receive support	79.2	83.0	69.8
Percentage of Entitled Who Actually Received Support	61.4	59.6	66.4
Mean Amount Received by Recipients in 1981	$1,440	$1,499	$1,320

SOURCE: U.S. Bureau of the Census, "Child Support and Alimony: 1981," *Current Population Reports,* series P-23, no. 124 (Washington, DC: U.S. Government Printing Office, 1984), table 1.

Not surprisingly, child support awards are much more rare among women in poverty than among women in general—which is part of the reason these women and their families are in poverty. Only 40 percent of poor women with dependents are awarded child support compared with 59 percent of all unmarried women with dependents. The chances of women in poverty receiving support and the average amounts received also are considerably lower than for the population in general. Whereas receiving full support would often not raise these women and children out of poverty, the lack of full payment, and even more so the lack of an award of payment, contributes to the poverty situation of women and their dependent children.

Finally, the lack of financial support is only part of the problem faced by unmarried mothers. These women also suffer from excessive demands on their time, what Vickery has referred to as "time poverty."[20] They very often do not receive nonmonetary assistance

[20]Clair Vickery, "The Time-Poor: A New Look at Poverty," *Journal of Human Resources* 12 (Winter 1977):27–48.

in caring for the day-to-day needs of their family either. Their shortage of time as well as money limits the labor force options and economic well-being of female family householders.

Economic Well-Being of Women and Men

In chapter 6, we discussed the substantial inequality which exists in the earnings of women and men as well as the difficulty in determining the causes of these differences. In this chapter we have focused on the relation between women's labor market and family roles because women's financial well-being is conditional on their marital and family living arrangements as well as their own human capital and labor force participation.

One might argue that it is overall, or lifetime, economic well-being, more so than earnings, that should be independent of gender. Just as it is "unfair" that life expectancy is lower for a male child so, also, it would seem "unfair" if one sex more so than the other can expect a lower standard of living on average throughout life. Earnings differentials may exaggerate the inequality between men and women, given that most adult women marry and, as wives, benefit not only from their own labor force activity and income but also from that of their husband. But the problems women face in the labor market and in raising children alone suggest that the expected level of economic well-being is lower for women than men.

In reality, it is quite difficult, if not impossible, to quantify all aspects of economic well-being in order to compare the lifetime standard of living of women and men. However, in order to provide a somewhat more complete picture of the economic situation of adult women compared with adult men than is afforded by earnings differentials alone, we turn to a look at the per capita, family, and household income of men and women aged 15 and over. While earnings differences are an important focus, the income at the disposal of individuals is also important.

By allocating a family income to an individual in Table 7.5, we are assuming the sharing of income within families and/or within households. In looking at per capita income, we are refining our focus to a per person measure of money income available. This assumes equal division of income among persons sharing a household. Unlike the poverty measure, no adjustments for economies of scale

TABLE 7.5

Changes in Income of Women and Men (1980 dollars)

Income	1960	1970	1980	1960–70 Percent Change	1970–80 Percent Change
PER CAPITA INCOME					
Women	$4,943	$7,103	$7,540	43.7%	6.2%
Men	5,122	7,629	8,287	48.9	8.6
Ratio (W/M)	0.96	0.93	0.91		
FAMILY INCOME					
Women	$15,137	$21,429	$19,536	41.6	−8.8
Men	16,090	23,251	21,466	44.5	−7.7
Ratio (W/M)	0.94	0.92	0.91		
HOUSEHOLD INCOME					
Women	$15,729	$22,022	$21,490	40.0	−2.4
Men	16,733	23,937	23,848	43.1	−0.4
Ratio (W/M)	0.94	0.92	0.91		

SOURCE: 1960, 1970, 1980 Census 1/1,000 Public Use Microdata Sample.

for larger households are included in these calculations. More refined measures can be constructed, but there is no single agreed-upon procedure for equating needs of households of different size and composition.[21] Per capita income is easily calculated and a frequently used measure of economic well-being.

As can be seen in Table 7.5 which shows mean per capita, family, and household income amounts in 1960, 1970, and 1980 (adjusted to 1980 dollars), the relative income position of women and men is not as divergent as the relative earnings of male and female workers. This is, of course, because the majority of adults are married, with women benefiting from the income of their spouse. In 1960 per capita income of adult women was 96 percent of that of adult men ($4,900 on average compared with $5,100). Household and family income was about $1,000 less for women or about 94 percent of what it was for men. The difference arose because of the smaller

[21]For a discussion of some of the issues involved in developing a needs measure, see Suzanne M. Bianchi, *Household Composition and Racial Inequality* (New Brunswick, NJ: Rutgers University Press, 1981), chap. 2 and appendix. For another procedure for equating needs of households of differing size, see Edward P. Lazear and Robert T. Michael, "Family Size and the Distribution of Real Per Capita Income," *American Economic Review* 70 (March 1980):91–107.

proportion of women who were married and the lower level of income in female-maintained households.

In the subsequent two decades, as the proportion of men and women who were married declined, the relative well-being of women compared with men deteriorated. By 1980 the per capita income of men and women had risen substantially, with most of the real increase coming in the 1960s. But on average income rose slightly faster for men than for women, so that by 1980 the dollar gap separating the per capita income of men and women was about $750 and the per person income of women was 91 percent of that of men. Trends are similar for household and family income except that these measures suggest that real income actually declined in the 1970s, whereas per person income continued to grow as households became smaller.

Table 7.6 documents the per capita income differences between men and women by marital status. It is assumed that married men and women benefit equally from household income in these calculations. Per capita income levels of married men and women differ slightly because the proportion of married persons with an absent spouse is slightly higher for women than for men.

Focusing on the unmarried, the largest differences between men and women are for divorced or separated persons. In 1960 the per capita income of divorced women was only 62 percent of that of divorced men. Divorced women have lower household income and larger households than men, since women usually retain custody of children following a divorce.[22]

After 1960 the relative income position of divorced women deteriorated. By 1970 per capita income of divorced women was only 52 percent of that of divorced men, subsequently increasing to 56 percent in 1980 although still below the 62 percent level in 1960. Throughout the 1960–80 period, per capita income increased for both sexes, but the increase was only 56 percent for divorced women compared with 72 percent for divorced men. As a greater proportion of divorced women came to live independently and support themselves

---

[22]Child support amounts have not been subtracted from the household income of men and are presumably included in the household income of women. But as we have seen, these amounts are fairly modest and often not paid. Cain adjusts for child care payments and finds that this affects ratios of female to male income amounts by a trivial amount (that is, 1 percent). See Glen Cain, "Welfare Economics of Policies Toward Women," *Journal of Labor Economics* 3 (January 1985 supplement):S375–96, table 3.

TABLE 7.6

Changes in Per Capita Income of Black and White Women and Men by Marital Status (1980 dollars)

Marital Status	Total			White			Black		
	1960	1970	1980	1960	1970	1980	1960	1970	1980
TOTAL, 15 Years and Over									
Women	$4,943	$7,104	$7,540	$5,207	$7,472	$8,024	$2,610	$4,068	$4,673
Men	5,172	7,629	8,287	5,411	7,950	8,715	2,903	4,744	5,592
Ratio (W/M)	0.96	0.93	0.91	0.96	0.94	0.92	0.90	0.86	0.84
MARRIED [Including Spouse Absent]									
Women	$5,087	$7,509	$8,077	$5,296	$7,760	$8,388	$2,774	$4,696	$5,573
Men	5,149	7,580	8,139	5,354	7,829	8,448	2,824	4,786	5,676
Ratio (W/M)	0.99	0.99	0.99	0.99	0.99	0.99	0.98	0.98	0.98
WIDOWED									
Women	$4,385	$6,230	$6,924	$4,679	$6,625	$7,355	$2,326	$3,377	$4,173
Men	5,279	8,203	8,694	5,585	8,849	9,396	3,342	4,379	4,925
Ratio (W/M)	0.83	0.76	0.80	0.84	0.75	0.78	0.70	0.77	0.85
DIVORCED/SEPARATED									
Women	$4,034	$5,578	$6,386	$4,524	$6,255	$7,058	$2,622	$3,576	$4,377
Men	6,516	10,711	11,440	7,181	11,664	12,386	4,183	7,229	7,787
Ratio (W/M)	0.62	0.52	0.56	0.63	0.54	0.57	0.63	0.49	0.56
NEVER MARRIED									
Women	$5,040	$6,872	$7,011	$5,391	$7,394	$7,781	$2,348	$3,601	$4,044
Men	5,030	7,158	7,795	5,349	7,629	8,419	2,622	4,021	4,858
Ratio (W/M)	1.00	0.96	0.90	1.01	0.97	0.92	0.90	0.90	0.83

SOURCE: 1960, 1970, 1980 Census 1/1,000 Public Use Microdata Sample.

and dependents solely on their own earnings or income,[23] their economic well-being vis-à-vis divorced men deteriorated.

Widowed women are relatively better off than divorced women. In 1960 widows had a per capita income 83 percent of that of widowers. This also declined to 76 percent by 1970, but in 1980 the ratio stood at 80 percent. The decline in relative well-being occurred only among Whites, however. The ratio of per capita income of Black widows to widowers increased from 70 to 85 percent between 1960 and 1980.

Per capita income of the never married was quite similar for both males and females in 1960. White women and men had almost equal levels of well-being and Black women's per capita income was 90 percent of that of Black men. This appearance of equality in part arises from the fact that the calculations include persons aged 15 to 19, which heavily weights the never-married population by persons in their teens, many of whom were still living in their parental homes. In 1960, in particular, unmarried young adults were much less likely to leave the parental home to form independent households. As the composition of the never-married population has shifted with delayed marriage and more young men and women living on their own and supporting themselves, the lower earnings of women relative to men has become a more important variable in the well-being of this group. Between 1960 and 1980 the relative well-being of never-married women deteriorated. By 1980 the per capita income levels of White women had declined to 92 percent of those of men. Among Black women they were down to 83 percent.

Estimates of gender differences in lifetime household and per capita income by Cain suggest a more unequal picture of well-being for men and women than the cross-sectional estimates of per capita income presented in Tables 7.5 and 7.6.[24] Cain assumes that husbands and wives share income equally, but differences arise from the dissimilar household incomes and household sizes of men and women in the unmarried state and from the sex difference in the proportion of the lifetime spent in the unmarried state. He estimates that over a lifetime, the per capita well-being of women is about 67

[23]See Suzanne M. Bianchi and Reynolds Farley, "Racial Differences in Family Living Arrangements and Economic Well-Being: An Analysis of Recent Trends," *Journal of Marriage and the Family* 41 (August 1979):537–51, table 2.

[24]Cain, "Welfare Economics," table 3.

percent of that of men and the household income of women about 81 percent of that of men.

Cain shows that the relative income position of women vis-à-vis men is better than their relative earnings position over their lifetime—that is, the household income and per capita income of women are much more equal to that of men than are earnings. But he notes that leisure inequities no doubt exist since unmarried women maintain larger households on average than unmarried men. However, these are not explicitly considered in his calculations.

These lifetime income estimates are hypothetical but illustrative. Women benefit from income other than their own earnings, making their economic well-being less dire than earnings differences alone would suggest. Still, women spend enough years supporting themselves and their dependents that the earnings inequalities between them and men have serious implications for lifetime well-being. Women on average probably do not enjoy the level of income and economic well-being that men do. And the situation of unmarried women may have deteriorated somewhat relative to men over the past two decades.

Summary

We have reviewed the economic significance of women's labor force participation and earnings for families. Husband-wife couples have come to rely on the earnings of both husband and wife. The proportion of family income contributed by the wife has increased, and in a significant and growing minority of couples the wife's earnings are the major source of income in any given year.

As husband-wife couples have come to rely on earnings from both partners, female-maintained households have become less likely to have earnings from anyone other than the householder. The relative income of female-maintained households to husband-wife households has declined, and an increasing proportion of the poverty population live in households managed by a woman. Racial differentials are extremely large, and a majority of the black poverty population lives in female-maintained families.

The economic problems of women maintaining families without a spouse present stem from the low average earnings of these women, which ill-equip them to support a family by themselves. Furthermore, many are never awarded child support or do not receive it when awarded.

When measured by per capita income, women's economic well-being over a lifetime is more equal to that of men than are their earnings. But women are less well-off than men because they have lower incomes than men during the years they spend outside a marital relationship, they spend a somewhat greater proportion of their lives living on their own, and they are often supporting children during those years.

From a purely economic standpoint, given the relatively high economic well-being of wives, it benefits women to marry and remain married. The fact that more and more women are divorcing or separating suggests either that changes in marital status are frequently not the result of women's choice or that the psychic costs of remaining in some marriages are so high that women are willing to accept the economic loss that accompanies a divorce. As long as the earnings of women are less than those of men and as long as the care and support of children following a divorce disproportionately fall to women, marital disruption will have a more adverse effect on the economic well-being of women and children than on men.

8

WORK, HOME, AND CHILDREN:
THE BALANCING ACT

P REVIOUS chapters have summarized the ways in which women's lives are more complex now than they were in the past. Among young women, rising educational attainment and later age at marriage have interacted to produce a wider range of occupational choices and accumulation of work experience. Among married women, fertility has declined and labor force participation has risen. There have always been wives and mothers who worked outside the home, but until the last several years they were the exceptions rather than the rule. Now approximately half of all wives combine traditional family responsibilities with employment obligations. How women balance these competing demands on their time is the topic of this chapter.

One initial strategy may be to delay marriage or childbearing until some work experience is gained. Women today can control their fertility in ways their grandmothers could not, and delayed childbearing is a choice made by increasing numbers of women. Women with children may balance competing demands by working part time or by choosing occupations with hours compatible with childrearing. Chapter 5 showed that 52 percent of all employed women work part time or part year, and half of all professionally employed women are school teachers or nurses—jobs which permit some amount of flexibility in scheduling.

Hiring household help, eating at restaurants, and making child care arrangements are other ways in which the conflict between women's dual roles as caregivers and wage earners is resolved. But employed wives continue to perform the major share of household tasks, and adequate child care arrangements are not always easy to make.

A common lament among many working mothers is that they sometimes feel guilty. When they are at work they worry about not spending enough time with their children, and when they are at home with a sick child they are worried about not being on the job. These psychological side-effects of labor force participation are less well documented than the demographic facts which lead to their occurrence. We know how many mothers work, but it is more difficult to assess the effects of work on women and their families.

One change that may help reconcile possible role conflict is the shift in attitudes about what constitutes proper sex role behavior. Stereotypes have eased with time, and many more men and women now approve of women working outside the home. As it becomes increasingly acceptable for women to be employed, some of the psychological pressure on women and their families should be alleviated.

Historically, most married women have raised children, but they have never been in the labor force in their current numbers. Smaller families are associated with higher rates of employment, but it is not clear which comes first—lower fertility or greater propensity to work.

Labor Force Participation and Fertility

In 1970 Bumpass and Westoff asked, "Do women limit their fertility in order to have time to pursue their non-family-oriented interests, or do women work if their fertility permits them to do so?"[1] This question has become the demographic equivalent of Freud's classic "What do women want?" After years of research the answer is still not clear.

[1]Larry L. Bumpass and Charles F. Westoff, *The Later Years of Childbearing* (Princeton, NJ: Princeton University Press, 1970).

Women who work outside the home have fewer children than women who are not employed.[2] In 1983 employed women aged 18 to 34 had an average of 0.8 children while women not in the labor force had an average of 1.7 children. Thirteen percent of employed women expect to remain childless compared with only 6 percent of women not in the labor force.[3]

On one side of the debate are those who argue that the strongest causal relationship is the effect of fertility on labor force participation: The presence of and the ages of children determine whether a woman will be in the labor force.[4] The greater the number of children and the younger their ages, the less likely it is that a woman will work outside the home. Women are most likely to work before marriage, less likely to work between marriage and first birth, and least likely to work between their first and second births. They then return to the labor force when their children are in preschool or school.[5] At least one researcher, however, has pointed out that after two or three births, the financial needs of the family can create significant pressure for the woman to work.[6]

Others argue that the strongest causal direction is from labor force participation to completed fertility. Young women who plan to work reduce their fertility in order to achieve labor force goals.[7] Representative of this side of the debate are the findings that women's

[2]Theodore H. Groat, Randy L. Workman, and Arthur G. Neal, "Labor Force Participation and Family Formation: A Study of Working Mothers," *Demography* 13 (February 1976):115–26; and Robert H. Weller, "Wife's Employment and Cumulative Family Size in the United States, 1970 and 1960," *Demography* 14 (February 1977):43–65.

[3]U.S. Bureau of the Census, "Fertility of American Women: June 1983 (Advance Report)," *Current Population Reports*, series P-20, no. 386 (Washington, DC: U.S. Government Printing Office, 1984), table 2.

[4]Lynne Smith-Lovin and Ann R. Tickamyer, "Nonrecursive Models of Labor Force Participation, Fertility Behavior, and Sex Role Attitudes," *American Sociological Review* 43 (August 1978):541–57; Lynne Smith-Lovin and Ann R. Tickamyer, "Models of Fertility and Women's Work: Comment on Cramer, ASR, April 1980," *American Sociological Review* 47 (August 1982):561–66; and James Sweet, *Women in the Labor Force* (New York: Seminar Press, 1973).

[5]National Center for Health Statistics, "Patterns of Employment Before and After Childbirth," *Vital and Health Statistics*, series 23, no. 4 (Washington, DC: U.S. Government Printing Office, 1980), p. 2.

[6]Elise F. Jones, "Ways in Which Childbearing Affects Women's Employment: Evidence from the U.S. 1975 National Fertility Study," *Population Studies* 36 (March 1982):5–14.

[7]Linda J. Waite and Ross M. Stolzenberg, "Intended Childbearing and Labor Force Participation of Young Women: Insights from Nonrecursive Models," *American Sociological Review* 41 (April 1976):235–52; and Ross M. Stolzenberg and Linda J. Waite, "Age, Fertility Expectations, and Plans for Employment," *American Sociological Review* 42 (October 1977):769–83.

plans to participate in the labor force at age 35 have a substantial effect on the total number of children they expect to have, while number of children expected has little effect on future labor force plans.[8] In general, working depresses fertility by competing for a woman's time. Women who work after marriage tend to delay the birth of the first child and may either delay the second birth or have another child quickly with an eye toward compressing time out of the labor force.[9]

Models that allow for reciprocal causation between fertility and labor force participation have not fully resolved the controversy. Cramer found that fertility affects employment in the short run and employment affects fertility in the long run.[10] Bean, Stephen, and Burr report that early employment reduces intended but not unintended fertility, while unintended childbearing deters subsequent working more than intended fertility.[11] Finally, some argue that the relationship between employment and fertility is spurious and caused by antecedent variables such as education and age at first marriage.[12] Whatever the relationship, childbearing must be a matter of individual, rational choice before any mechanism can operate.[13]

The inherent chicken-and-egg nature of this debate may explain why it is so hard to resolve. And which comes first probably matters more to academic researchers than to the women actually involved. This may be a case where correlation is more important than causation, and the best explanation for the negative correlation between employment and fertility seems to be that the role of mother often conflicts with the role of paid employee in our society.[14]

[8]Waite and Stolzenberg, "Intended Childbearing."

[9]Elise F. Jones, "The Impact of Women's Employment on Marital Fertility in the U.S., 1970–75," *Population Studies* 35 (July 1981):161–73.

[10]James C. Cramer, "Fertility and Female Employment," *American Sociological Review* 45 (April 1980):167–90; and James C. Cramer, "Models of Fertility and Women's Work: Reply" *American Sociological Review* 47 (August 1982):566–67.

[11]Frank D. Bean, Elizabeth H. Stephen, and Jeffrey A. Burr, "The Temporal Relationship between Labor Force Participation and Intended and Unintended Fertility: Racial and Religious Comparisons in the United States," *Texas Population Research Center Papers*, no. 6.007 (Austin: University of Texas, 1984).

[12]Geraldine B. Terry, "Rival Explanations in the Work-Fertility Relationship," *Population Studies* 29 (July 1975):191–205; and Jacob Mincer, "Market Prices, Opportunity Costs, and Income Effects," in Carl F. Christ, ed., *Measurement in Economics, Studies in Mathematical Economics, and Econometrics in Memory of Yehuda Grunfeld* (Stanford, CA: Stanford University Press, 1973), pp. 67–82.

[13]Jones, "The Impact," p. 172.

[14]Steven D. McLaughlin, "Differential Patterns of Female Labor Force Participation Surrounding the First Birth," *Journal of Marriage and the Family* 44 (May 1982):407–20; and William B. Clifford and Patricia Tobin, "Labor Force Participation of Working Mothers and Family Formation: Some Further Evidence," *Demography* 14 (August 1977):273–84.

Cross-cultural studies find no such negative relationship in developing countries where mothers work at home or have others in the household to share child care.[15] However, in the United States and in industrialized countries in general, the majority of paid employment opportunities are outside the home and child care is primarily the responsibility of the mother. Thus, there is an incompatibility of roles for American women that necessitates a choice between a large family and strong labor force attachment. The primary reason most women give for not working is their home responsibilities,[16] and many mothers report that they would look for work or work more hours if better child care arrangements were available.[17]

Child Care Arrangements

The proportion of mothers in the labor force has grown dramatically since the 1950s, from 18 to 57 percent. Increases for mothers of preschoolers have been particularly striking. As Figure 8.1 shows, only 12 percent of married women who had children under age 6 were working in 1950 compared with nearly 50 percent by 1980. In each decade the rates have increased, but the increases among those with preschoolers were greater in the 1960s than in the 1950s and greater yet in the 1970s.

Mothers of school-age children are also increasingly likely to work outside the home. In 1950 only 28 percent of women whose youngest child was over age 6 were in the labor force. Today it is over 60 percent. Looked at from the children's perspective, 54 percent of all children under age 18 in 1981 had mothers in the labor force; 45 percent of all preschoolers had working mothers.[18]

In actual numbers, 6 million women aged 18 to 44 with a preschooler were in the labor force in 1982, an increase of 1.3 million

---

[15]J. Mayone Stycos and Robert H. Weller, "Female Working Roles and Fertility," *Demography* 4 (1967):210–17; and Robert H. Weller, "The Employment of Wives, Role Incompatibility and Fertility," *Milbank Memorial Fund Quarterly* 46 (Fall 1969):507–26.

[16]U.S. Department of Labor, *Perspectives on Working Women: A Databook*, bulletin 2080 (Washington, DC: U.S. Government Printing Office, 1980), table 14.

[17]Martin O'Connell and Carolyn C. Rogers, "Child Care Arrangements of Working Mothers: June 1982," *Current Population Reports*, series P-23, no. 129 (Washington, DC: U.S. Government Printing Office, 1983); and Harriet B. Presser and Wendy Baldwin, "Child Care as a Constraint on Employment: Prevalence, Correlates, and Bearing on the Work and Fertility Nexus," *American Journal of Sociology* 85 (March 1980):1202–13.

[18]Allyson S. Grossman, "More Than Half of All Children Have Working Mothers," *Monthly Labor Review* 105 (February 1982):41–43.

FIGURE 8.1

*Trend in Labor Force Participation Rates of Mothers
With Children Under 18*

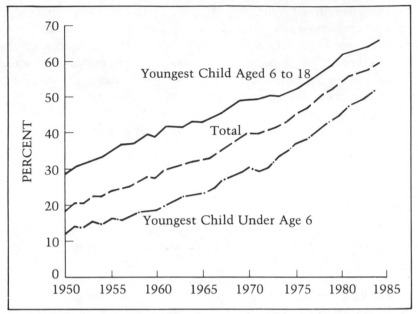

NOTE: Rates are given for married women only.

SOURCE: Elizabeth Waldman, "Labor Force Statistics from a Family Perspective," *Monthly Labor Review* 106 (December 1983), table 2; Howard Hayghe, "Working Mothers Reach Record Number in 1984," *Monthly Labor Review*, vol. 107 (December 1984), table 1.

women since 1977.[19] The involvement of such large numbers of women means that child care arrangements are of increasing importance. What was once an individual concern for a minority of mothers is rapidly becoming an issue for the majority.

Trends in child care arrangements show that fewer children were being cared for in their homes in the 1980s than in the 1950s (see Table 8.1). In 1958 just over one-half of all mothers employed full time relied on day care in the home; by 1982 that proportion had dropped to about one-quarter. Use of care in another home rose from 27 to 44 percent, and use of group care centers rose from 4 to 19 percent among mothers employed full time. Mothers who work part time are more likely to use home care than full-time workers, but

[19]O'Connell and Rogers, "Child Care Arrangements," p. 1.

TABLE 8.1
Child Care Arrangements of Working Mothers, Selected Years

Type of Child Care Arrangement	Worked Full Time				Worked Part Time			
	1958	1965	1977	1982	1958	1965	1977	1982
Total	100.0%	100.0%	100.0%	100.0%	(N/A)	100.0%	100.0%	100.0%
Care in Child's Home	56.6	47.2	28.6	25.7	(N/A)	47.0	42.7	39.3
By Father	14.7	10.3	10.6	10.3	(N/A)	22.9	23.1	20.3
By Other Relative	27.7	18.4	11.4	10.3	(N/A)	15.6	11.2	12.7
By Nonrelative	14.2	18.5	6.6	5.1	(N/A)	8.6	8.4	6.3
Care in Another Home	27.1	37.3	47.4	43.8	(N/A)	17.0	28.8	34.0
By Relative	14.5	17.6	20.8	19.7	(N/A)	9.1	13.2	15.6
By Nonrelative	12.7	19.6	26.6	24.1	(N/A)	7.9	15.6	18.4
Group Care Center	4.5	8.2	14.6	18.8	(N/A)	2.7	9.1	7.5
Child Cares for Self	0.6	0.3	0.3	—	(N/A)	0.9	0.5	—
Mother Cares for Child While Working	11.2	6.7	8.2	6.2	(N/A)	32.3	18.5	14.4
All Other Arrangements	—	0.4	0.8	0.3	(N/A)	—	0.4	0.1
Don't Know/No Answer	—	—	—	5.3	(N/A)	—	—	4.7

NOTE: Data for children under age 6 of ever-married women, 1958 and 1965; data for youngest two children under age 5 of ever-married women in 1977; data for youngest child under age 5 of all women in 1982.

SOURCE: Marjorie Lueck, Ann C. Orr, and Martin O'Connell, "Trends in Child Care Arrangements of Working Mothers," *Current Population Reports*, series P-23, no. 117, U.S. Bureau of the Census (Washington, DC: U.S. Government Printing Office, 1982), table A; Martin O'Connell and Carolyn C. Rogers, "Child Care Arrangements of Working Mothers: June 1982," *Current Population Reports*, series P-23, no. 129, U.S. Bureau of the Census (Washington, DC: U.S. Government Printing Office, 1982), table A.

the shift away from home care to other arrangements has also characterized part-time workers.

In 1982, 10 percent of mothers who worked full time relied on the child's father as the principal caregiver while they were at work. Child care by the father was most common among women who worked part time: About 20 percent of mothers who worked part time reported fathers as the caregivers.

Presser and Cain estimate that one-third of dual-earner couples with children in which both the husband and wife work full time have at least one spouse working a schedule other than a regular daytime shift. For 15 percent of these couples there is very little overlap between the work schedules of the husband and wife, which suggests that shift work may be the couple's solution to child care.[20] Women may choose part-time work in an attempt to stagger their work hours for compatibility with the husband's hours, so that the family's total work day is tailored to child care demands.[21]

Of course, a woman may be working part time (instead of not at all) because her husband is out of work. Among husbands who were the principal child caregivers in 1982 while their wives worked, 24 percent were unemployed.[22] Thus, fathers who take care of their children may be doing so only temporarily while looking for work.

Concern with adequate child care is a necessary component of women's work decisions. The younger the child, the greater are the constraints. Managing the child care–career nexus appears to play a large role in specific employment decisions of many mothers. Women work closer to home than men, partly because their family responsibilities increase the costs of a longer commute.[23] "Convenient" work (that is, working at home, within walking distance of home, or part time) reduces the constraints of children on employed mothers.[24] It is not only personal choices, but area characteristics that determine the convenience factor. Stolzenberg and Waite found that children affected their mother's likelihood of working in direct

[20]Harriet B. Presser and Virginia Cain, "Shift Work Among Dual-Earner Couples with Children," *Science* 219 (February 18, 1983):876–78.

[21]Steven L. Nock and Paul W. Kingston, "The Family Work Day," *Journal of Marriage and the Family* 46 (May 1984):333–43.

[22]O'Connell and Rogers, "Child Care Arrangements," table C.

[23]Janice F. Madden, "Why Women Work Closer to Home," *Urban Studies* 18 (June 1981):181–94.

[24]Jean Darian, "Convenience of Work and the Job Constraint of Children," *Demography* 12 (May 1975):245–58.

proportion to the cost and availability of child care, and the "convenience" of jobs where the family lived.[25]

One constraint on working mothers in organizing child care is the need for multiple arrangements. Approximately 17 percent of employed mothers in 1982 used more than one type of child care. Women employed part time are slightly more likely to use multiple child care arrangements than women who work full time (19 versus 16 percent), possibly due to more erratic work hours or temporary work. Women are most likely to rely on several sources of child care when the principal caregiver is the father, and the most frequent type of secondary care is in another person's home.[26]

A substantial minority of mothers not in the labor force say they would look for work if reasonably priced child care were available. In 1982 one-quarter of mothers not in the labor force said they would look for work if they could find good child care. Nearly half of unmarried mothers and one-third of low-income mothers said they would look for work if they could get child care.[27] These are the women with the greatest need to work and the fewest resources to enable them to work. About one mother in ten employed full-time and one mother in five employed part time say they would work more hours per week if satisfactory child care were available.[28] These statistics suggest that the child care needs of American women are not being fully met, due to either a lack of facilities or prohibitive costs.

Although finding good child care may be a problem, successful arrangements can be used to reconcile the role conflict women may feel between mothering and working. Transferring some child care responsibilities to others helps the "mothers of young children mediate the conflicting obligations of their maternal and other social and economic roles."[29] Limiting fertility expectations is another means by which women reduce role conflict. Powers and Salvo found that regular child care use was negatively associated with future birth expectations. A desire to work on the part of young moth-

---

[25]Ross M. Stolzenberg and Linda J. Waite, "Local Labor Markets, Children, and Labor Force Participation of Wives," *Demography* 21 (May 1984):157–70.

[26]O'Connell and Rogers, "Child Care Arrangements," pp. 13 and 14.

[27]O'Connell and Rogers, "Child Care Arrangements," table H.

[28]O'Connell and Rogers, "Child Care Arrangements," table F.

[29]Mary G. Powers and Joseph J. Salvo, "Fertility and Child Care Arrangements as Mechanisms of Status Articulation," *Journal of Marriage and the Family* 44 (February 1982):21–34.

ers not in the labor force was also negatively associated with future birth expectations. These findings suggest that labor force experience and plans affect fertility behavior. Since working is often an economic necessity, particularly for unmarried mothers, limiting fertility may be the easiest way to reduce potential conflicts between family and employment obligations.

International Comparisons

The United States is not alone in facing the increasing importance of alternate child care arrangements. Many other industrialized nations have seen recent rises in the number of women in the labor force.[30] For example, approximately 70 percent of Scandinavian women worked outside the home in the 1970s. In addition, a higher proportion of Scandinavian mothers of young children were in the labor force than American mothers. In 1975, 61 percent of Swedish women with children under age 7 were in the labor force compared with 39 percent of American women with children under age 6.[31]

The Swedish government provides a wide variety of social services which include many child care benefits and facilities. Nearly 50 percent of all Swedish children under age 7 with a working "guardian" were in municipal day care in 1980. Although the form of data collection prevents perfect comparison, 13 percent of American preschoolers with employed mothers were in group day care in 1977.[32]

The Federal Republic of Germany (FRG) does not encourage female labor force participation because fertility is below replacement level. Yet 35 percent of West German women with children under age 6 were in the labor force in 1979. Family child care is the predominant arrangement in the FRG, with 74 percent of children under age 3 cared for in their homes in 1975. Nearly 50 percent of that care was provided by grandparents. Only 15 percent of working mothers used a public day care arrangement.[33]

[30]Jacob Mincer, "Intercountry Comparisons of Labor Force Trends and Related Developments: An Overview," *Journal of Labor Economics* 3 (January 1985 supplement), table 1.

[31]Marjorie Lueck, Ann C. Orr, and Martin O'Connell, "Trends in Child Care Arrangements of Working Mothers," *Current Population Reports, Special Studies*, series P-23, no. 17, U.S. Bureau of the Census (Washington, DC: U.S. Government Printing Office, 1982), table O.

[32]Lueck, Orr, and O'Connell, "Trends in Child Care," table P.

[33]Lueck, Orr, and O'Connell, "Trends in Child Care," table T.

The rate of female labor force participation shows no sign of declining in industrialized nations. Meeting the child care needs of families to enable women to resolve some of the inherent role conflicts between mothering and working is a challenge in other countries as well as in the United States.

Employment and Household Chores

"A woman's work is never done" is a cliché most girls hear while growing up, but they probably fail to appreciate the homily until they start to work, marry, and have children. They find that a 20- or 40-hour work week outside the home does not exempt them from tasks inside the home. Individual couples may resolve the "chore wars" to their satisfaction, but most employed wives do more housework than most employed husbands.

Regardless of the sample or methodology used, every study to date on the household division of labor has found that women perform more household tasks than men.[34] This relationship applies to couples in which the wife works full time and those in which she works part time or not at all. The relationship also appears to be relatively stable over time despite increased numbers of women entering the labor force. Data gathered in the 1970s do not differ significantly from data for the 1960s.

Geerken and Gove found only one group of household tasks in which husbands participated more than wives: "handyman" and yard maintenance. Paying the bills was about equally divided between husbands and wives, while four other tasks were shouldered mainly by the wife: cleaning house, meal preparation, doing dishes, and child care (of these four, child care was most often shared). Among

---

[34]Sarah F. Berk, "Husbands at Home: Organization of the Husband's Household Day," in Karen Wolk Feinstein, ed., *Working Women and Families* (Beverly Hills, CA: Sage, 1979), pp. 125–58; Richard Berk and Sarah Berk, *Labor and Leisure at Home: Content and Organization of the Household Day* (Beverly Hills, CA: Sage, 1979); Michael Geerken and Walter R. Gove, *At Home and at Work: The Family's Allocation of Labor* (Beverly Hills, CA: Sage, 1983); Sar A. Levitan and Richard S. Belous, "Working Wives and Mothers: What Happens to Family Life?" *Monthly Labor Review* 104 (September 1981):26–30; Suzanne Model, "Housework by Husbands: Determinants and Implications," *Journal of Family Issues* 2 (June 1981):225–37; Sharon Y. Nickols and Edward Metzen, "Impact of Wife's Employment upon Husband's Housework," *Journal of Family Issues* 3 (June 1982):199–216; and Joanne Vanek, "Time Spent in Housework," *Scientific American* 231 (November 1974):116–20.

families in which the wife was not employed, just over 25 percent of wives were solely responsible for cleaning compared with fewer than 1 percent of husbands. Nearly 50 percent of nonworking wives were the only ones who prepared meals and 33 percent did dishes alone compared with fewer than 2 percent of husbands who tackled either task alone.[35]

Among families in which the wife was employed, proportionately fewer wives had sole responsibility for these tasks, but husbands showed no greater propensity to help. Working wives' responsibilities for traditionally female chores are relieved, if at all, by children or paid help. When children are available, their fathers make the smallest contributions on all measures of housework.[36]

Diary methods of recording household tasks show that wives allocate more time than husbands do to a wide range of household and child care activities. Morning routines for husbands are characterized by getting ready for work, while morning routines for wives involve kitchen and child care duties. Wives averaged almost 50 percent more morning activities than husbands did. There was little difference in activities between husbands with employed wives and those with wives not in the labor force, except that husbands with employed wives were more likely to make the bed.[37]

When the actual difference in hours spent on housework is compared, the figures can be discouraging for women. A six-year panel study of time allocation from 1968 to 1973 found that husbands averaged 2 hours a week in household chores compared with 35 hours a week for wives. Among couples in which both spouses were employed, the wife's time spent doing housework dropped to an average of 23 hours per week but the husband's time did not increase.[38] Presumably the difference was being made up by children, paid help, or lower standards of housekeeping.

Other data from the late 1960s and early 1970s show that working wives averaged 65 hours a week on combined jobs inside and outside the home versus about 57 hours per week for husbands. Data from the mid-1970s show more similarity between total work time of wives and husbands, but husbands performed only about 3

[35]Geerken and Gove, *At Home and at Work.*
[36]Model, "Housework by Husbands."
[37]Berk, "Husbands at Home"; and Berk and Berk, *Labor and Leisure.*
[38]Nickols and Metzen, "Impact of Wife's Employment."

hours of housework per week compared with 18 hours a week for wives.[39]

Husbands are most likely to participate in housework when their wives are highly educated and employed. However, the effect of education on attitudes toward the appropriate division of labor is influenced by the husband's income: As husband's income goes up, his chore involvement goes down. High-income men do more housework only if their wives earn comparable incomes; otherwise they do the least.[40]

Berk sees husbands as an "untapped potential for social change" which could ease the conflicting role demands women face.[41] Model is not so optimistic.[42] She proposes that family duties interfere with women's career development. Women's family roles intrude on their work roles, whereas men's work roles are more likely to intrude on their family roles. Husbands can "take work home" in ways that advance their careers, while "taking home to work" limits wives' career development.[43] As long as men have relatively few household responsibilities and women have so many, a cycle may be set up whereby women choose or accept lower occupational status and earnings, which in turn affects their "bargaining power" at home. This type of cycle and the discrepancy in household chores on which it feeds may affect the psychological well-being of women and their families.

Employment and Psychological Well-Being

Until recently, most people considered it "natural" for women to take care of the home and for men to work outside the home. Sociologist Talcott Parsons is famous for his theory of sex role differentiation, in which he proposed that the success of the marriage institution depends on role complementarity between husband and

---

[39]Sandra L. Hofferth and Kristin A Moore, "Women's Employment and Marriage," in Ralph W. Smith, ed., *The Subtle Revolution* (Washington, DC: Urban Institute, 1979), pp. 99–124; and Frank P. Stafford, "Women's Use of Time Converging with Men's," *Monthly Labor Review* (December 1980):57–58.

[40]Model, "Housework by Husbands."

[41]Berk, "Husbands at Home."

[42]Model, "Housework by Husbands."

[43]Joseph Pleck, "The Work-Family Role System," *Social Problems* 24 (April 1977):417–27.

wife.[44] That is, marriage works best when men perform the "instrumental" functions of earning a living and women perform the "expressive" functions of homemaking. The husband's occupation links the family to the larger socioeconomic system, while the wife's caretaking fulfills the family's emotional needs. Parsons proposed that such a sexual division of labor within the family leads to marital solidarity.

Parsons was more concerned with the survival of the family unit as a system than with the marital satisfaction of individual husbands and wives. He was also writing during a pronatalist period of unusually high fertility, low divorce rates, and low rates of labor force participation by women. But Parsons merely cast in academic terms what many people believe is the natural order of the universe. Popular wisdom suggests that when that order is violated, people will be unhappy, marriages will dissolve, and society will suffer.

Have society and individuals suffered as a result of more women entering the labor force? The divorce rate has risen over the last twenty years, but the fact that divorce is correlated with higher female labor force participation does not mean that it is caused by working women. There is also evidence that the divorce rate has recently leveled off in a period when the highest proportion of women are working. And most divorced people eventually remarry, indicating that the institution of marriage is not at risk.

Most studies have shown that working women and their families are doing quite well. Although there are no longitudinal data on marital satisfaction or adjustment before and after the wife enters the labor force, cross-sectional studies show that couples and families can benefit from working wives and mothers. Women themselves seem to be physically healthiest when working. Data from the National Health Interview Survey of 1977–78 revealed that working women had fewer days of illness and felt better than non-working women. Women who combine marriage, children, and work tend to be healthier than unmarried or unemployed women.[45]

[44]Talcott Parsons, "The Social Structure of the Family," in Ruth N. Anshen, ed., *The Family: Its Function and Destiny* (New York: Harper, 1949), pp. 173–201; and Talcott Parsons, "The American Family: Its Relations to Personality and to the Social Structure," in Talcott Parsons and Robert F. Bales, eds., *Family, Socialization, and Interaction Process* (New York: Macmillan, 1955), pp. 3–33.

[45]Lois M. Verbrugge and Jennifer H. Madans, "Women's Roles and Health," *American Demographics* 7 (March 1985):36–39.

Effects of Wife's Employment on Marriage

Simpson and England found that wives' employment actually improves marital interaction in the opinion of both spouses.[46] Marital solidarity was greatest for wives with high-status occupations married to husbands with high-status occupations. Simpson and England propose a theory of "role homophily" to replace Parsons' "role differentiation." That is, similarity of roles between husband and wife builds greater marital solidarity than role complementarity.

Houseknecht and Macke found that it is not actual employment that determines the marital adjustment of professional women, but the extent to which the family can accommodate to that employment.[47] Having a supportive husband who shares similar work values and having freedom from childrearing responsibilities contribute to higher marital adjustment among professionally employed women.

Houseknecht and Macke's sample of highly educated women is unique because it is a sample of women married to men of either similar or lesser educational status. There was no relationship between educational similarity and overall marital adjustment, suggesting that educational "superiority" of the wife is not a significant indicator of marital dissatisfaction. Similarly, Richardson found no support for the hypothesis that marital stress and dissatisfaction are associated with a wife's having a higher occupational status than her husband.[48] However, a study by Hornung and McCullough suggests that adverse effects on marital and life satisfaction result from incompatible educational and occupational statuses of spouses, and Pearlin makes a similar claim about incompatible social class backgrounds of husbands and wives.[49]

The best chances for marital satisfaction occur when both partners agree on the wife's employment status. That is, if both husband

[46]Ida Harper Simpson and Paula England, "Conjugal Work Roles and Marital Solidarity," *Journal of Family Issues* 2 (June 1981):180–204.

[47]Sharon K. Houseknecht and Anne S. Macke, "Combining Marriage and Career: The Marital Adjustment of Professional Women," *Journal of Marriage and the Family* 43 (August 1981):651–62.

[48]John G. Richardson, "Wife Occupational Superiority and Marital Troubles: An Examination of the Hypothesis," *Journal of Marriage and the Family* 41 (February 1979):63–72.

[49]Carl A. Hornung and B. Clair McCullough, "Status Relationships in Dual-Employment Marriages: Consequences for Psychological Well-Being," *Journal of Marriage and the Family* 43 (February 1981):25–41; and Leonard I. Pearlin, "Status Inequality and Stress in Marriage," *American Sociological Review* 40 (June 1975):344–57.

and wife want the wife to stay home and she does, or if both want her to work and she does, the level of depression for both spouses is lower than if the couple disagrees on the wife's employment.[50] What may be closest to the truth is that both work outside the home and full-time household work have costs and benefits. A study of six large national surveys found no consistent or significant differences in patterns of life satisfaction between women who work outside the home and those who do not.[51]

Studies on women's employment and mental health generally find evidence of the positive effects of employment. Gove and Geerken found that employed married men are in the best mental health, and housewives who are not in the labor force are in the worst mental health.[52] The mental health of employed wives was intermediate between the other two. Kessler and McRae found improved mental health among working wives but psychological distress among their husbands. This relationship is not associated with greater child care responsibilities, wives' earnings, or being replaced as sole provider. The psychological distress is significantly associated only with the husband's age, which may reflect traditional sex role attitudes or a change in the personal life cycle which affects psychological well-being more than wife's actual employment.[53]

Effects of Mother's Employment on Children

Concerns about working women causing more divorces go along with concerns about the effects on their children. There are more mothers in the labor force now than there were in the past, but there is no consistent evidence that their children are being harmed or helped by it. The National Academy of Sciences (NAS) Panel on Work, Family, and Community concluded that "existing research has not demonstrated that mothers' employment *per se* has consis-

[50]Catherine E. Ross, John Mirowsky and Joan Huber, "Dividing Work, Sharing Work, and In-Between: Marriage Patterns and Depression," *American Sociological Review* 48 (December 1983):809–23.

[51]James D. Wright, "Are Working Women Really More Satisfied? Evidence from Several National Surveys," *Journal of Marriage and the Family* 40 (May 1978):301–13.

[52]Walter R. Gove and Michael Geerken, "The Effect of Children and Employment on the Mental Health of Married Men and Women," *Social Forces* 56 (September 1977):66–76.

[53]Ron C. Kessler and James A. McRae, Jr., "The Effect of Wives' Employment on the Mental Health of Married Men and Women," *American Sociological Review* 47 (April 1982):216–27.

tent direct effects, either positive or negative, on children's development and educational outcomes."[54]

The research on which the NAS report was based presents a mixed picture. Mother's employment is sometimes associated with positive outcomes (for Blacks and children of lower-status families) and sometimes associated with negative effects on academic achievement (for children in two-parent White families). Effects of mother's employment also differ depending on the child's sex. There is evidence of achievement benefits for daughters of working mothers, and there is also evidence of lowered achievement among sons of middle-class working mothers. Daughters of mothers employed in high-status jobs are more likely to plan to work than daughters of mothers not employed, and both sons and daughters of working mothers tend to have the most egalitarian sex role attitudes.[55]

Conspicuous by its absence in the research literature is a concern with the effects of father's employment on children. Much of the effect of mother's work is probably mediated by the couple's ability to share child care responsibilities. Berk and Berk, for example, found that a husband performed more child care tasks in the evening if his wife worked at night.[56]

Concern with the mother's employment ignores the potential contributions that could be made by fathers. Just as with the cycle discussed earlier in regard to household chores and women's employment, there is a cycle of child care responsibility and employment. As long as social norms prescribe that mothers are the only appropriate caregivers for children, women will limit their labor force involvement or will experience conflict if they work outside the home. But attitudes about appropriate sex role behavior are changing, as the following section demonstrates.

Sex Role Attitudes

In a decade in which Geraldine Ferraro was nominated by the Democratic party to run for Vice President of the United States, it is

[54]Cheryl D. Hayes and Sheila B. Kamerman, eds., *Children of Working Parents: Experiences and Outcomes* (Washington, DC: National Academy Press, 1981).

[55]For a review of this literature, see Kristen A. Moore, Daphne Spain, and Suzanne M. Bianchi, "The Working Wife and Mother," *Marriage and Family Review* 7 (Fall-Winter 1984):77–98.

[56]Berk and Berk, *Labor and Leisure*.

clear that sex role attitudes in this country have changed. Men's and women's perceptions of appropriate behavior for women have become increasingly egalitarian. In the political arena alone, the proportion of Americans who say they would vote for a qualified woman for president rose from one-third in 1937 to four-fifths in 1983.[57] Cherlin and Walters found that a great deal of recent change occurred between 1972 and 1975, when the proportion of White men who said they would vote for a woman for president rose from 73 to 83 percent.[58]

Most women's concerns have not been with election to public office, but simply with whether to work outside the home. In 1937 82 percent of the population disapproved of a married woman working if she had a husband capable of supporting her; by 1972 about 68 percent of Americans *approved* of married women working, and by 1982 the proportion had risen to 75 percent.[59]

There is, of course, a reciprocal relationship between attitudes and behavior. When few women worked, public opinion was negative. Even now, there is evidence that husbands hold more negative attitudes toward wives' employment when they have a nonemployed wife at home.[60] As women entered the job market in increasing numbers, attitudes changed to meet new realities. Several studies have found that husbands' and wives' attitudes toward married women working are positively influenced by wives' employment.[61] It is often easier to adapt attitudes to changing necessities or preferences for women's labor force participation than to live with the conflict created by attitudes and behavior at odds with one another.

As attitudes toward married women working have become less

[57]Gallup Poll results as reported in *Time* Magazine, July 23, 1984.

[58]Andrew Cherlin and Pamela B. Walters, "Trends in United States Men's and Women's Sex-Role Attitudes: 1972 to 1978," *American Sociological Review* 46 (August 1981):453–60.

[59]Valerie K. Oppenheimer, *The Female Labor Force in the United States* (Westport, CT: Greenwood Press, 1970); Cherlin and Walters, "Sex-Role Attitudes"; and unpublished 1982 data from the National Opinion Research Center.

[60]Marianne A. Ferber, "Labor-Market Participation of Young Married Women: Causes and Effects," *Journal of Marriage and the Family* 44 (May 1982):457–68.

[61]Henry A. Gordon and Kenneth C. W. Kammeyer, "The Gainful Employment of Women with Small Children," *Journal of Marriage and the Family* 42 (May 1980):327–36; Joan Huber and Glenna Spitze, "Wives' Employment, Household Behaviors, and Sex Role Attitudes," *Social Forces* 60 (September 1981):150–69; Linda D. Molm, "Sex Role Attitudes and the Employment of Married Women: The Direction of Causality," *Sociological Quarterly* 19 (Autumn 1978):522–33; and Glenna Spitze and Linda J. Waite, "Wives' Employment: The Role of Husbands' Perceived Attitudes," *Journal of Marriage and the Family* 43 (February 1981):117–24.

traditional, so have attitudes toward working mothers. The prevailing assumption was that children would suffer from their mother's employment. Those attitudes have changed as the proportion of working mothers has risen.[62] People now say they think child care is a joint responsibility for fathers and mothers (even though actual time allocation studies show mothers still have ultimate responsibility). A 1980 Harris Poll reported that only 19 percent of men and women think "raising children should be the responsibility of the mother, not the father, whether or not she works."[63] Even though behavior has not yet caught up with professed beliefs, joint responsibility is an ideal among most Americans.

Public opinion polls from 1964 to 1974 show a sharp decline in the proportion of women who believe maternal employment is harmful to children's well-being.[64] Thornton, Alwin, and Camburn found more egalitarian sex role attitudes among daughters in 1980 than their mothers expressed in 1962, and mothers had also become more egalitarian over time.[65] Another study found that mother's employment was a crucial variable in influencing the daughter's work orientation.[66] Change thus occurs through both intergenerational and intragenerational channels.

Summary

Married women and mothers who work outside the home have shifted from a minority into the majority in the last decade. Thus, the concern of balancing home and work responsibilities is a relatively new social issue. Some of the strategies useful in reconciling competing uses of a woman's time are delayed marriage, delayed childbearing, part-time work, or working in occupations with hours compatible to childrearing.

[62]U.S. Department of Labor, Women's Bureau, *Time of Change: 1983 Handbook on Women Workers*, bulletin 298 (Washington, DC: U.S. Government Printing Office, 1983), table 1–15.

[63]Louis Harris and Associates, *Families at Work: Strengths and Strains*, General Mills American Family Report, 1980–81 (Minneapolis: General Mills, 1981).

[64]Karen O. Mason, John L. Czajka, and Sara Arber, "Change in U.S. Women's Sex Role Attitudes, 1964–1974," *American Sociological Review* 41 (August 1976):573–96.

[65]Arland Thornton, Duane F. Alwin, and Donald Camburn, "Causes and Consequences of Sex-Role Attitudes and Attitude Change," *American Sociological Review* 48 (April 1983):211–27.

[66]Anne S. Macke and William R. Morgan, "Maternal Employment, Race, and Work Orientation of High School Girls," *Social Forces* 57 (September 1978):187–204.

At the core of the balancing act is the attempt to combine child-rearing and paid employment. Women who work have lower fertility than women who are not in the labor force, yet an increasing proportion of mothers are employed outside the home. The proportion of working mothers rose significantly between 1950 and 1981. This shift in the labor force activity of mothers has created increased demands for child care, and the percentage of children in group day care facilities has risen. The United States is similar to other industrialized nations in the proportion of mothers in the labor force, although the primary type of day care varies by country.

Studies of the household division of labor indicate that employed wives perform the majority of housework and child care activities, while husbands contribute to the household mainly through paid employment. Time-use studies consistently report that wives take primary responsibility for household work whether or not they are employed outside the home.

Research has also shown that women and their families experience few negative effects from their employment. Wives' work can improve the marital satisfaction of both spouses, especially if they agree about the employment choice, and psychological well-being is greater for working women. The effects of mother's work on children is inconclusive, some studies finding positive effects and some finding negative effects. Lack of clear evidence is partly a result of the lack of sufficient longitudinal data to assess the long-term consequences of mothers' employment.

Sex role attitudes have become more egalitarian as women's labor force experience has increased. The majority of Americans now approve of married women working and think childrearing should be shared jointly by husbands and wives.

Women are still primarily responsible for housework and child care and are now increasingly responsible for a paycheck as well. This means that their time is split between work and home in ways that men do not experience. No longer an issue for just a few women, the balancing act now engages a large number of American women. Some have support (financial or emotional) from husbands, but an increasing proportion of mothers are unmarried. How American society meets women's and families' new needs is the challenge for the future.

CONCLUSION

HE NOTION of "cultural lag," developed by sociologist William
F. Ogburn, is useful in understanding the changing roles of
American women during this century. A cultural lag "occurs
when one of two parts of culture which are correlated changes before
or in greater degree than the other part does, thereby causing less
adjustment between the two parts than existed previously."[1]

The period before 1940 can be viewed as a time in which wom-
en's actual economic behavior and society's norms and institutions
for supporting that behavior were in close adjustment. Women's primary economic contribution was within the family as wife and
mother and the ideology of the era supported that role. Between 1900
and 1940 only 20 to 26 percent of women worked outside the home,
and they were mainly unmarried women or wives without children.
During this period there was general agreement that "woman's place
is in the home" because that is where most women were. At that
time over half of Americans did not approve of married women
working. Divorce rates were low and the majority of adult women
lived in married-couple households.

[1]William F. Ogburn, *On Culture and Social Change* (Chicago: University of Chicago
Press, 1964), p. 86.

Between 1940 and 1950 there was an increase in the proportion of women working outside the home, from one-quarter to one-third, which constituted a larger increase in one decade than had occurred in the previous forty years. But, as we have documented, increased labor force participation occurred primarily among older women whose children were grown or in school.

During the 1950s, when fertility hit its peak at over three children per woman, the increase in labor force participation slowed. In 1960 only 28 percent of wives with children were in the labor force. The majority of mothers who worked full time arranged for child care in their own home. The family-oriented 1950s were perhaps the last decade in which women's behavior and social norms were in agreement.

Women's labor force participation continued to increase in the 1960s and experienced the most rapid growth of any single decade during the 1970s. By 1980 just over one-half of all women were working outside the home. Even though Americans are now in favor of women working, the necessary adjustments have not been made to accommodate the greater demands on women's time. For example, employed wives continue to do the majority of household tasks. Day care facilities are not always adequate to meet the needs of working women, and when they are available they are often so expensive that they are beyond the means of many working mothers (especially unmarried mothers). Finally, wages of women remain low in comparison with men. These three issues—wages, child care, and housework—are all examples of society's delay in recognizing the changing status of women.

The shift of women out of the home and into the labor force and out of marriages and into independent living arrangements represents changes which are out of step with the ability of social institutions to support the changing economic role of women. In particular, we have shown that the market does not provide women with wages equal to those of men. Adequate child care, an equitable division of labor within the home, and the flexibility of the workplace have not evolved rapidly enough to facilitate women's market work and career development.

When only a minority of women worked outside the home, and prior to the rising divorce rate, lower wages for women were more "socially acceptable" and even legal before the Equal Pay Act of 1963. If one must attach a date to the point at which women's wages were in adjustment with social norms, it would probably be the period before the Equal Pay Act (1963) and before the years of high inflation, when the majority of women were not in the labor force. Now the majority of women are working, their educational attainment has risen, and an increasing proportion of women are maintaining their own households. Married women are also contributing increasingly more income to their households. Yet, wage inequalities persist.

Over the past twenty years wage inequalities have come under increased scrutiny. Some are beginning to question why men and women with equivalent years of schooling and those working in the same detailed occupation should earn different salaries. The very discussion of the issue of "comparable worth" would not have occurred thirty years ago when only a third of all women were working for wages. Now that half of all women are affected by wage inequalities, it is no longer just a personal problem for a few women, but an issue that affects a majority of all families.

Will it always be that women, more so than men, put the needs of children and family ahead of their own labor force advancement? Probably, at least for the foreseeable future. In two-parent families, until such time as wives command salaries equal to their husbands' salaries, on average, it is unlikely that men will devote as much time and energy to the nurturance of the family. Because of the difficulty of combining work and family roles, women will more often work part time or part year. However, women's labor market adjustments to accommodate children, which are often made within a two-parent family context and seem economically rational at the time, cause difficulty later when these same women find themselves divorced and in great need of supporting themselves and their children. In a world of high divorce rates and in which care and support of children following divorce fall disproportionately to women, specialization of men in the labor force and women in the home no longer provides the security it once did.

One might view the 1970s as a decade in which individual women made personal adjustments in order to establish themselves in the labor market and achieve wage parity with men. They delayed marriage and children, attended college in record numbers, began to major in nontraditional fields, and entered male-dominated professional and managerial ranks. The 1980s and 1990s may hold the answer as to how effective these individual acts by the baby boom cohort of women were. As they have their children and attempt to combine raising them with the responsiblities of mid-level positions in organizations, we will have the opportunity to see if they emerge from their childbearing years with earnings and labor force attachment that are more equal to those of men than has been true for past generations of women.

There are limits to how far individual adjustments can take women, however. We, as a society, have embarked on a road toward equality between the sexes to which there is no turning back. If we want a productive labor force of female and male workers, but also value the family, work hours must be flexible, day care available and affordable, and work within the home equitably divided. Until there is widespread recognition that day care, equal wages, and housework are not just "women's issues" but are much broader family issues affecting all persons, the balancing act women are engaged in currently will be just that—a delicate, fragile juggling always subject to breaking down.

Women are in the work force because they need to be there. They need to be able to earn a living, to support themselves and those dependent on them. The time has come to deal with this reality and to bring norms and institutions into line with society as it exists in the 1980s.

Bibliography

Aguirre, B. E., and W. C. Parr "Husbands' Marriage Order and the Stability of First and Second Marriages of White and Black Women." *Journal of Marriage and the Family* 44 (August 1982):605–20.

Alexander, Karl L., and Bruce K. Eckland "Sex Differences in the Educational Attainment Process."*American Sociological Review* 39 (October 1974):668–82.

Alexander, Karl L.; Bruce K. Eckland; and Larry J. Griffin "The Wisconsin Model of Socioeconomic Achievement: A Replication." *American Journal of Sociology* 81 (September 1975):324–42.

Alexander, Karl L., and Thomas W. Reilly "Estimating the Effects of Marriage Timing on Educational Attainment: Some Procedural Issues and Substantive Clarifications." *American Journal of Sociology* 87 (July 1981):143–56.

Angle, John, and David A. Wissman "Gender, College Major, and Earnings." *Sociology of Education* 54 (January 1981):25–33.

Bachrach, Christine A. "Childlessness and Social Isolation Among the Elderly." *Journal of Marriage and the Family* 42 (August 1980):627–36.

Bacon, Lloyd "Early Motherhood, Accelerated Role Transition, and Social Pathologies." *Social Forces* 52 (March 1974):333–41.

Badger, M. E. "Why Aren't Girls Better at Math? A Review of Research." *Educational Research* 24 (November 1981):11–23.

Bahr, Steven J. "The Effects of Welfare on Marital Stability and Remarriage." *Journal of Marriage and the Family* 41 (August 1979):553–60.

———— "Marital Dissolution Laws: Impact of Recent Changes for Women." *Journal of Family Issues* 4 (September 1983):455–66.

Baldwin, Wendy "Adolescent Pregnancy and Childbearing—Growing Concerns for Americans." *Population Bulletin*, vol. 31, no. 2. Washington, DC: Population Reference Bureau, 1980.

————, **and Virginia S. Cain** "The Children of Teenage Parents." *Family Planning Perspectives* 12 (January-February 1980):34–43.

Bancroft, Gertrude *The American Labor Force: Its Growth and Changing Composition.* New York: Wiley, 1958.

Bane, Mary Jo *Here to Stay: American Families in the Twentieth Century.* New York: Basic Books, 1976.

Barrett, John C. "Effects of Various Factors on Selection for Family Planning Status and Natural Fecundability: A Simulation Study." *Demography* 15 (February 1978):87–98.

Bayer, Alan E. "The College Drop-Out: Factors Affecting Senior College Completion." *Sociology of Education* 41 (Summer 1968):305–15.

———— "Marriage Plans and Educational Aspirations." *American Journal of Sociology* 75 (September 1969):239–44.

Bean, Frank D., and John P. Marcum "Differential Fertility and the Minority Group Status Hypothesis: An Assessment and Review." In Frank D. Bean and W. Parker Frisbie, eds., *The Demography of Racial and Ethnic Groups*. New York: Academic Press, 1978.

Bean, Frank; Elizabeth H. Stephen; and Jeffrey A. Burr "The Temporal Relationship between Labor Force Participation and Intended and Unintended Fertility: Racial and Religious Comparisons in the United States." *Texas Population Research Center Papers*, no. 6.007. Austin: University of Texas, 1984.

Becker, Gary S. "A Theory of Marriage." In Theodore W. Shultz, ed., *Economics of the Family*. Chicago: University of Chicago Press, 1974.

—— *A Treatise on the Family*. Cambridge, MA: Harvard University Press, 1981.

——; **Elizabeth M. Landes; and Robert T. Michael** "An Economic Analysis of Marital Instability." *Journal of Political Economy* 85 (December 1977):1141–87.

Beller, Andrea "Trends in Occupational Segregation by Sex: 1960–1981." In Barbara F. Reskin, ed., *Sex Segregation in the Workplace*. Washington, DC: National Academy Press, 1984.

Beresford, John C., and Alice M. Rivlin "Privacy, Poverty, and Old Age." *Demography* 3 (1966):247–58.

Berk, Richard, and Sarah F. Berk *Labor and Leisure at Home: Content and Organization of the Household Day*. Beverly Hills, CA: Sage, 1979.

Berk, Sarah F. "Husbands at Home: Organization of the Husband's Household Day." In Karen Wolk Feinstein, ed., *Working Women and Families*. Beverly Hills, CA: Sage, 1979.

Bianchi, Suzanne M. *Household Composition and Racial Inequality*. New Brunswick, NJ: Rutgers University Press, 1981.

—— "Changing Concepts of Households and Families in the Census and CPS." In *Proceedings of the Social Statistics Section*. Washington, DC: American Statistical Association, 1982.

—— "Wives Who Earn More Than Their Husbands." *Special Demographic Analyses*, CDS-80-9, U.S. Bureau of the Census. Washington, DC: U.S. Government Printing Office, 1983.

——, **and Reynolds Farley** "Racial Differences in Family Living Arrangements and Economic Well-Being: An Analysis of Recent Trends." *Journal of Marriage and the Family* 41 (August 1979):537–51.

Bianchi, Suzanne M., and Nancy F. Rytina "Occupational Change, 1970–80." Paper presented at the annual meeting of the Population Association of America, Minneapolis, May 1984.

Bianchi, Suzanne M., and Daphne Spain "American Women: Three Decades of Change." *Special Demographic Analyses*, CDS-80–8, U.S. Bureau of the Census. Washington, DC: U.S. Government Printing Office, 1983.

Bielby, Denise D. "Career Sex-Atypicality and Career Involvement of College Educated Women: Baseline Evidence from the 1960s." *Sociology of Education* 51 (January 1978):7–2C.

Bielby, William T., and James N. Baron "A Woman's Place Is with Other Women: Sex Segregation within Organizations." In Barbara F. Reskin, ed., *Sex Segregation in the Workplace: Trends, Explanations, Remedies*. Washington, DC: National Academy Press, 1984.

Bishop, Christine E. "The Demand for Independent Living by the Elderly: Effects of Income and Disability." Unpublished manuscript, 1983.

Blake, Judith "Can We Believe Recent Data on Birth Expectations in the United States?" *Demography* 11 (February 1974):25–44.

———, and Jorge H. Del Pinal "Negativism, Equivocation, and Wobbly Assent: Public 'Support' for the Prochoice Platform on Abortion." *Demography* 18 (August 1981):309–20.

Blanc, Ann K. "The Impact of Changing Family Patterns on Reproductive Behavior: Nonmarital Cohabitation and Fertility in Norway." Paper presented at the annual meeting of the Population Association of America, Minneapolis, May 1984.

Blau, Francine D. *Equal Pay in the Office.* Lexington, MA: Heath, 1977.

——— "Occupational Segregation and Labor Market Discrimination." In Barbara F. Reskin, ed., *Sex Segregation in the Workplace: Trends, Explanation, Remedies.* Washington, DC: National Academy Press, 1984.

———, and Wallace E. Hendricks. "Occupational Segregation by Sex: Trends and Prospects." *Journal of Human Resources* 14 (Spring 1979):197–210.

Blau, Francine D., and Larry Kahn "Race and Sex Differences in Quits by Young Workers." *Industrial and Labor Relations Review* 34 (July 1981): 563–77.

Blau, Peter M., and Otis Dudley Duncan *The American Occupational Structure.* New York: Wiley, 1967.

Bloom, David "What's Happening to the Age at First Birth in the United States? A Study of Recent Cohorts." *Demography* 19 (August 1982):351–70.

———, and Ann R. Pebley "Voluntary Childlessness: A Review of the Evidence and Implications." *Population Research and Policy Review* 1 (October 1982):203–24.

Bloom, David, and James Trussell "What Are the Determinants of Delayed Childbearing and Permanent Childlessness in the United States?" *Demography* 21 (November 1984):591–612.

Bogue, Donald *Principles of Demography.* New York: Wiley, 1969.

Bongaarts, John "A Method for the Estimation of Fecundability." *Demography* 12 (November 1975):645–60.

Bowden, Lee, and Frank Levy "The Economic Well-Being of Families and Individuals." In John L. Palmer and Isabel V. Sawhill, eds., *The Reagan Experiment.* Washington, DC: Urban Institute Press, 1982.

Bowen, William G., and T. Aldrich Finegan *The Economics of Labor Force Participation.* Princeton, NJ: Princeton University Press, 1969.

Brandwein, Ruth A.; Carol A. Brown; and Elizabeth M. Fox "Women and Children Last: The Social Situation of Divorced Mothers and Their Families." *Journal of Marriage and the Family* 36 (August 1974):498–514.

Bumpass, Larry L.; Ronald R. Rindfuss; and Richard B. Janosik "Age and Marital Status at First Birth and the Pace of Subsequent Fertility." *Demography* 15 (February 1978): 75–86.

Bumpass, Larry L., and James A. Sweet "Differentials in Marital Instability: 1970." *American Sociological Review* 37 (December 1972):754–66.

Bumpass, Larry L., and Charles F. Westoff *The Later Years of Childbearing.* Princeton, NJ: Princeton University Press, 1970.

Burch, Thomas K.; Kauser Thomas; and Marilyn McQuillan "Changing Household Headship in the United States, 1900 to 1970: A Preliminary Test of the Income Threshold Hypothesis." Paper presented at the annual meeting of the Population Association of America, Pittsburgh, April 1983.

Butz, William, and Michael Ward "The Emergence of Countercyclical U.S. Fertility." *American Economic Review* 69 (June 1979):318–27.

Cain, Glen "Women and Work: Trends in Time Spent in Housework." Discussion Paper no. 747–84. Madison: Institute for Research on Poverty, University of Wisconsin, 1984.

——— "Welfare Economics of Policies Toward Women." *Journal of Labor Economics* 3 (January 1985 supplement): S375–96.

———, **and Arlene Leibowitz** "Education and the Allocation of Women's Time." In F. Thomas Juster, ed., *Education, Income, and Human Behavior.* New York: McGraw-Hill, 1975.

Call, Vaughn R. A., and Luther B. Otto "Age at Marriage as a Mobility Contingency: Estimates for the Nye-Berardo Model." *Journal of Marriage and the Family* 39 (February 1977):67–79.

Card, Josefina J. "Long-Term Consequences for Children of Teenage Parents." *Demography* 18 (May 1981):137–56.

———, **and Lauress L. Wise** "Teenage Mothers and Teenage Fathers: The Impact of Early Childbearing on the Parent's Personal and Professional Lives." *Family Planning Perspectives* 10 (July-August 1978):199–205.

Carlson, Elwood, and Kandi Stinson "Motherhood, Marriage Timing, and Marital Stability: A Research Note." *Social Forces* 61 (September 1982):258–67.

Carter, Hugh, and Paul C. Glick *Marriage and Divorce: A Social and Economic Study,* Cambridge, MA: Harvard University Press, 1976.

Cherlin, Andrew "The Effects of Children on Marital Dissolution." *Demography* 14 (August 1977):265–72.

——— "Remarriage as an Incomplete Institution." *American Journal of Sociology* 84 (November 1978): 634–50.

——— "Postponing Marriage: The Influence of Young Women's Work Expectations." *Journal of Marriage and the Family* 42 (May 1980):355–65.

——— *Marriage, Divorce, Remarriage.* Cambridge, MA: Harvard University Press, 1981.

——— "Work Life and Marital Dissolution." In George Levinger and Oliver C. Moles, eds., *Divorce and Separation: Context, Causes, and Consequences.* New York: Basic Books, 1979.

———, **and Pamela B. Walters** "Trends in United States Men's and Women's Sex-Role Attitudes: 1972 to 1978." *American Sociological Review* 46 (August 1981):453–60.

Chester, R. "Is There a Relationship between Childlessness and Marriage Breakdown?" In Ellen Peck and Judith Senderowitz, eds., *Pronatalism: The Myth of Mom and Apple Pie.* New York: Crowell, 1974.

Chevan, Albert, and J. Henry Korson "The Widowed Who Live Alone: An Examination of Social and Demographic Factors." *Social Forces* 51 (September 1972):45–53.

Chilman, Catherine S. "Social and Psychological Research Concerning Adolescent Childbearing: 1970–1980." *Journal of Marriage and the Family* 42 (November 1980):793–806.

Clifford, William B., and Patricia Tobin "Labor Force Participation of Working Mothers and Family Formation: Some Further Evidence." *Demography* 14 (August 1977):273–84.

Clogg, Clifford C. "Cohort Analysis of Recent Trends in Labor Force Participation." *Demography* 19 (November 1982): 459–79.

Coleman, James S. "The Transition from School to Work." In Donald J. Treiman and Robert V. Robinson, eds., *Research in Social Stratification and Mobility,* vol. 3. Greenwich, CT: JAI Press, 1984.

Coombs, Lolagene C. "Reproductive Goals and Achieved Fertility: A Fifteen Year Perspective." *Demography* 16 (November 1979):523–34.

Cooney, Rosemary S. "Demographic Components of Growth in White, Black, and Puerto Rican Female-Headed Families: Comparison of the Cutright and Ross/Sawhill Methodologies." *Social Science Research* 8 (June 1979):144–58.

Corcoran, Mary "The Economic Consequences of Marital Dissolution for Women in the Middle Years." *Sex Roles* 5 (June 1979):343–53.

————, **and Greg J. Duncan** "Work History, Labor Force Attachment, and Earnings Differences Between the Races and Sexes." *Journal of Human Resources* 14 (Winter 1979):3–20.

Corcoran, Mary; Greg J. Duncan; and Michael Ponza "Work Experience and Wage Growth of Women Workers." In Greg J. Duncan and James N. Morgan, eds., *Five Thousand American Families: Patterns of Economic Progress*, vol. 10. Ann Arbor: Institute for Social Research, 1983.

Corcoran, Mary, and Martha S. Hill "Unemployment Income and Poverty." *Social Service Review* 54 (September 1980): 407–13.

Cramer, James C. "Fertility and Female Employment." *American Sociological Review* 45 (April 1980):167–90.

———— "Models of Fertility and Women's Work: Reply." *American Sociological Review* 47 (August 1982):566–67.

Cutright, Phillips "Components of Change in the Number of Female Family Heads Aged 15–44: United States, 1940–70." *Journal of Marriage and the Family* 36 (November 1974):714–21.

Danziger, Sheldon "Do Working Wives Increase Family Income Inequality?" *Journal of Human Resources* 15 (Summer 1980):444–51.

Darian, Jean "Convenience of Work and the Job Constraint of Children." *Demography* 12 (May 1975):245–58.

Davis, Howard "Employment Gains of Women by Industry, 1968–78." *Monthly Labor Review* 103 (June 1980):3–9.

Davis, Kingsley "The Theory of Change and Response in Modern Demographic History." *Population Index* 29 (October 1963): 345–65.

———— "The American Family in Relation to Demographic Change." In Charles F. Westoff and Robert Parke, eds., *Demographic and Social Aspects of Population Growth*, Commission on Population Growth and the American Future, vol. 1. Washington, DC: U.S. Government Printing Office, 1972.

————, **and Judith Blake** "Social Structure and Fertility: an Analytic Framework." *Economic Development and Cultural Change* 6 (1955–56):211–35.

Davis, Nancy J., and Larry L. Bumpass "The Continuation of Education after Marriage Among Women in the United States: 1970." *Demography* 13 (May 1976):161–74.

Daymont, Thomas, and Paul J. Andrisani "Job Preferences, College Major, and the Gender Gap in Earnings." *Journal of Human Resources* 19 (Summer 1984): 408–28.

DeJong, G. F., and R. R. Sell "Changes in Childlessness in the United States: A Demographic Path Analysis." *Population Studies* 31 (March 1977):129–41.

Devaney, Barbara "An Analysis of Variations in U.S. Fertility and Female Labor Force Participation Trends." *Demography* 20 (May 1983):147–62.

Dixon, Ruth B., and Lenore J. Weitzman "When Husbands File for Divorce." *Journal of Marriage and the Family* 44 (February 1982):103–15.

Draper, Thomas "On the Relationship between Welfare and Marital Stability: A Research Note." *Journal of Marriage and the Family* 43 (May 1981):293–99.

Duncan, Greg J. *Years of Poverty, Years of Plenty.* Ann Arbor: Institute for Social Research, 1984.

————, **and Saul D. Hoffman** "On-the-job Training and Earnings Differences by Race and Sex." *Review of Economics and Statistics* 61 (November 1979):594–603.

Duncan, Greg J., and Saul D. Hoffmann "The Economic Consequences of Marital Instability." Paper prepared for the NBER Income and Wealth Conference on Horizontal Equity, Uncertainty and Well-Being, Baltimore, December 1983.

Easterlin, Richard A. "Relative Economic Status and the American Fertility Swing." In Eleanor Sheldon, ed., *Family Economic Behavior.* Philadelphia: Lippincott, 1973.

———— "What Will 1984 Be Like? Sociological Implications of Recent Twists in Age Structure." *Demography* 15 (November 1978):397–432.

———— *Births and Fortune.* New York: Basic Books, 1980.

Ebaugh, Hallen R., and C. Allen Haney "Shifts in Abortion Attitudes: 1972–1978." *Journal of Marriage and the Family* 42 (August 1980):491–500.

England, Paula "Assessing Trends in Occupational Sex Segregation, 1900–1976." In Ivar Berg, ed., *Sociological Perspectives on Labor Markets.* New York: Academic Press, 1981.

———— "The Failure of Human Capital Theory to Explain Occupational Sex Segregation." *Journal of Human Resources* 17 (Summer 1982):356–70.

Espenshade, Thomas J. "The Economic Consequences of Divorce." *Journal of Marriage and the Family* 41 (August 1979):615–25.

———— "Marriage, Divorce, and Remarriage from Retrospective Data: A Multiregional Approach." *Environment and Planning A* 15 (December 1983):1633–52.

———— "Marriage Trends in America: Estimates, Implications, and Underlying Causes." *Population and Development Review* 11 (June 1985):193–245.

Farley, Reynolds "Recent Changes in Negro Fertility." *Demography* 3 (1966):188–203.

———— *Growth of the Black Population: A Study of Demograhpic Trends.* Chicago: Markham, 1970.

Featherman, David L., and Robert M. Hauser "Sexual Inequalities and Socioeconomic Achievement in the U.S., 1962–1973." *American Sociological Review* 41 (June 1976):462–83.

Ferber, Marianne A. "Labor-Market Participation of Young Married Women: Causes and Effects." *Journal of Marriage and the Family* 44 (May 1982):457–68.

————, **and Joe L. Spaeth** "Work Characteristics and the Male-Female Earnings Gap." *American Economic Review* 74 (May 1984):260–64.

Folger, John K.; Helen S. Astin; and Alan E. Bayer *Human Resources and Higher Education.* New York: Russell Sage Foundation, 1970.

Folger, John K., and Charles B. Nam *Education of the American Population: A 1960 Census Monograph.* Washington, DC: U.S. Government Printing Office, 1967.

Forrest, Jacqueline D., and Stanley K. Henshaw "What U.S. Women Think and Do About Contraception." *Family Planning Perspectives* 15 (July-August 1983):157–66.

Forrest, Jacqueline D.; Ellen Sullivan; and Christopher Tietze "Abortions in the United States 1977–1979." *Family Planning Perspectives* 11 (July-August 1983):157–66.

Freedman, Ronald; Deborah S. Freedman; and Arland D. Thornton "Changes in Fertility Expectations and Preferences between 1962 and 1977: Their Relation to Final Parity." *Demography* 17 (November 1980):365–78.

Freedman, Ronald; P. K. Whelpton; and Angus Campbell *Family Planning, Sterility, and Population Growth.* New York: McGraw-Hill, 1959.

Freshnock, Larry, and Phillips Cutright "Models of Illegitimacy: United States, 1969." *Demography* 16 (February 1979):37–48.

Fuchs, Victor *How We Live.* Cambridge, MA: Harvard University Press, 1983.

Galligan, Richard, and Steven J. Bahr "Economic Well-Being and Marital Stability: Implications for Income Maintenance Programs." *Journal of Marriage and the Family* 40 (May 1978):283–90.

Garfinkel, Irvin, and Sara McLanahan *Single-Mother Families and Public Policy: A New American Dilemma!* Washington, DC: Urban Institute, forthcoming.

Geerken, Michael, and Walter R. Gove *At Home and at Work: The Family's Allocation of Labor.* Beverly Hills, CA: Sage, 1983.

Glick, Paul C. "The Family Cycle." *American Sociological Review* 12 (April 1947): 164–74.

———— *American Families.* New York: Wiley, 1957.

———— "Updating the Life Cycle of the Family." *Journal of Marriage and the Family* 39 (February 1977):5–13.

———— "Marriage, Divorce, and Living Arrangements." *Journal of Family Issues* 5 (March 1984):7–26.

————, **and Hugh Carter** "Marriage Patterns and Educational Level." *American Sociological Review* 23 (June 1958):294–300.

Glick, Paul C., and Arthur J. Norton "Perspectives on the Recent Upturn in Divorce and Remarriage." *Demography* 10 (August 1973):301–14.

Glick, Paul C., and Arthur J. Norton "Marrying, Divorcing, and Living Together in the U.S. Today." *Population Bulletin*, vol. 32, no. 5. Washington, DC: Population Reference Bureau, 1977.

Glick, Paul C., and Robert Parke "New Approaches in Studying the Life Cycle of the Family." *Demography* 2 (1965):187–202.

Glick, Paul C., and Graham Spanier "Married and Unmarried Cohabitation in the United States." *Journal of Marriage and the Family* 42 (February 1980):19–30.

Goldin, Claudia "The Changing Economic Role of Women: A Quantitative Approach." *Journal of Interdisciplinary History* 13 (Spring 1983):707–33.

Goldman, Noreen and Graham Lord "Sex Differences in Life Cycle Measures of Widowhood." *Demography* 20 (May 1983):177–96.

Goldscheider, Calvin, and Peter Uhlenberg "Minority Group Status and Fertility." *American Journal of Sociology* 74 (January 1969):361–72.

Goldscheider, Frances K., and Julie DaVanzo "Living Arrangements and the Transition to Adulthood." *Demography* 22 (November 1985):545–63.

Goode, William F. *World Revolution and Family Patterns.* New York: Free Press, 1963.

Gordan, Henry A., and Kenneth C. W. Kammeyer "The Gainful Employment of Women with Small Children." *Journal of Marriage and the Family* 42 (May 1980):327–36.

Gove, Walter R., and Michael Geerken "The Effect of Children and Employment on the Mental Health of Married Men and Women." *Social Forces* 56 (September 1977):66–76.

Griffin, Larry J., and Karl L. Alexander "Schooling and Socioeconomic Attainments: High School and College Influences." *American Journal of Sociology* 84 (September 1978):319–47.

Groat, H. Theodore; Randy L. Workman; and Arthur G. Neal "Labor Force Participation and Family Formation: A Study of Working Mothers." *Demography* 13 (February 1976):115–26.

Grossman, Allyson S. "Women in Domestic Work: Yesterday and Today." *Monthly Labor Review* 103 (August 1980):17–21.

———— "More Than Half of All Children Have Working Mothers." *Monthly Labor Review* 105 (February 1982):41–43.

Gunter, B. G., and Doyle Johnson "Divorce Filing as Role Behavior: Effect of No-Fault Law on Divorce Filing Patterns." *Journal of Marriage and the Family* 40 (August 1978):571–74.

Haber, Sheldon E.; Enrique J. Lamas; and Gordon Green "A New Method for Estimating Job Separation by Sex and Race." *Monthly Labor Review* 106 (June 1983):20–27.

Halliday, Terence C. "Comment: Remarriage: The More Complete Institution?" *American Journal of Sociology* 86 (November 1980):630–35

Hampton, Robert "Marital Disruption: Some Social and Economic Consequences." In Greg J. Duncan and James D. Morgan, eds., *Five Thousand American Families: Patterns of Economic Progress*, vol. 3. Ann Arbor: Institute for Social Research, 1975.

Hannan, Michael T.; Nancy B. Tuma; and Lyle P. Groeneveld "Income and Marital Events: Evidence from an Income-Maintenance Experiment." *American Journal of Sociology* 82 (May 1977):1186–211.

Hannan, Michael T.; Nancy B. Tuma; and Lyle P. Groeneveld "Income and Independence Effects on Marital Dissolution: Results from the Seattle and Denver Income-Maintenance Experiments." *American Journal of Sociology* 84 (November 1978):611–33.

Hayes, Cheryl D., and Sheila B. Kamerman, eds. *Children of Working Parents: Experiences and Outcomes.* Washington, DC: National Academy Press, 1981.

Heer, David M. "The Measurement and Bases of Family Power: An Overview." *Journal of Marriage and the Family* 25 (May 1963):133–39.

———, and Amyra Grossbard-Schechtman "The Impact of the Female Marriage Squeeze and the Contraceptive Revolution on Sex Roles and the Women's Liberation Movement in the United States, 1960 to 1975." *Journal of Marriage and the Family* 43 (February 1981):49–66.

Hill, C. Russell, and Frank P. Stafford "Parental Care of Children: Time Diary Estimates of Quality, Predictability, and Variety." *Journal of Human Resources* 15 (Summer 1980):219–39.

Hofferth, Sandra L. "Some Long Term Economic Consequences for Women of Delayed Childbearing and Reduced Family Size." *Demography* 21 (May 1984):141–55.

———, and Kristin A. Moore "Early Childbearing and Later Economic Well-Being." *American Sociological Review* 44 (October 1979):784–815.

Hofferth, Sandra L., and Kristin A. Moore "Women's Employment and Marriage." In Ralph W. Smith, ed., *The Subtle Revolution*. Washington, DC: Urban Institute, 1979.

Hoffman, Saul "Marital Instability and the Economic Status of Women." *Demography* 14 (February 1977):67–76.

———, and John Holmes "Husbands, Wives and Divorce." In Greg J. Duncan and James N. Morgan, eds., *Five Thousand American Families: Patterns of Economic Progress*, vol. 4. Ann Arbor: Institute for Social Research, 1976.

Hogan, Dennis P. "The Variable Order of Events in the Life Course." *American Sociological Review* 43 (August 1978):573–86.

——— "The Transition to Adulthood as a Career Contingency." *American Sociological Review* 45 (April 1980):261–75.

———; Nan M. Astone; and Evelyn M. Kitagawa "The Impact of Social Status, Family Structure, and Neighborhood on Contraceptive Use Among Black Adolescents." Unpublished manuscript, Population Research Center, University of Chicago, April 1984.

Hogan, Dennis P., and Evelyn Kitagawa "The Impact of Social Status, Family

Structure, and Neighborhood on the Fertility of Black Adolescents." *American Journal of Sociology* 90 (January 1985):825–55.

Hornung, Carl A., and B. Clair McCullough "Status Relationships in Dual-Employment Marriages: Consequences for Psychological Well-Being." *Journal of Marriage and the Family* 43 (February 1981):25–41.

Horvath, Francis W. "Working Wives Reduce Inequality in the Distribution of Family Earnings." *Monthly Labor Review* 103 (July 1980):48–50.

Houseknecht, Sharon K., and Anne S. Macke "Combining Marriage and Career: The Marital Adjustment of Professional Women." *Journal of Marriage and the Family* 43 (August 1981):651–62.

Huber, Joan, and Glenna Spitze "Considering Divorce: An Expansion of Becker's Theory of Marital Instability." *American Journal of Sociology* 86 (July 1980):75–89.

Huber, Joan, and Glenna Spitze "Wives' Employment, Household Behaviors, and Sex Role Attitudes." *Social Forces* 60 (September 1981):150–69.

Jacobs, Jerry "Changes in Sex-Segregation in the 1970s." Unpublished manuscript, Department of Sociology, Harvard University, 1983.

Jacobson, Paul H. "Differentials in Divorce by Duration of Marriage and Size of Family." *American Sociological Review* 15 (April 1950):235–44.

Janssen, Susan G., and Robert Hauser "Religion, Socialization, and Fertility." *Demography* 18 (November 1981):511–28.

Johnson, Nan "Religious Differentials in Reproduction: The Effects of Sectarian Education." *Demography* 19 (November 1982):495–509.

Jones, Carol; Nancy Gordon; and Isabel V. Sawhill "Child Support Payments in the United States," Working Paper no. 992–03. Washington, DC: Urban Institute, 1976.

Jones, Elise F. "The Impact of Women's Employment on Marital Fertility in the U.S., 1970–75." *Population Studies* 35 (July 1981):161–73.

———— "Ways in Which Childbearing Affects Women's Employment: Evidence from the U.S. 1975 National Fertility Study." *Population Studies* 36 (March 1982):5–14.

————, **and Charles F. Westoff** "The End of 'Catholic' Fertility." *Demography* 16 (May 1979):209–18.

Kantner, John, and Melvin Zelnik "Sexual Experience of Young Unmarried Women in the U.S.." *Family Planning Perspectives* 4 (October 1972):9–17.

Kennedy, Robert "Minority Group Status and Fertility: The Irish." *American Sociological Review* 38 (February 1973):85–96.

Kerckhoff, Alan C., and Alan A. Parron "The Effect of Early Marriage on the Educational Attainment of Young Men." *Journal of Marriage and the Family* 41 (February 1979):97–107.

Kerckhoff, Alan C., and Robert A. Jackson "Types of Education and the Occupational Attainments of Young Men." *Social Forces* 61 (September 1982):24–25.

Kessler, Ron C., and James A. McRae, Jr. "The Effect of Wives' Employment on the Mental Health of Married Men and Women." *American Sociological Review* 47 (April 1982):216–27.

Klein, Deborah P. "Trends in Employment and Unemployment in Families." *Monthly Labor Review* 106 (December 1983):21–25.

Kleinbaum, Robert "Forecasting U.S. Age Specific Fertility Rates." Unpublished manuscript, Population Studies Center, University of Michigan, 1983.

Kobrin, Frances E. *"Components of Change in United States Household Headship."* Unpublished dissertation, University of Pennsylvania, 1971.

———— "Household Headship and Its Changes in the United States, 1940–1960, 1970." *Journal of the American Statistical Association* 68 (December 1973):793–800.

———— "The Fall of Household Size and the Rise of the Primary Individual." *Demography* 13 (February 1976):127–38.

———— "Family Extension and the Elderly: Economic, Demographic, and Family Cycle Factors." *Journal of Gerontology* 36 (May 1981):370–77.

Koo, Helen P., and Barbara K. Janowitz "Interrelationships between Fertility and Marital Dissolution: Results of a Simultaneous Logit Model." *Demography* 20 (May 1983):129–45.

Lazear, Edward P., and Robert T. Michael "Family Size and Distribution of Real Per Capita Income." *American Economic Review* 70 (March 1980):91–107.

Lee, Che-Fu, and Mohammad M. Khan "Factors Related to the Intention to Have Additional Children in the United States: A Reanalysis of Data from the 1965 and 1970 National Fertility Studies." *Demography* 15 (August 1978):337–44.

Lee, Ronald D. "Demographic Forecasting and the Easterlin Hypothesis." *Population and Development Review* 2 (September-December 1976):459–68.

———— "Target Fertility, Contraception, and Aggregate Rates: Toward a Formal Synthesis." *Demography* 14 (November 1977):455–79.

Levitan, Sar A., and Richard S. Belous "Working Wives and Mothers: What Happens to Family Life?" *Monthly Labor Review* 104 (September 1981):26–30.

Levy, Frank "The Intergenerational Transfer of Poverty." Working Paper, no. 1241–02. Washington, DC: Urban Institute, 1980.

Liker, Jeffrey, and Glen Elder "Economic Hardship and Marital Relations in the 1930s." *American Sociological Review* 48 (June 1983):343–59.

Lloyd, Cynthia B., and Beth T. Niemi *The Economics of Sex Differentials.* New York: Columbia University Press, 1979.

Lopata, Helena Z. *Widowhood in an American City.* Cambridge, MA: Schenckman, 1973.

———— *Women as Widows: Support Systems.* New York: Elsevier, 1979.

Louis Harris Associates *Families at Work: Strengths and Strains.* General Mills American Family Report, 1980–81. Minneapolis: General Mills, 1981.

Lueck, Marjorie; Ann C. Orr; and Martin O'Connell "Trends in Child Care Arrangements of Working Mothers." *Current Population Reports, Special Studies*, series P-23, no. 117, U.S. Bureau of the Census. Washington, DC: U.S. Government Printing Office, 1982.

Macke, Anne S., and William R. Morgan "Maternal Employment, Race, and Work Orientation of High School Girls." *Social Forces* 57 (September 1978):187–204.

Macklin, Eleanor D. "Heterosexual Cohabitation among Unmarried College Students." *Family Coordinator* 21 (October 1972):463–72.

———— "Nonmarital Heterosexual Cohabitation." *Marriage and Family Review* 1 (Spring 1978):1–12.

Madden, Janice F. "Why Women Work Closer to Home." *Urban Studies* 18 (June 1981):181–94.

Mallan, Lucy B. "Labor Force Participation, Work Experience, and the Pay Gap Between Men and Women." *Journal of Human Resources* 17 (Summer 1982):437–48.

Marini, Margaret M. "The Transition to Adulthood: Sex Differences in Educational Attainment and Age at Marriage." *American Sociological Review* 43 (August 1978):483–507.

—— "Effects of the Timing of Marriage and First Birth on Fertility." *Journal of Marriage and the Family* 43 (February 1981):27–48.

—— "Measuring the Effects of the Timing of Marriage and First Birth." *Journal of Marriage and the Family* 43 (February 1981):19–26.

—— "The Order of Events in the Transition to Adulthood." *Sociology of Education* 57 (April 1984):63–84.

——, **and Peter J. Hodsdon** "Effects of the Timing of Marriage and First Birth on the Spacing of Subsequent Births." *Demography* 18 (November 1981):529–48.

Marshall, Kimball P., and Arthur G. Cosby "Antecedents of Early Marital and Fertility Behavior." *Youth and Society* 9 (December 1977):191–21.

Masnick, George S. "The Continuity of Birth Expectations Data with Historical Trends in Cohort Parity Distributions: Implications for Fertility in the 1980's." In Gerry Hendershot and Paul Placek, eds., *Predicting Fertility: Demographic Studies of Birth Expectations*. Lexington, MA: Heath, 1981.

—— "Appendix B: Parity Projections." Final report prepared for the U.S. Department of Housing and Urban Development, 1985.

——, **and Mary Jo Bane** *The Nation's Families: 1960–1990*. Boston: Auburn House, 1980.

Masnick, George S., and John R. Pitken "The Baby Boom and the Squeeze on Multigenerational Households." Working Paper no. W83-6. Cambridge, MA: Joint Center for Urban Studies, Harvard University and Massachusetts Institute of Technology, 1983.

Mason, Karen O.; John L. Czajka; and Sara Arber "Change in U.S. Women's Sex Role Attitudes, 1964–1974." *American Sociological Review* 41 (August 1976):573–96.

McCarthy, James "A Comparison of the Probability of the Dissolution of First and Second Marriages." *Demography* 15 (August 1978):345–59.

——, **and Jane Menken** "Marriage, Remarriage, Marital Disruption and Age at First Birth." *Family Planning Perspectives* 11 (January-February 1979):21–30.

McClendon, McKee J. "The Occupational Status Attainment Processes of Males and Females." *American Sociological Review* 41 (February 1976):52–64.

McFalls, Joseph A., Jr. "Frustrated Fertility: A Population Paradox." *Population Bulletin*, vol. 34, no. 2. Washington, DC: Population Reference Bureau, 1979.

McLaughlin, Steven D. "Differential Patterns of Female Labor Force Participation Surrounding the First Birth." *Journal of Marriage and the Family* 44 (May 1982):407–20.

——, **and Michael Micklin** "The Timing of the First Birth and Changes in Personal Efficacy." *Journal of Marriage and the Family* 45 (February 1983):47–56.

Menken, Jane "Seasonal Migration and Seasonal Variation in Fecundability: Effects on Birth Rates and Birth Intervals." *Demography* 16 (February 1979):103–20.

—— "Age and Fertility: How Late Can You Wait?" *Demography* 22 (November 1985):469–83.

——; **James Trussell; Debra Stempel; and Ozer Babakol** "Proportional Hazards Life Table Models: An Illustrative Analysis of Socio-Demographic Influences on Marriage Dissolution in the United States." *Demography* 18 (May 1981):181–200.

Michael, Robert T. "Education and Fertility." In F. Thomas Juster, ed., *Education, Income and Human Behavior*. New York: McGraw-Hill, 1975.

—— "The Rise in Divorce Rates, 1960–1974: Age-Specific Components." *Demography* 15 (May 1978):177–82.

—— "Consequences of the Rise in Female Labor Force Participation Rates: Questions and Probes." *Journal of Labor Economics* 3 (January 1985 supplement):S117–46.

——; **Victor R. Fuchs; and Sharon R. Scott** "Changes in the Propensity to Live Alone: 1950–1976." *Demography* 17 (February 1980):39–56.

Milkovich, George T. "The Male-Female Pay Gap: Need for Reevaluation." *Monthly Labor Review* 104 (April 1981):42–44.

Mincer, Jacob "Market Prices, Opportunity Costs, and Income Effects." In Carl F. Christ, ed., *Measurement in Economics, Studies in Mathematical Economics, and Econometrics in Memory of Yehuda Grunfeld.* Stanford, CA: Stanford University Press, 1973.

—— *Schooling, Experience, and Earnings.* New York: Columbia University Press, 1974.

—— "Intercountry Comparisons of Labor Force Trends and of Related Developments: An Overview." *Journal of Labor Economics* 3 (January 1985 supplement):S1–32.

——, **and Haim Ofek** "Interrupted Work Careers: Depreciation and Restoration of Human Capital." *Journal of Human Resources* 17 (Winter 1982):3–24.

——, **and Solomon Polachek** "Family Investment in Human Capital: Earnings of Women." In Theodore W. Schultz, ed., *Marriage, Family Human Capital, and Fertility.* Chicago: University of Chicago Press, 1974.

Model, Suzanne "Housework by Husbands: Determinants and Implications." *Journal of Family Issues* 2 (June 1981):225–37.

Modell, John "Normative Aspects of American Marriage Timing Since World War II." *Journal of Family History* 5 (Summer 1980):210–34.

——; **Frank Furstenberg; and Douglas Strong** "The Timing of Marriage in the Transition to Adulthood: Continuity and Change, 1860–1975." In John Demos and Sarane Spence Boocock, eds., *Turning Points.* Chicago: University of Chicago Press, 1978.

Molm, Linda D. "Sex Role Attitudes and the Employment of Married Women: The Direction of Causality." *Sociological Quarterly* 19 (Autumn 1978):522–33.

Moore, Kristin A.; Daphne Spain; and Suzanne M. Bianchi "Working Wives and Mothers." *Marriage and Family Review* 7 (Fall-Winter 1984):77–98.

Moore, Kristin A., and Linda J. Waite "Marital Dissolution, Early Motherhood, and Early Marriage." *Social Forces* 60 (September 1981):20–40.

Morgan, James; Katherine Dickinson; Jonathan Dickinson; Jacob Benus; and Greg Duncan *Five Thousand American Families: Patterns of Economic Progress,* vol. 1. Ann Arbor: Institute for Social Research, University of Michigan, 1974.

Morgan, Leslie A. "A Re-Examination of Widowhood and Morale." *Journal of Gerontology* 31 (November 1976):687–95.

—— "Economic Change at Mid-Life Widowhood: A Longitudinal Analysis." *Journal of Marriage and the Family* 43 (November 1981):899–908.

Morgan, S. Philip "Intention and Uncertainty at Later Stages of Childbearing: The United States, 1965 and 1970." *Demography* 18 (August 1981):267–86.

—— "Parity-Specific Fertility Intentions and Uncertainty: The U.S., 1970 to 1976." *Demography* 19 (August 1982):315–34.

——, **and Ronald R. Rindfuss** "Marital Disruption: Structural and Temporal Dimensions." *American Journal of Sociology* 90 (March 1985):1055–77.

Mosher, William D. "Infertility Trends Among U.S. Couples: 1965–1976." *Family Planning Perspectives* 14 (January-February 1982):22–27.

———— "Fecundity and Infertility in the United States, 1965–1982." Paper presented at the annual meeting of the Population Association of America, Minneapolis, May 1984.

————, **and Christine A. Bachrach** "Childlessness in the United States: Estimates from the National Survey of Family Growth." *Journal of Family Issues* 3 (December 1982):517–44.

Mosher, William D., and Gerry E. Hendershot "Religion and Fertility: A Replication." *Demography* 21 (May 1984):185–91.

Mosher, William D., and Gerry E. Hendershot "Religious Affiliation and the Fertility of Married Couples." *Journal of Marriage and the Family* 46 (August 1984):671–78.

Mott, Frank, and Sylvia F. Moore "The Tempo of Remarriage Among Young American Women." *Journal of Marriage and the Family* 45 (May 1983):427–36.

Mueller, Charles W., and Hallowell Pope "Divorce and Female Remarriage Mobility: Data on Marriage Matches after Divorce for White Women." *Social Forces* 58 (March 1980):726–38.

National Center for Education Statistics *Digest of Education Statistics 1982.* Washington, DC: U.S. Government Printing Office, 1982.

National Center for Health Statistics "Patterns of Employment Before and After Childbirth." *Vital and Health Statistics*, series 23, no. 4. Washington, DC: U.S. Government Printing Office, 1980.

———— "Trends in Contraceptive Practice: United States, 1965–76." *Vital and Health Statistics*, series 23, no. 10. Washington, DC: U.S. Government Printing Office, 1982.

———— "Annual Summary of Births, Deaths, Marriages, and Divorces: United States, 1982." *Monthly Vital Statistics Report*, vol. 31, no. 13. Washington, DC: U.S. Government Printing Office, 1983.

———— "Advance Report of Final Divorce Statistics, 1981." *Monthly Vital Statistics Report*, vol. 32, no. 9, supplement. Washington, DC: U.S. Government Printing Office, 1984.

———— "Advance Report of Final Marriage Statistics, 1981." *Monthly Vital Statistics Report*, vol. 32, no. 11, supplement. Washington, DC: U.S. Government Printing Office, 1984.

———— "Advance Report of Final Mortality Statistics, 1982." *Monthly Vital Statistics Report*, vol. 33, no. 9, supplement. Washington, DC: U.S. Government Printing Office, 1984.

———— "Advance Report of Final Natality Statistics, 1982." *Monthly Vital Statistics Report*, vol. 33, no. 9, supplement. Washington, DC: U.S. Government Printing Office, 1984.

———— "Annual Summary of Births, Deaths, Marriages, and Divorces: United States, 1983." *Monthly Vital Statistics Report*, vol. 32, no. 9. Washington, DC: U.S. Government Printing Office, 1984.

———— "Use of Contraception in the United States, 1982." *Advance Data From Vital and Health Statistics*, no. 102. Washington, DC: U.S. Government Printing Office, 1984.

National Committee on Pay Equity *Who's Working for Working Women? A Survey of State and Local Government Pay Equity Initiatives.* Washington, DC: National Committee on Pay Equity, 1984.

———— "Pay Equity Newsnotes," May 1985.

Nickols, Sharon Y., and Edward Metzen "Impact of Wife's Employment upon Husband's Housework." *Journal of Family Issues* 3 (June 1982):199–216.

Nock, Steven L., and Paul W. Kingston "The Family Work Day." *Journal of Marriage and the Family* 46 (May 1984):333–43.

Norton, Arthur J. "The Family Life Cycle Updated: Components and Uses." In Robert F. Winch and Graham B. Spanier, eds., *Selected Studies in Marriage and the Family*. New York: Holt, Rinehart & Winston, 1974.

—— "Family Life Cycle: 1980." *Journal of Marriage and the Family* 45 (May 1983):267–76.

Nye, F. Ivan, and Felix M. Berardo *The Family*. New York: Macmillan, 1973.

O'Connell, Martin "Comparative Estimates of Teenage Illegitimacy in the United States, 1940–44 to 1970–74." *Demography* 17 (February 1980):13–24.

—— "Countercyclical Fertility: A View from the Trough." Unpublished manuscript, U.S. Bureau of the Census, Population Division, 1983.

——, **and Carolyn C. Rogers** "Assessing Cohort Birth Expectations Data from the Current Population Survey, 1971–1981." *Demography* 20 (August 1983):369–84.

O'Connell, Martin, and Carolyn C. Rogers "Child Care Arrangements of Working Mothers: June 1982." *Current Population Reports*, series P-23, no. 129, U.S. Bureau of the Census. Washington, DC: U.S. Government Printing Office, 1983.

O'Connell, Martin, and Carolyn C. Rogers "Out-of-Wedlock Births, Premarital Pregnancies, and their Effect on Family Formation and Dissolution." *Family Planning Perspectives* 16 (July-August 1984):157.

O'Connell, Martin, and Maurice Moore "New Evidence on the Value of Birth Expectations." *Demography* 14 (August 1977):255–64.

O'Connor, James F. "A Logarithmic Technique for Decomposing Change." *Sociological Methods and Research* 6 (August 1977):91–102.

Ogburn, William F. *On Culture and Social Change*. Chicago: University of Chicago Press, 1964.

O'Neill, June "The Trend in the Sex Differential in Wages." Paper presented at the Conference on Trend in Women's Work, Education, and Family Building, White House Conference Center, Cherwood Gate, Sussex, England, June 1983.

—— "The Trend in the Male-Female Wage Gap in the United States." *Journal of Labor Economics* 3 (January 1985 supplement):S91–116.

——, **and Rachel Braun** "Women and the Labor Market: A Survey of Issues and Policies in the United States." United States Country Report to the Conference on "Regulation of the Labor Market: International Comparison of Labor Market Policy Related to Women." IIMV/LMP, Berlin, 1981.

Oppenheimer, Valerie K. *The Female Labor Force in the United States*. Westport, CT: Greenwood Press, 1970.

—— "The Life-Cycle Squeeze: The Interaction of Men's Occupational and Family Cycles." *Demography* 11 (May 1974):237–45.

—— "The Sociology of Women's Economic Role in the Family." *American Sociological Review* 42 (June 1977):387–405.

—— *Work and the Family*. New York: Academic Press, 1982.

Osterman, Paul "Affirmative Action and Opportunity: A Study of Female Quit Rates." *Review of Economics and Statistics* 64 (November 1982):604–12.

Pampel, Fred C. "Changes in the Propensity to Live Alone: Evidence from Consecutive Cross-Sectional Surveys, 1960–1976." *Demography* 20 (November 1983):433–48.

Parsons, Talcott "The Social Structure of the Family." In Ruth N. Anshen, ed., *The Family: Its Function and Destiny*. New York: Harper, 1949.

_____ "The American Family: Its Relation to Personality and to the Social Structure." In Talcott Parsons and Robert F. Bales, eds, *Family, Socialization, and Interaction Process.* New York: Macmillan, 1955.

Pearlin, Leonard I. "Status Inequality and Stress in Marriage." *American Sociological Review* 40 (June 1975):344–57.

Pleck, Joseph "The Work-Family Role System." *Social Problems* 24 (April 1977):417–27.

Polachek, Solomon W. "Occupational Self-Selection: A Human Capital Approach to Sex Differences in Occupational Structure." *Review of Economics and Statistics* 63 (February 1981):60–69.

Posten, Dudley L., Jr., and Kathryn B. Kramer "Patterns of Childlessness Among Catholics and Non-Catholics in the United States." Texas Population Research Center Papers, no. 6.006. Austin: University of Texas, 1984.

Potter, R. G., and F. E. Kobrin "Some Effects of Spouse Separation on Fertility." *Demography* 19 (February 1982):79–95.

Powers, Mary G., and Joseph J. Salvo "Fertility and Child Care Arrangements as Mechanisms of Status Articulation." *Journal of Marriage and the Family* 44 (February 1982):21–34.

Pratt, William F., and Gerry E. Hendershot "The Use of Family Planning Services by Sexually Active Teenage Women." Paper presented at the annual meeting of the Population Association of America, Minneapolis, May 1984.

Pratt, William F.; William D. Mosher; Christine A. Bachrach; and Marjorie C. Horn "Understanding U.S. Fertility: Findings from the National Survey of Family Growth, Cycle III." *Population Bulletin,* vol. 39, no. 5. Washington, DC: Population Reference Bureau, December 1984.

Presser, Harriet B. "The Timing of the First Birth, Female Roles and Black Fertility." *Milbank Memorial Fund Quarterly* 49 (July 1971):329–61.

_____, **and Wendy Baldwin** "Child Care as a Constraint on Employment: Prevalence, Correlates, and Bearing on the Work and Fertility Nexus." *American Journal of Sociology* 85 (March 1980):1202–13.

Presser, Harriet B., and Virginia Cain "Shift Work Among Dual-Earner Couples with Children." *Science* 219 (February 18,1983):876–78.

Preston, Samuel H. "Estimating the Proportion of American Marriages that End in Divorce." *Sociological Methods and Research* 3 (May 1975):435–60.

_____, **and John McDonald** "The Incidence of Divorce Within Cohorts of American Marriages Contracted Since the Civil War." *Demography* 16 (February 1979):1–25.

Preston, Samuel H., and Alan T. Richards "The Influence of Women's Work Opportunities on Marriage Rates." *Demography* 12 (May 1975):209–22.

Price-Bonham, Sharon, and Jack Balswick "The Noninstitutions: Divorce, Desertion, and Remarriage." *Journal of Marriage and the Family* 42 (November 1980):959–72.

Pullum, Thomas "Separating Age, Period, and Cohort Effects in White U.S. Fertility, 1920 to 1970." *Social Science Research* 9 (September 1980):225–44.

Rainwater, Lee *Behind Ghetto Walls.* Chicago: Aldine, 1970.

Reid, John "Black America in the 1980s." *Population Bulletin,* vol. 37, no. 4. Washington, DC: Population Reference Bureau, 1982.

Reskin, Barbara F., ed. *Sex Segregation in the Workplace: Trends, Explanations, Remedies.* Washington, DC: National Academy Press, 1984.

_____, **and Heidi Hartmann, eds.** *Women's Work, Men's Work: Sex Segregation on the Job.* Washington, DC: National Academy Press, 1985.

Richardson, John G. "Wife Occupational Superiority and Marital Troubles: An

Examination of the Hypothesis." *Journal of Marriage and the Family* 41 (February 1979):63–72.

Rindfuss, Ronald R., and Larry L. Bumpass "Age and the Sociology of Fertility: How Old Is Too Old?" In Karl E. Taeuber, Larry L. Bumpass, and James A. Sweet, eds., *Social Demography.* New York: Academic Press, 1978.

Rindfuss, Ronald R.; Larry L. Bumpass; and Craig St. John "Education and Fertility: Implications for the Roles Women Occupy." *American Sociological Review* 45 (June 1980):431–47.

Rindfuss, Ronald R.; S. Philip Morgan; and C. Gray Swicegood "The Transition to Motherhood: The Intersection of Structural and Temporal Dimensions." *American Sociological Review* 49 (June 1984):359–72.

Rindfuss, Ronald R., and James A. Sweet *Postwar Fertility Trends and Differentials in the United States.* New York: Academic Press, 1977.

Ritchey, P. Neal, and C. Shannon Stokes "Correlates of Childlessness and Expectations to Remain Childless." *Social Forces* 52 (March 1974):349–56.

Robinson, J. Gregory "Labor Force Participation Rates of Cohorts of Women in the United States: 1880 to 1979." Paper presented at the annual meeting of the Population Association of America, Denver, April 1980.

Rodgers, Willard L., and Arland Thornton "Changing Patterns of First Marriage in the United States." *Demography* 22 (May 1985):265–79.

Roos, Patricia A. "Sex Stratification in the Workplace: Male-Female Differences in Economic Returns to Occupation." *Social Science Research* 10 (September 1981):195–224.

Rosen, Bernard C., and Carol S. Aneshensel "Sex Differences in the Educational-Occupational Expectation Process." *Social Forces* 57 (September 1978):164–86.

Ross, Catherine E.; John Mirowsky; and Joan Huber "Dividing Work, Sharing Work, and In-Between: Marriage Patterns and Depression." *American Sociological Review* 48 (December 1983):809–23.

Ross, Heather L., and Isabel V. Sawhill *Time of Transition: The Growth of Families Headed by Women.* Washington, DC: Urban Institute, 1975.

Rossi, Alice "Transition to Parenthood." *Journal of Marriage and the Family* 30 (February 1968):26–39.

Ryder, Norman B. "The Future of American Fertility." *Social Problems* 26 (February 1979):359–70.

―――, and Charles F. Westoff *Reproduction in the United States 1965.* Princeton, NJ: Princeton University Press, 1971.

Rytina, Nancy F. "Tenure as a Factor in the Male-Female Earnings Gap." *Monthly Labor Review* 105 (April 1982):32–34.

―――, "Comparing Annual and Weekly Earnings from the Current Population Survey." *Monthly Labor Review* 106 (April 1983):32-36.

―――, and Suzanne M. Bianchi "Occupational Reclassification and Changes in Distribution by Gender." *Monthly Labor Review* 107 (March 1984):11–17.

Sabagh, Georges, and David Lopez "Religiosity and Fertility: The Case of Chicanos." *Social Forces* 59 (December 1980):431–39.

Sandell, Steven H., and David Shapiro "The Theory of Human Capital and the Earnings of Women: A Reexamination of the Evidence." *Journal of Human Resources* 13 (Winter 1978):103–17.

Schaffer, Kay *Sex Roles and Human Behavior.* Cambridge, MA: Winthrop, 1981.

Schoen, Robert "California Divorce Rates by Age at First Marriage and Duration of First Marriage." *Journal of Marriage and the Family* 37 (August 1975):548–55.

———— "Measuring the Tightness of a Marriage Squeeze." *Demography* 20 (February 1983):61–78.

————; Harry N. Greenblatt; and Robert B. Mielke "California's Experience with Non-Adversary Divorce." *Demography* 2 (May 1975):223–44.

Schoen, Robert; William L. Urton; Karen Woodrow; and John Baj "Marriage and Divorce in Twentieth Century American Cohorts." *Demography* 22 (February 1985):101–14.

Schwartz, Saul; Sheldon Danziger; and Eugene Smolensky "The Choice of Living Arrangements by the Elderly." Washington, DC: Brookings Institution, 1983.

Seal, Karen "A Decade of No-Fault Divorce: What It Has Meant Financially for Women in California." *Family Advocate* 1 (Spring 1979):10–15.

Sewell, William H.; Robert M. Hauser; and David L. Featherman *Schooling and Achievement in American Society.* New York: Harcourt Brace Jovanovich, 1976.

Sewell, William H.; Robert M. Hauser; and Wendy C. Wolf "Sex, Schooling and Occupational Status." *American Journal of Sociology* 86 (November 1980):551–83.

Shah, Farida, and Melvin Zelnik "Parent and Peer Influence on Sexual Behavior, Contraceptive Use, and Pregnancy Experience of Young Women." *Journal of Marriage and the Family* 43 (May 1981):339–48.

Shanas, Ethel "A National Survey of the Aged." Final report to the Administration on Aging, U.S. Department of Health, Education and Welfare, 1978.

————; Peter Townsend; Dorothy Wedderburn; Henning Friis; Paul Milhoj; and Jan Stehouwer *Old People in Three Industrial Societies.* New York: Atherton Press, 1968.

Siegel, Jacob S., and Maria Davidson "Demographic and Socioeconomic Aspects of Aging in the United States." *Current Population Reports, Special Studies,* series P-23, no. 138, U.S. Bureau of the Census. Washington, DC: U.S. Government Printing Office, 1984.

Simpson, Ida Harper, and Paula England "Conjugal Work Roles and Marital Solidarity." *Journal of Family Issues* 2 (June 1981):180–204.

Sklar, Judith "Marriage Regulation and the California Birth Rate." In Kingsley Davis and Frederick G. Styles, eds., *California's Twenty Million: Research Contributions to Population Policy.* Berkeley: Institute of International Studies, University of California, 1971.

Sloane, Douglas M., and Che-Fu Lee "Sex of Previous Children and Intentions for Further Births in the United States, 1965–1976." *Demography* 20 (August 1983):353–67.

Smith, D. P. "A Reconsideration of Easterlin Cycles." *Population Studies* 35 (July 1981):247–64.

Smith, James P. "The Distribution of Family Earnings." *Journal of Political Economy* 87 (October 1979):S162–92.

————, and Michael P. Ward "Women's Wages and Work in the Twentieth Century." Report prepared for the National Institute of Child Health and Human Development, R-3119-NICHD. Santa Monica, CA: Rand Corporation, 1984.

Smith, James P., and Michael P. Ward "Time Series Growth in the Female Labor Force." *Journal of Labor Economics* 3 (January 1985 supplement):S59–90.

Smith, Shirley J. "New Worklife Estimates Reflect Changing Profile of Labor Force." *Monthly Labor Review* 105 (March 1982):15–20.

———— "Revised Worklife Tables Reflect 1979–80 Experience." *Monthly Labor Review* 108 (August 1985):23–30.

————, and Francis W. Horvath "New Developments in Multistate Working Life Tables." Paper presented at the annual meeting of the Population Association of America, Minneapolis, May 1984.

Smith-Lovin, Lynne, and Ann R. Tickamyer "Nonrecursive Models of Labor Force Participation, Fertility Behavior, and Sex Role Attitudes." *American Sociological Review* 43 (August 1978):541–56.

———— "Models of Fertility and Women's Work: Comment on Cramer, ASR, April 1980." *American Sociological Review* 47 (August 1982):561–66.

Soldo, Beth J., and Patience Lauriat "Living Arrangements Among the Elderly in the United States: A Loglinear Approach." *Journal of Comparative Family Studies* 7 (Summer 1976):351–66.

Soldo, Beth J.; Mahesh Sharma; and Richard T. Campbell "Determinants of the Community Living Arrangements of Older Unmarried Women." *Journal of Gerontology* 39 (July 1984):492–98.

Spanier, Graham "Married and Unmarried Cohabitation in the United States: 1980." *Journal of Marriage and the Family* 45 (May 1983):277–88.

————, and Paul C. Glick "Paths to Remarriage." *Journal of Divorce* 3 (Spring 1980):283–98.

Spitze, Glenna, and Linda J. Waite "Wives' Employment: The Role of Husbands' Perceived Attitudes." *Journal of Marriage and the Family* 43 (February 1981):117–24.

Stafford, Frank P. "Women's Use of Time Converging with Men's." *Monthly Labor Review* 103 (December 1980):57–58.

Staples, Robert "Towards a Sociology of the Black Family: A Theoretical and Methodological Assessment." *Journal of Marriage and the Family* 33 (February 1971):119–38.

St. John, Craig "Race Differences in Age at First Birth and the Pace of Subsequent Fertility: Implications for the Minority Group Status Hypothesis." *Demography* 19 (August 1982):301–14.

————, and Harold Grasmick "Decomposing the Black/White Fertility Differential." *Social Science Quarterly* 66 (March 1985):132–46.

Stolzenberg, Ross M., and Linda J. Waite "Age, Fertility Expectations, and Plans for Employment." *American Sociological Review* 42 (October 1977):769–83.

Stolzenberg, Ross M., and Linda J. Waite "Local Labor Markets, Children, and Labor Force Participation of Wives." *Demography* 21 (May 1984):157–70.

Stycos, J. Mayone, and Robert H. Weller "Female Working Roles and Fertility." *Demography* 4 (1967):210–17.

Suter, Larry, and Herman Miller "Income Differences Between Men and Career Women." *American Journal of Sociology* 78 (January 1973):962–74.

Sweet, James A. *Women in the Labor Force.* New York: Seminar Press, 1973.

———— "Demography and the Family." In Alex Inkeles, ed., *Annual Review of Sociology*, vol. 3. Palo Alto: Annual Reviews, 1977.

———— "Recent Trends in the Household and Family Status of Young Adults." Working Paper no. 78-9. Madison: Center for Demography and Ecology, University of Wisconsin, 1978.

———— "Changes in the Allocation of Time of Young Women Among Schooling, Marriage, Work, and Childrearing: 1960–1976." Working Paper no. 79–15. Madison: Center for Demography and Ecology, University of Wisconsin, 1979.

———— "Components of Change in the Number of Households, 1970–80." *Demography* 21 (May 1984):129–40.

Tanfer, Koray, and Marjorie C. Horn "Contraceptive Use, Pregnancy, and Fertility Patterns Among Single American Women in Their 20s." *Family Planning Perspectives* 17 (January-February 1985):10–19.

Terry, Geraldine "Rival Explanations in the Work-Fertility Relationship." *Population Studies* 29 (July 1975):191–205.

Thomlinson, Ralph *Population Dynamics.* New York: Random House, 1965.

Thompson, Kenrick "A Comparison of Black and White Adolescents' Beliefs about Having Children." *Journal of Marriage and the Family* 42 (February 1980):133–40.

Thornton, Arland "Fertility Change after the Baby Boom: The Role of Economic Stress, Female Employment, and Education." Final Report prepared for National Institute of Child Health and Human Development. Ann Arbor: Institute for Social Research, 1976.

———— "Marital Dissolution, Remarriage and Childbearing." *Demography* 15 (August 1978):361–80.

———— "Marital Instability Differentials and Interactions: Insights from Multivariate Contingency Table Analysis." *Sociology and Social Research* 62 (July 1978):572–95.

————; **Duane F. Alwin; and Donald Camburn** "Causes and Consequences of Sex-Role Attitudes and Attitude Change." *American Sociological Review* 48 (April 1983):211–27.

Thornton, Arland, and Deborah Freedman "Changing Attitudes toward Marriage and Single Life." *Family Planning Perspectives* 14 (November-December 1982):297–303.

Thornton, Arland, and Deborah Freedman "The Changing American Family." *Population Bulletin,* vol. 38, no. 4. Washington, DC: Population Reference Bureau, 1983.

Thornton, Arland; Ronald Freedman; and Deborah S. Freedman "Further Reflections on Changes in Fertility Expectations and Preferences." *Demography* 21 (August 1984):423–29.

Thornton, Arland, and Willard Rodgers "Changing Patterns of Marriage and Divorce in the United States." Final Report prepared for the National Institute of Child Health and Human Development. Ann Arbor: Institute for Social Research, 1983.

Tissue, Thomas "Low Income Widows and Other Aged Singles." *Social Security Bulletin* 42 (December 1979):3–10.

————, **and John L. McCoy** "Income and Living Arrangements Among Poor Aged Singles." *Social Security Bulletin* 44 (April 1981):3–13.

Treiman, Donald J. "The Work Histories of Women and Men: What We Know and What We Need to Find Out." In Alice Rossi, ed., *Gender and the Life Course.* New York: Aldine, 1985.

————, **and Heidi I. Hartmann** *Women, Work, and Wages: Equal Pay for Jobs of Equal Value.* Washington, DC: National Academy Press, 1981.

Treiman, Donald J., and Kermit Terrell "Sex and the Process of Status Attainment." *American Sociological Review* 40 (April 1975):174–200.

Treiman, Donald J., and Kermit Terrell "Women, Work, and Wages—Trends in the Female Occupational Structure Since 1940." In Kenneth C. Land, ed., *Social Indicator Models.* New York: Russell Sage Foundation, 1975.

Tsui, Amy Ong "The Family Formation Process Among U.S. Marriage Cohorts." *Demography* 19 (February 1982):1–27.

United Nations *Demographic Indicators of Countries: Estimates and Projections as Assessed in 1980.* New York: United Nations, 1982.

U.S Bureau of the Census "Characteristics of the Population Below the Poverty Level: 1982." *Current Population Report,* series P-60, no. 144. Washington, DC: U.S. Government Printing Office, 1984.

———— "Childspacing among Birth Cohorts of American Women: 1905 to 1959."

Current Population Reports, series P-20, no. 385. Washington, DC: U.S. Government Printing Office, 1984.

—— "Child Support and Alimony: 1981 (Advanced Report)." *Current Population Reports, Special Studies*, series P-23, no. 124. Washington, DC: U.S. Government Printing Office, 1983.

—— "Detailed Occupation of the Experienced Civilian Labor Force by Sex for the United States and Regions: 1980 and 1970." *1980 Census of Population, Supplementary Report*, PC80–S1–15. Washington, DC: U.S. Government Printing Office, 1984.

—— "Earnings by Occupation and Education." *1980 Census of Population, Subject Report*, PC80–2–8B. Washington, DC: U.S. Government Printing Office, 1984.

—— "Educational Attainment in the United States: March 1981 and 1980." *Current Population Reports*, series P-20, no. 390. Washington, DC: U.S. Government Printing Office, 1984.

—— "Estimates of Poverty Including the Value of Noncash Benefits: 1979 to 1982." *Technical Paper 51*. Washington, DC: U.S. Government Printing Office, 1984.

—— "Families Maintained by Female Householders, 1970–79." *Current Population Reports, Special Studies*, series P-23, no. 107. Washington, DC: U.S. Government Printing Office, 1980.

—— "Fertility of American Women: June 1979." *Current Population Reports*, series P-20, no. 358. Washington, DC: U.S. Government Printing Office, 1980.

—— "Fertility of American Women: June 1980." *Current Population Reports*, series P-20, no. 375. Washington, DC: U.S. Government Printing Office, 1982.

—— "Fertility of American Women: June 1982 (Advance Report)." *Current Population Reports*, series P-20, no. 379. Washington, DC: U.S. Government Printing Office, 1983.

—— "Fertility of American Women: June 1982." *Current Population Reports*, series P-20, no. 387. Washington, DC: U.S. Government Printing Office, 1983.

—— "Fertility of American Women: June 1983." *Current Population Reports*, series P-20, no. 395. Washington, DC: U.S. Government Printing Office, 1983.

—— "Fertility of American Women: June 1983 (Advance Report)." *Current Population Reports*, series P-20, no. 386. Washington, DC: U.S. Government Printing Office, 1984.

—— *Historical Statistics of the United States, Colonial Times to 1970*, Bicentennial Edition. Washington, DC: U.S. Government Printing Office, 1975.

—— "Household and Family Characteristics: March 1980." *Current Population Reports*, series P-20, no. 366. Washington, DC: U.S. Government Printing Office, 1981.

—— "Household and Family Characteristics: March 1983." *Current Population Reports*, series P-20, no. 388. Washington, DC: U.S. Government Printing Office, 1984.

—— "Marriage, Divorce, Widowhood, and Remarriage by Family Characteristics: June 1975." *Current Population Reports*, series P-20, no. 312. Washington, DC: U.S. Government Printing Office, 1977.

—— "Marital Status and Living Arrangements: March 1982." *Current Population Reports*, series P-20, no. 380. Washington, DC: U.S. Government Printing Office, 1983.

—— "Marital Status and Living Arrangements: March 1983." *Current Population Reports*, series P-20, no. 389. Washington, DC: U.S. Government Printing Office, 1984.

—— "Money Income of Households, Families, and Persons in the United States: 1982." *Current Population Reports,* series P-60, no. 142. Washington, DC: U.S. Government Printing Office, 1984.

—— "Number, Timing, and Duration of Marriages and Divorces in the United States: June 1975." *Current Population Reports,* series P-20, no. 297. Washington, DC: U.S. Government Printing Office, 1976.

—— "Perspectives on American Fertility." *Current Population Reports, Special Studies,* series P-23, no. 70. Washington, DC: U.S. Government Printing Office, 1978.

—— "Population Profile of the United States: 1981." *Current Population Reports,* series P-20, no. 374. Washington, DC: U.S. Government Printing Office, 1982.

—— "Premarital Fertility." *Current Population Reports,* series P-23, no. 63. Washington, DC: U.S. Government Printing Office, 1976.

—— "School Enrollment—Social and Economic Characteristics of Students: October 1981 (Advance Report)." *Current Population Reports,* series P-20, no. 373. Washington, DC: U.S. Government Printing Office, 1983.

—— "School Enrollment—Social and Economic Characteristics of Students: October 1979." *Current Population Reports,* series P-20, no. 360. Washington, DC: U.S. Government Printing Office, 1981.

—— "A Statistical Portrait of Women in the United States: 1978." *Current Population Reports, Special Studies,* series P-23, no. 100. Washington, DC: U.S. Government Printing Office, 1980.

—— "Trends in Childspacing: June 1975." *Current Population Reports,* series P-20, no. 315. Washington, DC: U.S. Government Printing Office, 1978.

U.S. Department of Health and Human Services, Center for Disease Control "Abortion Surveillance 1979–1980." Atlanta, GA: U.S. Department of Health and Human Services, 1983.

U.S. Department of Labor, Bureau of Labor Statistics *Handbook of Labor Statistics,* bulletin 2175. Washington, DC: U.S. Government Printing Office, 1983.

—— *Perspectives on Working Women: A Databook,* bulletin 2080, Washington, DC: U.S. Government Printing Office, 1980.

—— Press Release, June 26, 1984.

U.S Department of Labor, Women's Bureau *Time of Change: 1983 Handbook on Women Workers,* bulletin 298. Washington, DC: U.S. Government Printing Office, 1983.

Vanek, Joanne "Time Spent in Housework." *Scientific American* 31 (November 1974):116–20.

Vaughn, Barbara; James Trussell; Jane Menken; and Louise Jones "Contraceptive Failure Among Married Women in the U.S., 1970–1973." *Family Planning Perspectives* 9 (November-December 1977):251–57.

Veevers, J. E. "Voluntarily Childless Wives: An Exploratory Study." *Sociology and Social Research* 57 (April 1973):356–65.

Verbrugge, Lois M., and Jennifer H. Madans "Women's Roles and Health." *American Demographics* 6 (March 1985):36–39.

Vickery, Clair "The Time-Poor: A New Look at Poverty." *Journal of Human Resources* 12 (Winter 1977):27–48.

Viscusi, W. Kip "Sex Differences in Worker Quitting." *Review of Economics and Statistics* 62 (August 1980):388–98.

Waite, Linda J. "Working Wives and the Family Life Cycle." *American Journal of Sociology* 86 (September 1980):272–94.

————, and **Kristin A. Moore** "The Impact of an Early First Birth on Young Women's Educational Attainment." *Social Forces* 56 (March 1978):845–65.

Waite, Linda J., and Glenna D. Spitze "Young Women's Transition to Marriage." *Demography* 18 (November 1981):681–94.

Waite, Linda J., and Ross Stolzenberg "Intended Childbearing and Labor Force Participation of Young Women: Insights from Nonrecursive Models." *American Sociological Review* 41 (April 1976):235–52.

Waldauer, Charles "The Non-Comparability of the "Comparable Worth" Doctrine: An Inappropriate Standard for Determining Sex Discrimination in Pay." *Population Research and Policy Review* 3 (June 1984):141–66.

Ward, Michael, and William Butz "Completed Fertility and Its Timing." *Journal of Political Economy* 88 (October 1980):917–40.

Watson, Joellen "Higher Education for Women in the United States: A Historical Perspective." *Educational Studies* 8 (Summer 1977):133–44.

Weed, James A. "National Estimates of Marriage Dissolution and Survivorship: United States." National Center for Health Statistics. *Vital and Health Statistics*, series 3, Analytic Studies, no. 19. Washington, DC: U.S. Government Printing Office, 1980.

Weitz, Shirley *Sex Roles: Biological, Psychological, and Social Foundations.* New York: Oxford University Press, 1977.

Weitzman, Lenore J. "The Economics of Divorce: Social and Economic Consequences of Property, Alimony, and Child Support Awards." *UCLA Law Review* 28 (August 1981):1181–268.

Welch, Charles E., and Sharon Price-Bonham "A Decade of No-Fault Divorce Revisited: California, Georgia and Washington." *Journal of Marriage and the Family* 45 (May 1983):411–18.

Weller, Robert H. "The Employment of Wives, Role Incompatibility and Fertility." *Milbank Memorial Fund Quarterly* 46 (Fall 1969):507–26.

———— "Wife's Employment and Cumulative Family Size in the United States, 1970 and 1960." *Demography* 14 (February 1977):43–66.

————, and **Frank B. Hobbs** "Unwanted and Mistimed Births in the United States: 1968–1973." *Family Planning Perspectives* 10 (May-June 1978):168–72.

Westoff, Charles F. "The Decline of Unplanned Births in the United States." *Science* 191 (January 9, 1976):38–41.

———— "Marriage and Fertility in the Developed Countries." *Scientific American* 239 (June 1978):51–57.

———— "Some Speculations on the Future of Marriage and Fertility." *Family Planning Perspectives* 10 (March-April 1978):79–83.

————, and **Norman B. Ryder** *The Contraceptive Revolution.* Princeton: Princeton University Press, 1977.

Westoff, Charles F., and Norman B. Ryder "The Predictive Validity of Reproductive Intentions." *Demography* 14 (November 1977):431–54.

Whelpton, Pascal K.; Arthur A. Campbell; and John E. Patterson *Fertility and Family Planning in the United States.* Princeton, NJ: Princeton University Press, 1966.

Wilkie, Jane R. "The Trend Toward Delayed Parenthood." *Journal of Marriage and the Family* 43 (August 1981):583–92.

———— "The Decline in Occupational Segregation Between Black and White Women." In Cora B. Marrett and Cheryl Leggon, eds., *Research in Race and Ethnic Relations*, vol. 4. Greenwich, CT: JAI Press, 1985.

Williams, Gregory "The Changing U.S. Labor Force and Occupational Differentiation by Sex." *Demography* 16 (February 1979):73–88.

Wilson Kenneth L., and Eui Hang Shen "Reassessing the Discrimination Against Women in Higher Education." *American Education Research Journal* 20 (Winter 1983):529–51.

Winsborough, Halliman "Statistical Histories of the Life Cycle of Birth Cohorts: The Transition from Schoolboy to Adult Male." In Karl E. Taeuber, Larry L. Bumpass, and James A. Sweet, eds., *Social Demography.* New York: Academic Press, 1978.

Wolf, Douglas A. "Kinship and the Living Arrangements of Older Americans." Final report to the National Institute of Child Health and Human Development. Washington, DC: Urban Institute, January 1983.

———— "Kin Availability and the Living Arrangements of Older Women." *Social Science Research* 13 (March 1984):72–89.

Wolf, Wendy C., and Neil D. Fligstein "Sex and Authority in the Workplace: The Causes of Sexual Inequality." *American Sociological Review* 44 (April 1979):235–52.

Wolf, Wendy C., and Rachel Rosenfeld "Sex Structure of Occupations and Job Mobility." *Social Forces* 56 (March 1978):823–44.

Wright, James P. "Are Working Women Really More Satisfied? Evidence from Several National Surveys." *Journal of Marriage and the Family* 40 (May 1978):301–13.

Yankelovich, Skelly, & White *The General Mills American Family Report, 1974–75.* Minneapolis: General Mills, 1975.

Zelnik, M., and J. Kantner "First Pregnancies to Women Aged 15–19: 1971–1976." *Family Planning Perspectives* 10 (January-February 1978):10–20.

Index